Alone But Together

Adult Distance Study Through Computer Conferencing

Alone But Together

Adult Distance Study Through Computer Conferencing

Daniel V. Eastmond
SUNY Empire State College

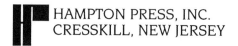

HAMPTON PRESS, INC.
CRESSKILL, NEW JERSEY

Library of Congress Cataloging-in-Publication Data

Eastmond, Daniel V.
    Alone but together : adult distance study through computer conferencing / Daniel V. Eastmond.
        p.   cm.
    Includes bibliographical references and index.
    ISBN 1-57273-030-7 (cloth). -- ISBN 1-57273-031-5 (pbk.)
    1. Distance education--United States--Computer-assisted instruction. 2. Computer conferencing--United States. I. Title.
    LC5803.C65E27   1995
    371.3'34--dc20   95-35058
                                                                       CIP

Hampton Press, Inc.
23 Broadway
Cresskill, NJ 07626

Contents

Preface

When I read a book, I always want to know who the author is, and why the book was written. So, in case you carry these thoughts in the back of your mind, too, I will quickly put your curiosity to rest. Several aspects of my background relate to the subject of this book: using computer conferencing for adult distance study. First, I have used computer technologies for the past fifteen years, particularly personal computer applications in education and training. I've worked as an instructional technologist, with a graduate degree in that field and six years of experience in developing training programs for business and industry, particularly about computer subjects. I've developed courses that rely on the computer as their main medium for delivery—both with computer-based training and interactive videodisc.

Because of my intense interest in both adult and distance education, I determined to make them the focus of my doctoral studies at Syracuse University in 1990. Although I had been an electronic mail user for over five years, it was only at Syracuse that I began to participate in network discussion groups. I moderated one of these, the Adult Education Network (AEDNET), for some time and "lurked" on several other listserves. Also, I was editor for an on-line electronic journal, *New Horizons in Adult Education*.

At the time I began the fieldwork that forms the basis of this book, I had limited exposure to computer conferencing through organizing two informal electronic study groups and in writing an article on computer conference facilitation. However, since then my involvement with computer conferencing for distance education has expanded. I took a position whose duties included the technical development and instructional support for a distance education initiative which offered four adult education graduate courses using computer conferencing (Eastmond & Rohfeld, 1993). I developed training materials and conducted workshops on computer networking to assist students and faculty in acquiring the necessary skills to study and instruct on-line.

I took a course halfway through this study, "On-line Education and Training," taught by computer conferencing from the British Open University. The course gave me firsthand experience with being a distance student using this medium, as well as course materials and discussions which enable educators to develop and implement instruction for computer conferencing. Notes that I kept about my own learning experiences on-line remind me that I was once up at 2:00 AM and slaved all night long reading up on the conference, finally quitting at 9:00 AM in exasperation at not being able to upload a response. These notes showed me how easily I forgot the intense frustration of a novice. As the technical barriers disappeared, I gained new skills, and conference participation became routine.

So, I experienced most of the themes I discuss in this book. I'm aware that my attitudes affected the perspective with which I approached this research. For instance, I had a vested interest in making sure that the computer conferencing courses I developed were successful. In addition, I was aware that I've enjoyed participating in computer conferencing through various electronic study groups. However, I also consider myself a skeptic about this technology—I don't favor it necessarily above other distance education media or classroom courses. I believe it has advantages, but the design of instruction for this medium must incorporate off-line experiences which use other modalities and social experiences, if possible, to compensate for its limitations.

My experiences give me a unique point-of-view, one which improved this study. First, I included myself as a "pseudo" subject and dutifully wrote regular fieldnotes about my own experiences and impressions. These I contrasted and compared with the other students I studied for additional insights into their experience. By making my perspective explicit, I was able to more effectively gather data and analyze it. Also, by holding the perspective of trainer, administrator, and technical support person, I was aware of the institutional constraints that learners and staff have to face.

I've often felt that being a qualitative researcher and a distance learner have much in common. Both roles require a great deal of inner drive and self-discipline, since it is only the individual who is pushing the project forward. These are solitary ventures for the most part; the researcher may meet with informants or the learner may come together with other "classmates" on-line, but for the most part the routine of

fieldwork or off-line study is done alone. And, if the person is conduct-
ing research at a distance, as I was, the dynamics are much the same.
For instance, during one of my early interviews, I explored with a
woman who lived out West, her visual impressions of the instructor and
other students in the on-line course. We laughed as I revealed the dis-
crepancy between her descriptions and images I had formed from in-
person associations with these people. But, I also created images of
those research colleagues of mine whom I had only met by email or
over the phone. I awoke from a startling dream one Saturday morning
at 4:00 AM, toward the end of this project with the distinct visual image
of a woman I had collaborated with in Canada but never met face-to-
face. I hurried to the computer in my study to relay these impressions,
only to receive her Monday email response that my image of her was
totally off-base. We both laughed over the phone about this later, and I
am still curious what she looks like.

I mention these experiences with distance qualitative research
because they capture the essence of my position—that the central
meaning of adult learning through on-line study lies in more than
descriptions of course structures, on-line characteristics, and relationships between demographic variables. Rather, computer conferencing is
experienced individually by real adults, and it touches their lives differently, based on the larger context and personal philosophies from which
they approach distance study. Perhaps it is because of the distance and
isolation involved in distance learning and distance research that I've
felt compelled to explain in this book who these people are, the meaning that online learning has for them, and the lengths to which they
have gone in making this novel instructional experience effective for
them. Moreover, it is the search for more humanness in an environment
"where people are reduced to lines on a screen" that drove me to seek
out dimensions of human qualities on-line: friendship, emotion, pas-
sion, and learning. And, this concern begged that I expand these dimensions to address larger societal issues of an ensuing information technology, of which computer conferencing for adult distance study is but
one example. My hope is that this book not only reveals how solitary
adult learners are able to gather for distance study by use of computer
conferencing, but causes greater reflection upon the subtle ways that
technologies influence each of us in becoming more alone but together.

Dan Eastmond
Saratoga Springs, New York

1

Introducing the Conference

CLASS MEMBERS MEET

On September 12, 1991, just before noon, David Engles, the instructor for the distance course, "The Constitution: The Judiciary and Public Policy," began discussion to branches of the computer conference from his office at Hawks College. In the general conversation area, THE PUB, he posted this opening note:

> THE PUB. Pull up a chair; grab a beer or seltzer. In the pub, we can relax and talk about anything and everything.

And, in the next note he started the conversation with a current news item:

> Judge Clarence Thomas is now undergoing the Senate confirmation process for his nomination to the Supreme Court. What do you think of the process? What do you think of Judge Clarence Thomas—should he be seated on the Court?

As the students gradually began to "assemble" online, Len Parker made the first response several days later, at 1:18 AM, just before leaving to work a night shift:

Well, he does seem to have been prepared quite well . . . To
sum up: I personally prefer "liberal" rulings. At the same time, I
don't want to see an anti court backlash. I oppose any attempt
to pack the court.

David, who had been eagerly monitoring the conference,
replied at 9:38 AM that same morning, just after arriving to work at his
Hawks office in the Distance Education Center. But, it was not until the
next day at 7:10 PM when another student, Dennis Weather, joined the
conversation, logging in from his work computer after hours:

Clarence Thomas is doing just what any astute politician would
do, and that is to answer only those questions that may not
jeopardize his chances of confirmation. . . .

There were enough people online at this point for a lively conversation to take off. Each of these three made comments the next day,
September 20—David and Len had posted their earlier notes at roughly
the same time, but Dennis sent his note from work at the end of his
lunch hour:

I think the JC committee should reject Thomas on the basis that
he is not experienced enough and has shown too much variation in past judgements[sic]. . . I, too, want to see INTELLECTU-
AL GIANTS on the Court!

Craig Brooks, working at home from his personal computer, two
hours before leaving for his swing-shift work as a security guard, made
his first contribution at 1:14 PM, without having read the earlier discussion:

Hey bartender, how about a couple of shots for me and the
Professor. Yes, that one over there, the tequila. The bottle with
the worm in it. Yes, a slice of lemon and a little salt would be
good. OK Professor let's go, lick, slurp, such ahh. Hey Doc, I
see you got the worm. Good Man! Let me tell you, I haven't
been in one of these college pubs since 1971. And if I remember right, I was singing a song by Jethro Tull at the time.
"Sitting on a park bench, da ta da." Hey, let's see if we can find
some fellow female students. There is only one thing I have to
remember. I promised my wife, that if I visited this pub, I'm not
allowed to do any adjudicating . . . Oh, oh, oh, oh, Aqualung
da, da, da, ta, da.

As Craig went on to read the other people's notes, he became
horrified by what he had just done; he told me about it later:

I wrote something awfully stupid [on the computer conference] and I had to call [David] up. When I first got on. It was my first time using the modem and it was my first time where I was actually communicating with somebody. I got on to the system, into CONFER and all, and I see this notice, "The Pub." And there is this message, "Respond." So, I say, "I'll buy this drink for everybody; this one's on me" Right? . . .

So, I start reading and its got people debating on the courts. So, here is my response, "Here, everybody, have a drink." So, I got panicky so I called to tell David, "Hey, you've got to get this out of here; people are going to think I'm crazy." But, he said not to worry.

I think that broke the ice, because after that people started saying, "Yeah, I think I will have a drink, too." It started to humanize this instead of just posturing. . . . This is when people started relaxing. Now, sometimes I will (or somebody will) when you are in the pub section, someone will say, "I'll have another drink." And we all relax.

However, Craig did apologize, posting this note about a half hour later:

Sorry about my responce [sic] above. I'm very new at this. I responded to an item without reading any of the outher[sic] responces[sic]. Please ignor[sic] me while I go back and reread this [CONFER] Guide.

Maybe Craig was right—the group seemed to completely ignore his outburst at first as Len, David, and a new participant—Lyn Vaughn, joining on September 27 at midnight from home—continued this conversation as if nothing had happened. Kerry Jones wrote his first message on October 2 from his work computer after hours in the same serious tone, as did Randy Fox from his office after work on October 4. Kris joined the group, dialing into Hawks College's 800 number from a western state. There were also 17 similarly serious notes during this period, but the conversation started to loosen up, with others starting to incorporate "drinking" references into their writing:

Len (Oct. 6): When you wrapped yourself in the flag, you knocked my beer over!

Dennis (Oct. 7): This is the first class I ever took where they handed beers around. Must say that I enjoy it as much as anyone. By the way, I drink Miller Lite, so if anyone wants to place a bet on Bills vs. Chiefs game tonite, I'll take the Bills and give six.

Len (Oct. 8): I don't bet but here's a Miller Lite. Here, I'll pass it through the screen. I hope your graphics are good, otherwise it will end up being a Pabst.

David (Oct. 8): This pub metaphor is getting out of hand. I may have to move our seminar to a coffee house. Actually, the best times and most interesting discussions I ever had in college and grad school were in pubs and cafes, so I rather like the metaphor.

Len (Oct. 9): So do I. Here, have a beer.

It finally looked like the group was forming and relaxing, and class was now in session.

OVERVIEW

Many adults pursue formal education programs in spite of full-time employment, marriage, childrearing, and community activity. Some seek degrees, having only limited access to institutional resources because of remoteness or schedule conflicts. Or, perhaps they have had frustrating or humiliating classroom experiences that led them to seek education through different conventions. Perhaps their unique way of inquiry leads them to other modes of learning. Whatever the reasons, adult students have increasingly been attracted to adult-focused, independent degree programs that offer experiential credit and are delivered at a distance through telecommunications technologies.

This book explores the lives of a group of these adult students, their rationale for pursuing an independent study degree at a distance, and their perceptions of computer conferencing. It helps to fill a void about these issues in the literature on distance learning. I primarily used the qualitative research methods of unstructured interviews and participant observation to gather data and analyzed it from a symbolic interaction perspective. These methods, not commonly used in distance education research, reveal important aspects of this learning experience and the adult students—their lives and perceptions of the computer conferencing medium. The book explains their learning approaches with this new instructional environment and explores the nature of online polarities and relationships. The study fits this type of experience into the greater social context to explore the meaning of learning and living in an information technology age. Finally, the book presents a model of adult distance study through computer conferencing and discusses the implications of these research findings for distance education practice.

I set out to study adult students who were seeking their baccalaureate degree, concentrating on their involvement in a course on the Constitution, taught using computer conferencing. The university that offers this course, Hawks College,[1] located in the Northeastern United States, specializes in independent university degree programs for adult students. This upper division course required students to read three texts, watch a 13-part video series, write four papers, and contribute at least twice weekly to a computer conference on the Constitution.

With approval from Hawks, the professor, and nine students, I began observations and unstructured interviews near the beginning of the course in late September 1991. These sessions continued through February 1992, shortly after the course ended. I met in person with the three participants who lived within a 2-hour drive of my home; these three I actually watched access the computer conference and interact with the online session. The other six I interviewed by phone, some several times. I kept detailed notes, wrote personal reflections, and amassed relevant documents. Later, I pursued thematic fieldwork, following up with some of these students months later, and interviewed 11 students enrolled in summer session courses on telecommunications, ethical use of computers, and communications. A couple of these students had taken other online courses earlier on environmental issues and writing. Finally, I interviewed Hawks College personnel—a computer conferencing course instructor, the technical support person for these courses, and two advisors—to obtain their perspectives of this experience for these adult students and the role they play. In total I conducted 38 interviews and observation sessions.

This chapter sets the stage for the rest of the book by establishing a context within which it can be understood. To begin with, it describes the emergence of nontraditional higher education, using Hawks College as an example to explain programmatic initiatives that facilitate college study in adulthood. Second, it defines distance education and the salient attributes that distinguish the concept as used in this study. Third, it describes the emergence of distance courses that rely on computer conferencing for instructional delivery, looking at important definitional attributes, concepts, and terms. It traces its brief educational history, discusses its advantages and limitations, and portrays the educational promise writers ascribe to it. Finally, the chapter closes by addressing the overall theme of the book: alone but together.

---

[1]All names of individuals and institutions given in this book are pseudonyms, used to maintain the anonymity with which they consented to participate in the study.

EMERGENCE OF ADULT HIGHER EDUCATION

In the past three decades, adults[2] have increasingly replaced traditional age students at universities and colleges. Students over 25 years of age made up 39% of total enrollments in 1982 and an estimated 49% for 1992. Similar census figures show that 85% of adult students study part time (Apps, 1989).

Over the past century, evening schools typically accommodated the lifestyles and learning needs of adult students. However, universities and education agencies recognized the adult student growth trend in the late 1960s and 1970s and responded accordingly, either by establishing purpose-built nontraditional institutions, such as the British Open University and Nova University, or by developing nontraditional programs within existing institutions (Darkenwald & Merriam, 1982). Apps (1989, pp. 122-145) describes many of these programs and institutions. A mid-1970s survey found 300 nontraditional degree-granting institutions (Darkenwald & Merriam, 1982), but the number is now "indeterminate" (Hatfield, 1989, p. 309).

Nontraditional seems to be the favored term to describe these institutions and programs, with *universities without walls, adult-focused higher education, open universities,* and *external degree programs,* often being used synonymously, although these terms emphasize different features. What characterizes nontraditional education? Philosophically, it is the breaking down of barriers for adult learners and shifting the emphasis from how or where that learning took place to learner outcomes. Also, characteristics of these institutions include credit for prior learning, open entry and exit, individualized study, various administrative options, instructor variation, augmented resource access, and distance education (Apps, 1989; Darkenwald & Merriam, 1983; Hatfield, 1989; Rose, 1989).

Nontraditional Study at Hawks College

Hawks College manifests each of the elements of a nontraditional adult institution. Established in the early 1970s, Hawks is a well-known college aimed at accommodating the busy lifestyles of adult learners. It was one of the first U.S. nontraditional colleges to become fully accredited, and it is open to both state residents and out-of-state students (at

---

[2]Adult educators do not typically rely on age as the primary definitional characteristic of adulthood. They look more at social role characteristics instead (Darkenwald & Merriam, 1982). Age often predicts life-phase progression and is used her to show trends in higher education.

a higher cost). The College offers associate, bachelor's, and master's degrees. The master's is the only degree not available through distance study.

Hawks College consists of many offices scattered throughout the state. There are 1 to 5 full- and part-time faculty members at most of these units and some support staff. These unit offices are administered by eight centers, which have more faculty members, located in larger metropolitan areas. The headquarters is in Parnel Acres. Because the college sites are dispersed throughout the state, students may study at Hawks's facilities in all metropolitan areas and in many small towns, too.

Hawks's mission is to meet the needs of a diverse population of adult students through a wide variety of programs. It allows for easy entry, exit, and reentry into formal education as the individual feels the need for retooling and life-long learning. Goals of the college include:

- to increase access for those unable to study on a campus by providing other alternatives;
- to develop academic content responsive to individual purposes and emerging social needs; and
- to ensure program quality at reasonable cost.

Their philosophy is that college-level learning occurs at many places and times outside of the college classroom, and that education should be based on the individual's life, not on a traditional curriculum or institutional schedule.

During 1992 the average enrollment was 6,500 students. By 1994, Hawks had graduated over 24,000 students. Their attrition rate at 55% is comparable to other adult programs. Students range from 18 to 80 years old, but the typical student ranges from 35 to 45. The average student is 37, female (60%), employed, and has prior college experience (80%). Eighty-two percent study part time, given their other career, family, and community obligations.

Hawks College awards credit for college-level learning, often gained through experience, regardless of where those skills and knowledge were obtained. Besides accepting transfer credit from accredited institutions, Hawks evaluates students' learning from other settings and will award appropriate credit as that learning fits within each student's individual program of study. This may entail taking examinations such as College Level Examination Program (CLEP), submitting military or work transcripts of courses or certificates previously determined to be of college level, or demonstrating that learning through essays, products, and through interviews with a qualified evaluator.

Guided independent study is the mainstay of Hawks's instruction. Students work closely with a faculty advisor to develop their individual degree program in one of many broad areas of study such as business, human services, history, science, and the arts. This process of degree program planning, which also includes determining possible credits for prior learning, is the only required course at the college. Students work one on one with a faculty advisor to create this component and thereafter use mutually developed learning contracts to guide each semester's study until degree completion. This study is often done one on one with the advisor and other faculty in tutorial fashion.

However, Hawks also offers a wide range of instructional formats besides guided independent study with an advisor: group studies; study at a distance, including contact by mail, telephone, and computer conferencing; and cross-registration for traditional courses at area colleges. They may also draw on a full variety of resources in designing their learning contracts: textbooks, video- and audiotapes, computer tutorials, and integration of work or community experiences, such as learning from a corporate training program or internships with a social service agency.

Distance Education at Hawks College

Distance delivery systems, such as correspondence study and televised instruction, are common features of nontraditional study (Darkenwald & Merriam, 1982), increasing their accessibility to adult students. Ehrmann (1990) described various distance technologies and case studies that have "opened up the college" for greater access by adult students. Garrison (1989) further stated: "most distance learners do not have the luxury of choosing between distance and conventional methods. . . . For many would-be-learners, the choice is distance education or nothing" (p. 225). Students take distance education courses from the institution of enrollment, as well as other ones, as needed.

For those who cannot meet at Hawks College's dispersed facilities, Hawks offers a distance learning option—taking courses in one's residence by mail, phone, or computer conferencing, with interactive video by satellite added in 1992 to some locations. Their Distance Education Center (DEC) offers courses in most academic areas and several bachelor degrees. In 1992, DEC had 2,000 students enrolled, 40% of whom lived out of state, and some in foreign countries. Up to 16 credit hours of the distance degree can be individually tailored to meet the needs and resources of the distance student through independent study courses. Audio- and videocassettes increasingly supplement course texts and correspondence materials as the typical mode of study. Tutors telephone students several times during each term for increased interactivity.

Success of Hawks College

Controversial among conventional higher education providers, nontra-ditional higher education may be a passing fad or harbinger for the mainstream of the next decade (Apps, 1988). If trends in nontraditional study continue, the distinctions between these adult education univer-sities and traditional higher education providers will blur and disap-pear (Apps, 1989).

The enrollment at Hawks College has steadily increased since its inception, primarily from word-of-mouth advertising by satisfied stu-dents and alumni. When the College began operating, the completion rate of adult students at traditional schools was only 20%, but that rate has risen to roughly 45% for those studying at Hawks College. More than half of Hawks students who complete their bachelor's degree enroll in graduate programs, in which they compete well. Eighty-five percent remain in their same community after graduation. Fifty percent of the graduates feel that their employment has improved by obtaining a Hawks degree, through increased status, pay increases, job enhance-ment, and job satisfaction. One quarter were promoted at work or found a new job based on their degree.

Because this study investigated a distance education environ-ment, the next section defines distance education and notes other characteristics that lead to a better understanding of this phenomenon.

DISTANCE EDUCATION: DEFINING THE FIELD

The term *distance education* suggests that learning takes place within an institutional context, even though teacher and students are spatially separated. However, this concept has many more subtle dimensions that impinge on the adult distant learner's experience with computer conferencing.

Traditional Definitional Criteria

Rumble (1986) discusses at length various aspects of attempts to define distance education. Central to his analysis are Keegan's (1986) seven principle characteristics, derived from attempts of other scholars to define the field. The first four (discussed next) are most central and less controversial:

- Separation of teacher and student—the learner may be separated in space or in time, or by both (as in computer conferencing). Moore's (1989) conception of transactional distance (discussed later in Chapter 3) fits within this criterion, which Rumble stated is "perhaps the most fruitful use of the term 'distance'" (p. 7).
- Influence of an educational organization—as noted earlier, learning takes place under the auspices of an institution and is formal or informal in nature, not incidental.
- Use of technical media—because of the distance, instructional exchanges must be mediated, thereby making economies of scale possible. Most distance education takes place through mail correspondence based on texts and perhaps supplemented by audio, video, computer-assisted instruction packages, and even lab materials. Electronic distance media use audio, video, and computer conferencing (Barker, Frisbie, & Patrick, 1989).
- Provision of two-way communication—students as well as instructors must be able to initiate dialogue at any time during the instructional process. Instructional systems that are self-contained and one-way represent educational technology but not distance education (Rumble, 1986, p. 12).

Other Important Characteristics

Keegan's (1986) final three principles are debatable, yet still important, as discussed here:

- Absence of group learning, with students largely taught as individuals—traditional forms of distance education, using correspondence or broadcast media, fit nicely into this criterion, but new distance learning technologies, particularly audio and video teleconferencing seem to be defined by group instruction instead (Barker et al., 1989).
- Participation in the most industrialized form of education— Keegan (1986) analyzed this aspect of distance education proposed by Otto Peters, which has now "been moved outside of the definition proper" (p. 48). Features of an industrialized process are division of labor, mechanization, assembly line, mass production, standardization, and monopolization (Keegan, 1986).
- Independent learning—this simply mirrors the absence of the group learning characteristic, that is, that learners learn in private, away from others—a characteristic challenged by new media (Barker et al., 1989).

Interactivity has also been proposed as an important dimension in understanding distance education, particularly in light of new distance education technologies (Barker et al., 1989; Moore, 1989). Chapter 3 discusses this dimension further.

Distance education, as used throughout this study, relies most heavily on the first four of Keegan's (1986) characteristics: (a) separation of teacher and student, (b) influence of an educational organization, (c) use of technical media, and (d) provision of two-way communication. It assumes some characteristics of industrialized processes,[3] but this attribute is not incorporated into the definition. Independent learning and lack of group study must be rejected because they are defied by the very nature of computer conferencing, as explained later. Interactivity remains an important feature of the new communications technologies, such as computer conferencing. However, it is not a definitional attribute of distance education.

But why do students engage in distance study? Usually adult commitments to work and/or family preclude them from traveling to campus and engaging in full-time study. Shift work, erratic schedules, or extensive travel—the characteristics of many jobs—make distance study attractive, indeed for many the only option available for obtaining a college education. Others may choose this more isolated form of study to avoid traditional classroom experiences in which they may not seem to fit. Enhanced media, interactivity, and exchange with other distance students improve the study experience for those engaged in this demanding and sometimes solitary form of education.

A NEW MEDIUM: COMPUTER CONFERENCING

Definition and Characteristics

Computer conferencing can be defined from both a technical and behavioral standpoint. From a computer standpoint, it refers to a type of networked mainframe software that facilitates structured asynchronous communications, accessed by a terminal or personal computer with a modem. As a social phenomena, it refers to a group of people who engage in communication, learning, or decision making, mediated by a computer network application. From either perspective, computer conferencing shares several key features, outlined by several authors (Eastmond, 1992; Florini, 1989; Harasim, 1990b; Hiltz, 1986), as follows:

---

[3]Possibly newer distance education technologies share more features with the emergent information age of developed nations than they do with industrial processes.

- asynchronicity—the ability for participants to be involved in the same online conversations at different times.
- structured communications—the computer software keeps multiple, concurrent discussions separate and provides participants with several means for engaging in select conversations.
- multiple sites—those involved in the computer conference may participate from many locations, sometimes worldwide, depending on site access to networked computer resources.
- interactivity—the online communication is continually shaped and depends on the input and feedback of its multiple participants.
- text-based environment—current mainframe computer systems, which permit distance and easy dial-up access, only allow conferencing systems to accept and display text.[4]
- group involvement—computer conferencing systems allow private, individual electronic message exchanges, but most communication takes place in larger, group discussion areas where each member can read and respond to each communiqué.

Online classes and *electronic seminars* are usually used synonymously with "computer conferencing," whereas *computer-mediated communications* or *electronic discussions* are typically used in a broader sense to denote any form of computer-networked conversation.

Computer conferencing shares characteristics with several other computer-based communication and information exchange technologies—computer-assisted instruction (CAI), electronic mail, network discussion groups, and bulletin board systems—yet it holds important distinctions. Unlike CAI, computer conferencing information is not preprogrammed, and it allows for deeper and shared group activity. Likewise, computer conferencing involves a circumscribed group and a structured conversational environment, unlike electronic mail in which exchanges take place between individuals in an open-ended personal environment. Network discussion groups—those handled by listserves—differ from computer conferencing because they distribute unstructured messages outward to individual users situated on multiple systems, who must sort and file these discussions themselves. Bulletin board systems, like Usenets, come closest to computer conferencing systems, but they are generally restrictive in the users' capability to form new discussion areas, and they are available publicly and not to private groups.

---

[4]Newer "desktop" conferencing technologies, which require special personal computer equipment and/or network connections, incorporate motion and still video, graphics, and audio besides text. These systems are expected to burgeon in the near future.

Computer conferencing systems often contain these features that facilitate group conversational activities:

- Branching—the capability to have subtopical discussions emerge and continue simultaneously with those of the main topic.
- Threading—the capability to keep an electronic audit trail of how current messages relate to past ones.
- Profiling—the capability for users to see the conference structure, participation, and contribution levels and obtain biographical information about other users.
- Review—participants can reread entire conversations by topic and private message exchanges, sometimes being able to modify and restructure these as well.
- Powers—different privilege levels can be given to categories of users, for example, some can only read certain topics, delete or modify messages, see survey responses, and so forth.

History

Several factors converged to make computer conferencing a viable distance education alternative. First, corporations, universities, and governments linked their mainframe computers into networks that extend across the globe. Also, the personal computer proliferated within home and office environments, making larger computer applications available through an inexpensive extension—the modem and a telephone line. Finally, telephone networks dedicated to electronic information exchange and access are becoming increasingly available and widespread. These developments make such activities as database searching, online discussion groups, electronic mail, and file transfers inexpensive and increasingly available to individuals located throughout the world.

The instructor for one of the courses I studied, Dave Engles, was instrumental in bringing computer conferencing to Hawks College. He described its genesis:

> The start was actually almost accidental. I guess it was about 1987 roughly, when the college was asked to be a beta-test site for the new conferencing software this company had just produced, CONFER.[5] So they loaded in CONFER 3.0 and got it on the system, and it just sat there.

---

[5]The brand name, CONFER, which is used to indicate the computer conferencing software in use by Hawks College, is also fictitious and does not refer to any actual or potential system that may use this name.

And, it happened one day in the middle of the lunch I was having with the user-support person. He was playing around with it, describing it to me, and I thought, "This could have some potential, . . ." A couple of folks down at the computer center were playing around with it and it was kind of fun. So, I decided to try it out, and I got online. There were only about five or six people involved at the time at the college, and mostly they were just the "techies."

Somebody (I'm not sure who now) said, "It is a shame that you can't think of how to use this thing productively." And it came to me as almost an intuitive thing at the time. I thought how this might be used for an electronic seminar; it fit the instructional mode I was thinking in at the time. . . . Anyway, I was teaching an American Diplomacy course in the spring, and I thought, "I'll take it on-line!". . .

So, that is how it all got started, almost by accident. And, in the two months in which I had to get ready, I tried to find out who else in the world had done this kind of thing, and literally couldn't find anyone in this country who had. I found some people elsewhere, Robin Mason at the British Open University and Morten Paulsen in Norway, who were doing it. But, at that time, these people had really just done what I was planning to do—just tried it out.

I really couldn't find anyone to show me how, so I was able to just discover things that would work on my own. . . . Since then I've found several people who have taught classes using computer conferencing, and when we compare dates, we find that we all started at about the same time. The technology was ready and apparent, and a lot of people tried it out at the same time. . . .We were on a panel at a conference at the University of Maine when this occurred to us. We started asking when each of us got started, and it was 1987. That is when it sort of hit me that there was this independent flowering in the area all at the same time. But, within a year, there was a lot of interest growing and a lot of conversations about what was going on. You would start to go to conferences, thinking that you would be the only one, and then there were five or six sessions all on computer conferencing.

His story appears to mirror the history Harasim (1991) outlined of computer conferencing, especially for education. Although developed in 1971, it was not used for instruction until a decade later. Major initiatives began in the mid- to late 1980s, and by the early 1990s, computer conferencing had been adopted by many colleges and universities. Eastmond (1992) lists three universities that operate entire degree programs through this instructional delivery system; Kaye, Mason, and Harasim (1989) provide major case studies of computer conference use by academic organizations, and a recent monograph lists over 200 organizations that are involved in computer-mediated communications for education (Wells, 1992). Kaye (1992b) discusses how computer communications are used for education—for virtual seminars, for online classrooms, for games and communications, for writing and language labs, for supporting multimedia distance education initiatives, or for an adjunct activity or resource to the typical lecture classroom.

Academic writing related to computer network use for education proliferated during this same time period. Journal articles appear from 1984, and three edited texts about the use of computer conferencing for education extend from 1989 (Harasim, 1990c; Kaye, 1992a; Mason & Kaye, 1989). Three bibliographies are available on the use of computer-mediated communications for education (Burge, 1992; Harasim, 1990a; Romiszowski, 1992); the most recent (Burge, 1992) lists approximately 385 references. What is evident is the rapid proliferation of computer conferencing use in various ways within education and the simultaneous burgeoning of scholarship around this phenomena, all within the last decade.

Advantages and Limitations

Using computer conferencing for education presents some pragmatic advantages over some other distance education media. Along with affording heightened interactivity, a crucial characteristic of electronic communications technologies (Barker et al., 1989), it does so at minimal expense. First, costs for operating computer conferencing are lower because it "piggy-backs" onto mainframe computers, networks, and personal computers that institutions and individuals have anyway, thus adding further value to these investments. There are no studio, classroom, or exorbitant equipment costs needed exclusively for this technology. Second, it represents a continually available instructional environment, one that learners can access at their own convenience, day or night, seven days a week. Third, computer conference systems can be accessible to students on campus or from as far as continents away.

There are instructional advantages for using computer conferencing as well. Harasim (1989) listed several of these—computer conferencing provides an "augmented environment for collaborative learning and teaching" (p. 60) because it is uniquely suited for group activities—seminars, working groups, learning partnerships, and debates. Active learning is another key advantage—by its very nature the online communications milieu promotes learner contributions. Another instructional factor she found is interactive learning—it provides more information exchange than a regular classroom in complex and nonlinear patterns. Also, computer conferencing brings a more equitable distribution of communication, she observed, because everyone has an equal opportunity to express themselves, and no one can easily dominate the conversation. Mason (1988) sees computer conferencing as promoting self-direction by encouraging greater learner autonomy. Later, Harasim (1990b) added that computer conferencing amplifies intellectual development by supporting divergent thinking through idea-generating activities. Other authors express many of these same themes (Davie, 1989; Florini, 1989, 1990; Hiltz, 1986).

However, these same scholars also mention drawbacks to computer conferencing. Hiltz (1986) was concerned that this environment is less personable because the nuances of socioemotional exchange are removed and students may feel socially awkward in communicating. Some difficulties Harasim (1987) reported students having were informational overload, asynchronicity, inconvenience of increased access following multiple, concurrent discussions, and the loss of visual cues. To these Davie (1989) added difficulties in using hardware and software, navigating one's way through the conversational environment with only a small screen with which to view it, timed-delayed exchanges leading to disjointed transactions and poorly referenced communiqués, and participation based on concern about one's written communications and typing ability. Mason (1988) expressed concern that nonparticipant "lurkers" and dominant personalities may present special problems. The text-only environment may not be appropriate to visually oriented subject matter, such as that found in the arts, math, and science (Florini, 1990). Also, Harasim (1990b) found the medium lacking in its support of the intellectual activities of idea linking and idea structuring—convergent thinking processes that future software enhancements through hypertext and hypermedia will make possible in computer conferencing.

Educational Promise

Despite the disadvantages just mentioned, the tone of the computer conferencing literature seems optimistic: Improved instructor facilitation, technical support, student training, and instructional design will overcome the limitations of computer conferencing-based instructional systems. Harasim (1989) proclaimed:

> On-line education is more than a new delivery mode. It is a new learning domain which enables us as educators and as learners to engage in learning interactions more easily, more often and perhaps more effec-

tively, but also to develop qualitatively new and different forms of educational interactions. If we approach this new domain from old mindsets . . . we may be applying metaphors that are not only limiting as a perspective but perhaps even misleading (p. 62).

These views of computer conferencing—its characteristics, advantages, and limitations—are expressed by innovative educators, usually from reflection on their own experience implementing and teaching through this medium, and are rarely based on research. They often represent the efforts of instructors seeking to develop successful learning experiences by experimenting with and thinking about computer conferencing courses and are barely informed by the expressed perceptions of actual distance students.

ALONE BUT TOGETHER

A lot of [the Constitution course members'] closing thoughts were how wonderful it was to use the computer because they were no longer alone. They felt this connection with other students, and they liked being able to talk back and forth and get different perspectives. And I think that's true for a lot of the Distance Education Center courses. You're usually on your own. You work with an instructor, and there may be other people taking the course, but you just have no contact with them. The only ideas you hear about the course are your own, with maybe a few comments from the tutor. This use of the computer conferencing is a nice way to bounce ideas off other people.—Kerry Jones (January 16, 1992)

This book studies adult college students involved in obtaining degrees through distance education, focusing on their computer conferencing experience. From fieldwork I discovered a variety of individuals pursuing degrees for personal and professional reasons and choosing the distance education option because of its convenience, its fit with their preferred learning style, or its ability to allow for selective anonymity during learning. I discovered them interacting and processing information in many different ways and questioned them about their learning approaches. Rich opinions emerged about their experience with computer conferencing and the purpose of education in their lives. They also provided insights into the formation of online relationships for collaborative learning.

I found these students alone but together, whether focusing on their personal and professional lives, their perceptions of computer conferencing, the means by which they came to learning in the online environment, or the relations they had with others in their course. Given Hawks's approach to adult education—one-on-one tutoring in independent study or the structured course taking of distance study— these students formerly had little contact with other students at their same institution. Their educational experience was individualized, as they could customize a degree program uniquely tailored to their interests, background, needs, and skills. Most of them had developed a personal portfolio to evidence prior college-level learning for which they received credit. Occasionally, some had met with other students in tutored study, and many spoke of feeling out of place in the few traditional college courses they had taken. Their primary relationship with Hawks College, particularly those who were solely distance students, had been with an advisor by telephone or through written feedback in their correspondence study—primarily a solitary experience. Computer conferencing came into these peoples' lives and serendipitously presented new possibilities to study with other student peers and to see their course instructor in a new light as he or she interacted with the other students online. For some, this brought the social advantage of being able to meet other students and explore common interests, backgrounds, and vocational aspirations. It made it possible to feel more a part of Hawks College, as an institution, by sharing that identity and peculiar study mode with other students similarly engaged.

Moreover, the connectedness of computer conferencing presented new learning possibilities for collaboration and group learning in an entirely new instructional format. The online environment brought opportunities to share intellectual insights and receive specific and in-depth feedback from others in a relatively nonthreatening environment. Students could interact with each other and the instructor in a setting in which immediate, physical presence did not enter into the construction of their contributions. Students in traditional college campuses come together as part of their study activities but are separated throughout the course as they continue the work of reading texts, fulfilling assignments, or carrying out projects. Being alone in distance study is qualitatively different, as is coming together in an electronic seminar—themes to be discussed in the chapters ahead.

2

The Distance Students

The whole reason I started back to school was because I got laid off at my job. I mean, I realized that I really had no employable skills, no trade that I could do. So, I needed to get a degree to be prepared for bad times again.—Craig Brooks

This chapter begins by explaining how qualitative studies, such as this one, can provide rich insights into distance students; the predilection of researchers who study distance education has been to use quantitative measures. Next, it presents a typology of these distance students, based on their educational orientation, and provides a rich description of the 20 students involved in this study, placing meat on the skeletal understanding given in the literature on distance learners. Then it provides insights into the shared characteristics, educational aims, and individual outlooks they hold about their adult college degree pursuits. Finally, this chapter presents related scholarship about distance students, especially those using computer conferencing. My hope is that by presenting some of the dynamics of each individual's career, lifestyle, and educational outlook, their lives will be seen as personal, independent pursuits, although they share features with other distance learners.

DIFFICULTIES IN CONDUCTING RESEARCH
ABOUT DISTANCE STUDENTS

One of the difficulties institutions that offer distance education courses have is obtaining a thorough, in-depth understanding of their individual clientele needs. Granger (1990a) stated:

> Personal factors such as background and learning styles, prior learning and experience, students' expectations, skills [sic] levels and motivation can vary widely in significance. For the most part, however, these are known by distance faculty almost intuitively at the level of "what might work" or "what to look out for." (p. 165).

By its very nature, these units are physically separated from those they serve, and their interactions with them are mediated—either by letter, telephone, or computer network. Ralph, a distance student who was asked to be on a special committee, spoke of visiting the Distance Education Center:

> I get up there and walk into the building and there's a lady at the copier in the hallway, and I'm looking kind of perplexed and, she says "You must be the student." I said "The student? Oh yeah." . . . And I was fussed over. It was kind of like being a foreigner. They don't ever see their students. It was quite interesting being the student and everybody taking this interest in me. It was kind of funny to me, yet enjoyable to be honest, the attention. I met David then, and we took a liking to each other. We've got a good relationship going. But it was just an odd thing. "You must be THE STUDENT" in big capital letters. I can see it coming out of her mouth. [both laugh]

The time and space separation involved in studying distance education students inclines researchers to favor quantitative measures—contacting hundreds of learners with a questionnaire or similar instrument using the mail system. It is difficult to travel to students' homes or work sites or have telephone discussions with them in probing, unstructured interviews (Morgan, 1984). The strength of quantitative approaches is that they can indicate the extent of some phenomena or attitude, but their drawback is that they seek to reduce personalities, relationships, and outlooks into a numerical analysis and predefined categories, without capturing the richness of what is going on in the setting.

"Studies adopting qualitative methodologies are under-represented in distance education," wrote Morgan (1984, p. 255). The following findings about the distance students in this study work to alleviate that concern.

TYPES OF DEGREE SEEKERS

Qualitative studies at the British Open University found "orientation" a more holistic concept to describe educational pursuit than the common psychological construct of "motivation." They defined it as "the collection of attitudes, aims, and purposes that express a students' relationship with a course and the university or college" (Morgan, 1984, p. 259). Although regular students had four orientations—vocational, academic, personal, and social—distance students only exhibited the first three. In conventional forms of distance education, group association was not possible, so adults seeking education for social reasons chose other learning formats (Morgan, 1984). Houle (1961) had previously used qualitative methods to discover three motivational orientation types of adults that were quite similar: goal-oriented, activity-oriented, and learning-oriented learners.

In examining the things these students told me about themselves and their lives, general patterns of orientation emerged. I developed a typology based on the reasons they gave me for becoming engaged in this degree quest at this phase of their lives (see Figure 2.1).

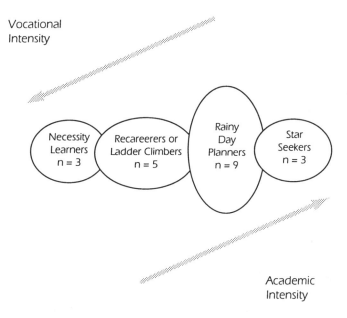

Figure 2.1. Adult student orientation to learning

Students in three of these categories—"necessity learners," "recareer or ladder climbers," and "rainy day planners"—all have career development as their orientation, with varying levels of vocational intensity. The "star seekers" are the small group of students I encountered with personal or academic orientations. Just like Morgan (1984), I found no one engaged in their education simply for social reasons, which was not surprising because those involved in distance study usually anticipate working in a personalized fashion (Keegan, 1986). Be aware that although I sought to place these learners in the categories of "best fit," individuals may share views with those in adjacent categories.

Necessity Learners

Those I have labeled "necessity learners" need to get their degrees in order to keep their position, advance further in management, or find a new job. Three of the students—Lyn Vaughn, Carl Winer, and Rick Turner—fall within this category.

Lyn Vaughn

Perhaps Lyn Vaughn best exemplifies a "necessity learner." Lyn was one of the few people I interviewed in person; I first met her in her office, a couple hours drive from my home. She is a bursar for a small community college. The following paragraphs from my fieldnotes capture some of her middle-class lifestyle:

> I had no difficulty finding the administration building once I arrived at the campus. It was small by university standards, but the people wandering the halls at 4:45 PM seemed about the same. There were young college students and older adults. . . . After getting some more directions, I finally found the door to her work area. It had a big sign on it saying, "Only Authorized Persons." I knocked, and a woman in her 30s, casually dressed, came to the door. I told her I had come to see Lyn Vaughn. She asked my name, propped the door open (but didn't motion for me to enter so I waited), while she went to get her. Presently she returned with an older woman. "Hello, Lyn Vaughn?" I asked. "Yes, you must be Dan Eastmond," she said smiling.
>
> She stepped forward and shook my hand. Lyn must be in her 50s. She was of average height, but slightly overweight. Her hair was completely gray, but her skin was still quite smooth and she looked young. She was wearing makeup and jewelry, but was wearing an oversized blue sweater, slacks, and shoes that looked less casual.

She escorted me past desks of women, sorting papers, chatting, and looking like they were getting ready to close up shop for the weekend. Whereas their work area was open, her office was enclosed, adjoining theirs, with the door open. It looked comfortable, fairly spacious, and clear of clutter (i.e., the desk was entirely clean, and papers weren't hanging out of folders and books in the one or two bookcase/files in the room.) An IBM PS/2 personal computer was central to the desk. The screen displayed a spreadsheet, possibly Lotus 1-2-3.

She explained her casual dress that day at work; their office had been doing some cleaning and moving. She led me in a white minivan to her home. It was situated in a tidy, modest neighborhood on the outskirts of town. After meeting her husband, a communications specialist, and her 10-year-old son, she told me about their family.

Her daughter recently got married, a wedding that impacted the family savings. She had considered recording the "Constitution" course's videotapes by connecting their VCR with the video camera they had purchased to photograph the wedding, but then decided it was too much bother. She keeps all of the family finances, and her husband does the cooking. She was a leader for her son's Cub Scout unit and was quite involved in the parent- teacher association of his school.

Lyn told me frankly that she had been told by the college where she worked that if she did not get her degree, she would lose her job, and they were giving her three years to do it. However, she had budgeted her time carefully, assumed an extra couple of classes a semester, and was keeping to a schedule that allowed her to finish in two years. She told me that although she does bursar work, the college gives her a lesser title so they can get by with paying her less.

Given all the demands on her time, she chose to do all of her degree through distance education. She works a regular 8 to 5 day and values her evening family time, so she opted for a format in which she would not have to spend her evenings tied up in class. She does most of her studying between 3:00 and 7:00 AM before her day starts, taking a short nap after work to compensate for lost sleep time.

She did not consider going to college after high school—the family needed her income—so she started out as an insurance auditor and has been working in progressively higher levels of accounting ever since.

Carl Winer

At 36 years old, Carl works as a general store manager of a supermarket where he puts in 50 hours a week. Add to that a 15-hour-a-week commute, parenting five children, and the 16-credit-hour course load he was taking the summer semester I interviewed him, and he appeared to be the busiest student I studied. His wife works during the day at a Monday to Friday bookkeeping job, whereas his schedule fluctuates throughout the week, making it difficult to take any regularly scheduled classes.

Carl's employer provided the incentive for his return to college:

> I never had a real push to do it [get a degree] because I was progressing through my career; I was still being promoted; I was still moving upward into fields and areas that I wanted to go into, and that kind of stuff. So, not having a degree was not holding me back from achieving anything. I continued to move forward. But, as late, what has happened is my company has taken the position that if you don't have your bachelor's degree, I am not able to move to the next level. They told me quite frankly that they wanted to put me in those positions, but I don't have a degree, so that is that. So, that is a big motivating factor.

The company also reimburses the cost of his degree, which he says helps.

Before he started at Hawks College, he tried taking a couple of classes through the years but had been so busy and tired then that he confessed getting little out of them. He considers himself a naturally good student, getting high marks throughout high school; nevertheless, he enrolled in basic reading and writing courses when he returned to school.

He feels that he now has some time and seniority to tackle his education, plus a very supportive wife, and older kids who can watch themselves and the youngest child in the evenings so he can study. The degree he has planned for himself has an emphasis on human resource development and psychology; with it he hopes the company will move him into training or labor relations.

Rick Turner

Rick is the director of data processing for a large department store chain, but that is changing:

> After 64 years the company went out of business unfortunately, so I'm in the process of looking for another job, soon to be unemployed. In my last class I made the statement that it took me and my family 26 years to earn a decent living, and now I'm going to become a college graduate, and I'm going to be unemployed [both laugh]. But I hope it doesn't last too long.

Rick sees the degree as enhancing his chances of finding a new position.

He started college at age 21, going full time for a year in California and taking classes during the day in New Jersey when he worked nights. But eventually he quit. His wife was the person who discovered Hawks College and convinced him to pursue it because the program fit him. He is on the board of his condo unit, has an 11-year-old daughter, and a cat. He is getting a management degree with a minor in computer science.

Recareerers or Ladder Climbers

Those I have labeled "recareerers/ladder climbers" do not have the same external necessity to complete their education, but these individuals were ambitiously achieving specific career ends and viewed education as an integral, enabling component for realizing those dreams. Of the five students, three were climbing career ladders (Kerry Jones, Ralph Briar, Miguel Lopez), and the other two were beginning in second careers (Harry Schwartz, Judy Wells).

Kerry Jones

Kerry is a good example of a "ladder climber." At 23 years old, he works as a bookkeeper/accountant in his town's governmental office. I was able to meet Kerry face to face; he lives in a rural community about a two-hour drive from my home. My fieldnotes tell of this visit:

> We agreed to meet at the combination ice cream, convenience store, and gas station in town. As he gave me fairly elaborate directions on how to get to Grantsville, I asked him if the store would be hard to find; he said, "No, it is at the only intersection with a traffic light in the town," and besides it was on the main highway. . . .
>
> It was dark by the time I arrived in Grantsville. . . . Because I was 15 minutes early, I decided to drive about town, after I had located our rendezvous point. It was very small; I guessed that the population was between 500 and 3,000. The main street was lined with a mix of storefronts and homes, mostly two-story. There were several restaurants, a liquor store, a small hotel, signs for a nursing home, and an elementary school (off the main drag). Near the center of town the homes were close together, lights beaming through windows, and the homes had larger yards surrounding them as you moved out of town. I only saw two sets of people out walking about (but it was a cold night). Everyone I saw and met on this visit was white (European-American).

I drove to the convenience store, parked, and walked into the store to await Kerry's arrival. As I came in, the store employee was talking to two college-age girls sitting at a booth who were laughing and chatting away over some milkshakes. Also, leaning against the counter and chatting with them was a rather tall, tubby fellow of the same age, dressed in blue sweat pants, and wearing a light-weight red plaid jacket. He was clean-shaven and had straight hair of conservative length parted to one side, similar to the way I wear my own. "This must be Kerry," I thought to myself, so I asked him, "Are you Kerry Jones?" He said, "Yes, you must be Dan Eastmond." He said an abrupt good-bye to his friends and we stepped outside.

Because he had walked from his nearby home, we got into my car to drive to the county office building, just a few blocks away. . . . When we arrived at the county building, he directed me to park up close in the assistant clerk's reserved spot. [I sensed he took pride in showing me his position.] The building was a converted Victorian mansion. We entered in the front door. . . . From there he led me to a back room and announced that this was the police office.

Kerry used the police chief's computer system for the online course. The police chief was observing his experience with this distance technology because he was also considering taking a course this way. Kerry read his texts at home and would watch the course videos late at night, as it bored the rest of the family.

Kerry took typing courses in high school and uses a computer at work a great deal, so it was easy for him to work online. He earned two associate degrees (one in accounting) at a community college, located about a 45-minute drive away. His ancestors immigrated from Lithuania, and he dabbles in family genealogy and oral history of the community in his free time.

Because Kerry ultimately wants to get his doctorate and teach political science at the college level, this distance course fit his vocational plans. However, he admitted that he took it partially because he was intrigued with the technology involved. The political science bachelor's degree he is now seeking will not help him in his current job but is an important step toward that ultimate goal.

Ralph Briar

Ralph Briar is young at 34 to be the deputy fire chief (second in command) for a large city; he worked his way up through the ranks there over the past 12 years. Married without children, both he and his spouse, a nurse, work regular day shifts. He earned an applied science associate degree in fire protection in three years right after high school and worked for a short time as a fire instructor, as well. As a rising star in the department, he aims to have a masters of public administration (MPA) degree upon retirement age in eight years so he can either stay on with the department (possibly as fire chief) or go into law or teaching. The generalist bachelor's degree he is currently working on emphasizes business and fire administration, so he can get tuition reimbursement.

Miguel Lopez

An immigrant from Argentina, Miguel manages the financial computer system for a business supply company located in a large metropolitan area. He is 31 years of age, married without children. He took five years of engineering courses before coming to the United States, and he took several English as a Second Language (ESL) courses at the community college before enrolling at Hawks, where he is getting a bachelor's degree in computer science. He expressed concern about the acceptance of a nontraditional degree but finds this is the only way he can pursue an education, given his busy work life and financial obligations. Although an avid computer network hobbyist, he must take most of his courses in tutorial format for lack of an advanced computer science curriculum in a distance education mode. Miguel wants to continue on for his doctorate and teach computer science at a university but is unsure how to pursue that dream through nontraditional education.

Harry Schwartz

A former professional guitarist for 20 years, Harry made a career change several years ago to work in bookkeeping at a national medical insurance company. He went to the Berkeley School of Music (in Boston, MA) just after high school for several years "until the money ran out." Now 38 years old, he started an accounting degree at Hawks College in 1988 and has been going part time ever since. He hopes to eventually move up into a more responsible managerial accounting position within his company or become a CPA with an accounting firm. His wife works as a receptionist/light accountant in an office of a major soft drink firm and also goes to school part time. They own their home, have children aged 13, 9, and 5, and the family is so busy that they rarely have meals together. He teaches guitar and still toys around with music on the side.

Judy Wells

> I decided to pursue [a Hawks degree] because it was at this
> point I had decided that I wanted to go to law school because
> it met all of my criteria which was I wanted a situation, skill, that
> I could take with me wherever I went, that I had something
> that would put me in greater economic control, abilities,
> power. And, I know there are a zillion lawyers out there, but
> with the background I have in real estate, and now the experi-
> ence of working in a law firm, when I finish it, I don't think I will
> have any problem in getting a job. Because, I have five years in
> real estate, and two years now but four years when I graduate
> of actual work experience in a law firm. The person I replaced
> who left was a lawyer.

Five years ago, at 32 years of age, Judy made a complete career change—going from a professional theater career with lots of travel to being a real estate agent. Since then she picked up a paralegal certificate while working full time, and she was recently hired at a law firm. This demanding job requires her to work 12-hour days, and although her job remains her first priority, her Hawks education remains a close second, enabling the ultimate career advancement she desires. Judy describes herself as a "take charge and control" type of person, one who can prove herself capable. She considers herself an ultra-liberal feminist, combating sexism in the workplace and in her studies. She dropped the Constitution course, her first (and last) distance education course, near the end of it, resolved that learning at a distance was not for her. However, afterward she continued to ardently pursue her degree through other instructional formats.

Rainy Day Planners

The "rainy day planners" have vocational reasons for pursuing their degrees, but they were gaining the credentials primarily to leverage them into a new career only if their current employment did not work out. The degree represents a "rainy day" insurance policy to use against a major career change sometime in the more distant future. The actual purpose to which they will put the degree seems less apparent (although they do have plans), and I did not get the sense that they thought they would move ahead in their current job if they had a degree. There were nine persons whom I placed in this category: Craig Brooks, Ted Gardener, Francis Jershon, Jack Last, Kris Barker, Melody Cook, Rose Miller, Len Parker, and Randy Fox.

Craig Brooks

Craig, age 39, works the swing shift at a psychiatric center as a security guard. He formerly worked in corrections and law enforcement, until he was laid off—the impetus for his return to school. Craig escorted me to his home, where he does most of his studies from his desk, which dominates the basement. These fieldnotes capture my first impressions:

> He told me it would take him 10 minutes to get [to the pay phone I was calling from] and to be on the "look out" for a 1960s Volkswagen van with a racing boat on the top.
>
> Sure enough, the van shortly appeared thereafter, and Craig stepped out to introduce himself. We sort of awkwardly shook hands and said, "Hello." He is a normal height, European-American male, on the slender side, though he appeared quite muscular and fit. He was wearing a T-shirt with a canoe race inscribed on it, faded but clean jeans, and tennis shoes. His hair was originally a dark brown, but was now graying. He had a mustache. I noticed his teeth—slightly yellow and possibly having had some work done on them. I don't think he was wearing a belt. I was more formally dressed in a dress shirt, slacks, and shoes; I apologized, explaining that I had come directly from a meeting.
>
> I mentioned that the canoe looked a lot like the ones folks use in triathlons. He said, yes it was. Craig had been a racer of just canoes for several years, but because of his smoking habit, he didn't compete anymore. But, his brother does race, and since he is a good runner and cycler, he has been able to place in the top three places nationally in many triathlon competitions. I was impressed.
>
> The parking lot conversation was that brief, as he invited me to follow his car. It seemed that he took me all over town getting there—through downtown (not much for this small town of 30-40,000 people), by some manufacturing, across the railroad tracks, through a residential neighborhood and local shops, churches, and a supermarket. The neighborhoods were tidy with landscaping, but with small homes. I'd say they were working and middle class. There were both European- and African-Americans present. Then, he steered me up a gradual hill on a road that appeared to lead out into the country. Several blocks later we pulled up into a steep, dirt driveway up beside a moderate sized home in a wooded, large lot.
>
> He led me into the house by the back door. The first room was like an enclosed patio with wood stacked for building projects. Craig said that he was doing lots of handiwork projects

before he started on this degree program. We entered into the main house area onto a split-level landing. He led me up another short flight into the living room. I saw a couch, stuffed chairs, and a large TV/VCR "home entertainment" center there.

Craig's wife works days at a nursing home, and his three children, aged 14, 11, and 3, are all in school or child care when he does his studying in the mornings and early afternoons. It takes both of their incomes to make house payments and keep the household running. He sees the family primarily on his days off. Craig also studies at work, against agency policy, but has never been officially reprimanded for it, although he feels it causes jealousy among the other workers. He is majoring in political science and business and hopes to go on for a master's degree, especially one offered by distance education. His exact career aims seemed unclear, but he has this hope:

> I worked in corrections and in law enforcement. I mean I don't like the job but that's all I could get. Hopefully this education will bring a lot of opportunities.

Ted Gardener

Ted, in his early 30s, works with Craig on the evening security shift of the psychiatric center. They enrolled at Hawks at about the same time:

> Ted: We work the evening shift and that's when most of your part-time classes are given. So that's why we opted for Hawks, so we could set the hours.
>
> Dan: It sounds like it was kind of a joint decision to do this. Did you put Craig onto it, or did he put you onto it?
>
> Ted: Well, I went to Hawks before but I didn't enroll. I just went to talk to the people there. I forget why I didn't enroll. Something else came up, and I didn't enroll then. Then Craig said he was going to one of the sessions, and I went with him, and that's when we both decided to enroll. For the most part it's been a positive experience. I've really enjoyed it because its not really school oriented, its individual oriented; its what you want to learn.

Ted's wife works days as a counselor in mental health or Catholic Charities; with his evening schedule, they can each cover the child care of their 4-year-old son during the other's work shift. Distance courses allow him to stay at home and provide child care, but next year when their son enters kindergarten, Ted plans to take most of his classes through the tutorial mode. He is concerned that civil service work like his is not very stable, so he is majoring in political science with a third-world emphasis so he will have other employment options if he is laid off, possibly as secondary school teacher or economic development specialist. Ted endured the computer conferencing course but shipped his modem right back as soon as it ended.

Francis Jershon

> Francis: My job is working as a school bus driver. You work really weird hours. You start, like this year my beginning road time is 6:30 a.m., but that is not the earliest road time. And you don't come off of the road until anywhere between 4 and 4:30, with break time in-between.
>
> Dan: I have always wondered in-between what bus drivers do.
>
> Francis: Well, sometimes they do nothing [laughs]. And sometimes they do the stuff people do at night, like by the time you have finished dinner, it is almost time to go to bed, you know. So, that is my schedule. It is more erratic than, say, an office worker's schedule.

Francis, age 46, became a widow this past year, but her entry into Hawks College, after a 26-year hiatus since high school, predates that event. She just completed her associate degree with Hawks College. She lives with her two daughters, 13 and 18 years old, in a modest home. She chose Hawks College because its various study formats allowed her to work on her schooling between bus runs and to be at home most evenings. Her daughters were initially excited by her being able to use computer networks for her study, until they realized that it occupied their single phone for hours at a time, so that has been a source of friction regarding her online course. Her bachelor's degree is a mixture of psychology and writing; she would like to work in human resources, counseling drug users and alcoholics.

Jack Last

Jack lives the closest to me, and he was the first student I interviewed:

> I pulled up to his house, a fairly nice one on a country road with a big yard. It appeared that they were doing some work on the driveway or entrance to the house. He met me at the door, and we introduced ourselves. He appeared to be of nor-

mal height and build for his age, which I guessed to be about 33 years old. His hairline was receding, he wore wire-rim glasses, and his hair was jet black. He was casually attired, as was I. His demeanor was friendly, softer spoken, outgoing, but task-directed. From there he ushered me into the kitchen through a well-kept house which had a family feel to it, given the pictures, library books, and homey ornaments which decorated the rooms. A stereo was softly blaring jazzy pop music in the other room.

Jack works as a machinist at a large manufacturing plant. When he was laid off for a brief period about six years ago, he determined that he would gain a university degree to have employable skills, should that happen again. He took classes at various local colleges as well as distance courses from several institutions, transferring them to or incorporating them within his Hawks College study program. He was in the last semester of his degree program when we met.

Kris Barker

Kris, age 40, works as a personnel specialist for a family service agency in a medium-size city of a western state. She is married with two sons, aged 7 and 11, and they are living in a new home they had just built in the suburbs. Her emphasis in personnel over the past six years has been in hiring and payroll, for which she was able to earn some experiential credit at Ohio State, and which she later transferred into Hawks. She has taken courses at the local college but does most of her course work at a distance. She has just three more classes (all of which she planned to take at once the semester after we spoke) to complete her degree in business management.

Melody Cook

A 26-year-old, Melody has worked for the past nine years as a secretary—a job she dislikes. Her husband (of seven years) just started a small business, and they are expecting their first child this year. She has been taking classes at community and business colleges for the past seven years—all of which she was able to transfer into Hawks a year ago. Those credits, plus a year of course work, along with credits she earned for prior experience, earned her a liberal arts associate degree last spring. She had difficulty specifying a vocational direction but chose social work as her aim in a recent career course. She enjoys taking courses through distance means because she can stay at home and especially sees this as an advantage with the new baby coming.

Rose Miller

Rose manages a store of a small children's clothing chain from April through November and then does bookkeeping and buying for the entire chain during the off season. Although the position is lucrative, retail seems more demanding each year; she sees a college degree as a future entree into a new career. Recently divorced, now in her 40s, she raises her three daughters as a single parent. She started college and dropped out several times before, but with two daughters in college, she finds her lifestyle (and family) more supportive—plus the three of them receive increased financial aid by her going to school—so she feels she will make it through this time. She enjoys taking distance education courses so she can stay at home, saying she is always out of the house at work as it is. She is majoring in human resources but is exploring other career options through her education because she eventually wants to get out of business.

Len Parker

Len, around 45 years old, works as a night security guard, a vocation that he finds enjoyable and unpressured; one that he has done continually since high school. He spoke of his decision to return to school:

> I guess what did it for me was watching the Iran-Contra Affair on Television. During those hearings, everyone was worried that the Sandinistas were smuggling dope into this country and giving it to American children. But, I said, "Bullshit." That can't be right.
>
> I was a part of the Peace Movement, back in 1964-65, but then dropped out. I wondered, what could I do to bring about better understanding in the world. And, I decided that I wanted to go back to school and learn about international relations and write about it for others. And, if I got a degree, someone might listen to what I had to say.

He lives at home with his mother and they share a car, which she takes to work each day. This situation seemed ideal for independent and distance study. Because of his limited access to library resources, he took out subscriptions to all the major international relations publications. He became an avid electronic network enthusiast with the connectivity he learned for this course by computer conferencing but eventually dropped the course for several reasons: preference for his network activity, philosophical differences with the instructor, inability to accept and conform to the required papers, and technical difficulties he experienced as a result of his extensive network activity.

Randy Fox

In his 40s, Randy works for a paper company, designing peripheral equipment for large machines, which requires much unscheduled travel to sites all over the eastern part of the country. He lives in the small, rural community in which the company plant is located. This has become a stable career for him, but his background is filled with job changes: professional keyboard musician, doing and managing auto repairs, and electrical work for a major defense contractor. His educational background is filled with starts and stops in a number of universities and programs. Hawks College provides one of the few formats flexible enough to accommodate his erratic schedule, but he wondered (in his first semester when I contacted him) whether they could provide enough technical electrical engineering courses to make the degree worthwhile. His employer will pay for the education, and he feels like he has time to pursue his studies. His oldest two sons entered college but quickly dropped out to take other jobs; he is hoping the two now in high school will continue on. He hopes someday to work his way up into management within the company.

Star Seekers

The "star seekers" are those who are primarily chasing a university diploma because of their desire to learn and fulfill a long-suppressed college education dream. There were three of them in my study: Betty Omgast, Vicky Harland, and Dennis Weather.

Betty Omgast

Betty, a 45-year-old Italian-American with a lively sense of humor, has worked all of her adult life in nursing, as a night obstetric nurse (delivering babies). She worked full time putting her lawyer-husband through school and helping him launch his career, choosing the night shift so she could cover their children's child care. But now her successful husband supports them, and she has cut back her work hours to just three days every two weeks, enough time she says to keep up on what is happening in the hospital. She explains why she returned to college:

> Even though I don't ever need to work full-time because my husband supports me, and I don't need to get a better job, I have reached a plateau in my life. My children are a certain age and I have time. And rather than just standing still asking my children what I can do for them, I say, "What can I do for

myself?" So now I say, "Yeah, I will advance." I say to my middle daughter who only has one semester to go, I said, "Gee, maybe we'll go get our masters together."

She explains that she was just too busy before in her life with the needs of her husband and children to pursue a college degree. Betty did go intensively to nursing school for a three-year certificate, but did not stay the extra year for the degree—she felt so pressured to get through and get out working that she saw no need. Later, because she valued education, she started a degree again, at Hawks 12 years ago, but was unable to see it through. But now she has the time. Betty explains that she is now "learning for learning's sake," "learning for myself, now." She has not decided yet in what field to get her bachelor's degree, telling her mentor, "I don't know how to bottle my enthusiasm to just one subject." And, the mentor's line of "What do you want to do?" does not fit her because she wants to do it all. She thinks she is good at directing and motivating others, perhaps in psychology or education.

Vicky Harland

Vicky, nearing age 50, has worked in management in a leading comput-er manufacturing firm for the past 14 years and currently heads a train-ing organization within the company. She lives apart from her Virginia-based family (except on weekends) on this 3-year special assignment. Her husband is an executive for the same corporation; they have a mar-ried daughter and 18-year-old son. At her managements' suggestion she embarked on a degree program in 1984, getting experiential credit for 54 hours. Then she "stopped out" while in Virginia for the next six years—the kids were having trouble adjusting and her career was too demanding. But, upon moving back to the northeast, Vicky has embarked again into a degree program, this time with Hawks College (who accepted all of her transfer credits). She spends a good deal of her time traveling around the country, with weekday evenings away from family, so distance education provides a flexible means for her to pro-ductively occupy her spare time.

Vicky suggests she is "learning for learning's sake" at this point because she will rise no further nor receive greater recognition for her bachelor's degree in her current, secure job. However, she dreams of working in career development or youth counseling as a second career upon retirement. Although she is just taking electives now, all of these courses tie in directly to her work, for that is where her interests lie: a business law class to help her with contract and licensing negotiations, a computer ethics course because of her strong ideas about how computers should be used within a company, and a psychology course to develop a more theoretical understanding of how to deal with those who work for her. She is also picking up a couple of intensive French courses, reviving a high school interest, by attending night classes at a nearby college.

Dennis Weather

Dennis, at age 46, is the superintendent of a waste treatment facility in a rural district. He has worked there for the past 21 years and feels too comfortably placed to consider a career change. Dennis took a year of college just after high school, but then was drafted, went overseas, came back and got married, and has been in his current occupation ever since. He has taken hundreds of courses and seminars over the years and reads 12 professional magazines in his field a month, so he was able to gain experiential credit for about half of his degree. Dennis took distance courses and doubled up on tutored assignments to avoid travel to the Hawks University unit in which he enrolled, one and a half miles from his home. He completed his degree in waste water management during our interview sessions.

For later reference, Table 2.1 summarizes some major characteristics of the students in this study.

UNIQUE AND SHARED FEATURES

It would be inaccurate to present these adult students as having a uniform outlook, but some themes arose in these discussions that help to understand them as a whole. This section explains the general characteristics they share: being first-generation college students, working adults whose education is a second priority, and being similar to other Hawks students. Next, it presents their instructional choices, degree-seeking dreams, the success of this type of educational system, the social connections of distance learners, the family valuing of education, and their views of education.

General Characteristics

As these students described their educational backgrounds, it became apparent that they were the first generation in their families to obtain a university degree. Judy explained:

Table 2.1. Student Characteristics

Name	Occupation	Family	Age	Sex	Ambition	Location
Barker, Kris	personnel specialist	married; 2 children	40	female	same; HRD position	medium city
Briar, Ralph	deputy fire chief	married; no children	34	male	fire chief, teacher, lawyer	suburb of large city
Brooks, Craig	security guard 3 children	married;	39	male	political science	large town
Cook, Melody	secretary	married; pregnant	26	female	social worker	suburb of city
Fox, Randy	paper mill equip. designer	married; 4 sons	42*	male	same; mgt position	small rural town
Gardener, Ted	security guard	married; 1 son	35*	male	teacher; econ. dev. specialist	large town
Harland, Vicky	training manager	married; 2 children	46*	female	same; retire as counselor	suburb of city
Jershon, Francis	bus driver	widowed; 2 children	46	female	drug/alcohol counselor	suburb of city
Jones, Kerry	town accountant	single; lives at home	23	male	professor of political science	small rural town
Last, Jack	machinist	married; *2 children	31*	male	same; business	rural suburb of small city

Table 2.1. Student Characteristics (cont.)

Name	Occupation	Family	Age	Sex	Ambition	Location
Miguel Lopez	computer system operations mgr	married; childless	31*	male professor	same; college	large city
Miller, Rose	clothes store manager	single parent; 3 daughters	43*	female business	HRD or non-	rural town
Omgast, Betty	part-time nurse; homemaker	married; 3 daughters	46	female	none	suburb of large city
Parker, Len	security guard	single; lives w. mother	45*	male	same; prof. of int'l relat'ns	small town
Schwartz, Harry	bookkeeping	married; 3 children	38*	male	mgt accountant or CPA	small town
Turner, Rick	computer mgr; being laid off	married; 1 child	44	male	find similar job	suburb of city
Vaughn, Lyn	bursar of college	married; 2 children	50*	female	same	large town
Weather, Dennis	superintendent of water treatment	married; unknown	45	male	same	rural town
Wells, Judy	paralegal	single	32	female	lawyer	small city
Winer, Carl	grocery store manager	married; 5 children	36	male	trainer or labor relations	suburb of city

*best estimate

When I graduated from high school, college wasn't really an option. They didn't ever encourage me. My parents didn't. We really didn't have the money in the family, so it was more or less understood by all of us (the four of us brothers, sisters, and myself) that we weren't going. So, we didn't.

My brother worked for IBM and put himself through school, working full time. It took about 16 years, but he finally got a degree. My sister got married and therefore became more economically able. So, therefore, she could go to school, which she did. She graduated summa cum laude, so she did really well. And, I am putting myself through school and working full time at the same time. So, all of us seem to have a desire to get this done, whether it is quickly or slowly.

Lyn expressed similar views:

When I graduated from high school times were different, socially and economically. My family needed my financial input. So, I worked. I don't know if I even wanted to go to college; I think I did; but, I can't remember back that far. But, not going was no great disappointment. It was not like today when everyone's parents just expect their kids will go to college.

But their parents may have been a factor in their current zeal to get an education themselves, as Betty described:

My father was a house painter and my mother was a housewife. That's why they sent me to a private school; to get a better education than they had. My father is not a dumb person. He just never had a formal education. All his life it held him back. My father was a shy person to strangers or people with a title. He was nervous thinking they'd say something that he wouldn't understand. All his life I saw that it held him back. He felt intimidated around people who had a better education. My father was warm and loving, unlike my girlfriend's father who was a doctor. My girlfriend's father was always very cold and she was never close to him. But my father was intimidated by people who had titles. So I always knew that I'd never let that happen to me.

Another characteristic that seemed to be universally shared is that of being working adults—school, however important to them, remains a lower priority than the job or family responsibilities. Rose explained:

The reason I chose Hawks College is because I'm in a rather remote area, the tip of [Beaver Island], so wherever I would go would mean traveling 50 minutes to an hour. With working full time and being responsible for the children, I just didn't feel I could take the time to drive somewhere and sit for several hours. I was needed at home. I heard about Hawks several years ago; maybe 10 or 12 years ago. I found that at the time my home was not quiet enough to be able to work independently. But this time it did work. I just have one child at home now and she'd be studying the same time I am.

Miguel explained why an alternative format university like Hawks College was all that he could consider:

I have been going to college since 1979. I have been working all of my career, full time. I have to pay the bills, and a mortgage, and all of that other stuff. For me, going to college, the university, was very difficult. In the beginning I went to a traditional university, but I found out that most of the classes, it was like a complete waste of time. Those students, they have a lot of time, and they are allowed to waste it. And, now you are a busy person, you have things to do, you have to go back to work, you are always late, you feel kind of out of place.

However, for some, the appeal of a university degree at this later period of life is that there was simply no time for it earlier. Carl explained:

Prior to going to school, there was no time for study. I'd go to work, I'd come home with the kids, and so forth. The career path had not slowed down to the point where there was some time for me to try to fit some studies in. And, of course, the difficult part of this is that in retail, your schedule is so varied—it fluctuates almost weekly, sometimes daily, so it would be very difficult for me to go to set classroom situations or set schedules that way. Because, I have to always be able to respond to the store when the need arises.

The students in my study do not seem to vary much from the typical Hawks student, profiled in Chapter 1. The age range in my study was from 23 to 50 years, with an average of 38 years old. Eight (40%) were women and 12 (60%) were men (just the reverse of the Hawks College makeup). These students were all employed, although two had only part-time positions, and they were in differing stages of completing their program—some were in their first semester and some had been going steadily for four years. Eighty percent of their student body, according to Hawks College documents, are involved for career progression reasons, although 20% are engaged for self-fulfillment. These same proportions seem to be reflected in my typology of learners presented earlier.

Instructional Choices

Not all of these individuals were solely distance students—several were only taking this distance course and usually attended classes or tutorial sessions instead. However, nine of the students (nearly half) whom I studied were taking courses primarily from a distance (mainly mail and phone interaction). They did so for several reasons: (a) their lifestyles fluctuated so much that they could not keep to a fixed class schedule, (b) their work schedule prevented them from attending courses when they were typically taught, or (c) they did not fit into class settings and had difficulty with that educational format. Vicky's comments are typical:

> I called up [Hawks College], and I'll tell you that was the best thing I've ever done. They are so wonderful because I'm a self-starter. I don't need anyone to tell me what to do. Just say the end result that you want and I'll go and I'll do it. That's the way I am in my work. So this is terrific for me because I can go in, review my degree plan, I pick certain subjects, I go off, and we simply agree on what I'm going to do in the next two to three weeks; I go off and do it, I come back, its done, its critiqued, then I get more to do. Then I do it. And that two weeks is up to me to manage my time. If I have to travel, I take my work with me. If I'm going on vacation, I take it with me.

Another 10 students took a variety of individually tutored, group tutored, regular classroom, and distance education courses, which were not only chosen to get the best subject matter match for their needs and interests, but also because the students enjoyed the variety and social aspects of the various formats. Only one student, Judy Wells, found this first distance experience so disconcerting that she will probably never take another course that is not face to face. She explained:

> I think my personality is such that I may do other tutored courses like a one-on-one kind of a situation or in a classroom. I think I need a person to get feedback from, to meet with, to register. And I cannot do it through the mail. I can't. To me its too far removed, and when somebody writes something, you don't have the opportunity to say I don't understand what you mean. You cannot get that immediate feedback. It takes too long for me. I don't have the time and I don't want to be bothered with it.

None of these students have to make major decisions about whether to do a significant amount of their course work through a computer conferencing medium, simply because there are not that many of these types of courses available at Hawks at the present time; it is not an option. However, several wished they could take many more courses using this technology and have been exploring ways they might obtain a master's degree through online education.

Perhaps mirroring the diversity of their backgrounds and present employment, these students were pursuing a myriad of degree titles—business, accounting, political science, psychology, management, computer science, international relations, communications, and so forth. Most of them, however, had practical, applied titles that meshed strongly with career aspirations.

Degree-Seeking Dreams

It surprised me to learn that these "late" college degree seekers had such ambitious dreams—11 of the 20 told me they planned to go on for a graduate degree, and 3 were interested in doctorates. In most of the other cases, it did not come up; only three students told me the bachelor's degree was as far as they were headed.

I am not sure what to make of this. It could be that they realize that a bachelor's degree is no longer sufficient for the new careers they have envisioned for themselves. Or, perhaps school-based learning has become addictive; now that they have taken and successfully completed college classes, it becomes an important part of their identity. Or, maybe Hawks advisors are strongly supporting and even pushing them on toward more education. I would have expected these students to be just holding on to finish their bachelor's degrees, but in most cases they were eager about further university study for potential careers.

The big question is whether this advanced education they seek will actually enable them to achieve their career aims—dreams of various sizes and clarity held by 18 of the 20 persons I interviewed. Perhaps my placement of them into these various categories reflects the way I would personally answer the question. The "necessity learners" will achieve their ends, as will the "recareerers or ladder climbers." I am not as sure with the "rainy day planners" because they possibly rely too heavily on the possession of an educational credential to bail them out of their current position, which they are not prepared to leave anyway unless they are laid off.

More realistically, it seems that nowadays bachelor's level education in adulthood primarily enhances related work experience or acts as a "foot in the door" to enter a new field. The discouraging perspective I would give to most of these "rainy day planners" is that important job experience is probably more important than advanced graduate degrees for realizing their career ends. Successful and mature careerists, such as Vicky or Dennis, will retain important positions and career possibilities, regardless of further education, because of those positions they have held in the past. Perhaps this sort of education works best for a "rainy day planner" like Kris Barker, whose achievement of it will secure her comfortable, current position.

How much importance is placed on a degree by an employer, especially an advanced one, when achieved as an adult through alternative formats, including distance education? Hawks College claims that about 60% of their graduates go into complete graduate programs, in which they compete well. Fifty percent of the graduates feel that their employment has improved after obtaining a Hawks degree through increased status, pay increases, job enhancement, and job satisfaction. One-quarter were promoted at work or found a new job, based on their degree. For example, Dennis, who got his degree for personal reasons, was nevertheless pleasantly surprised to get an unexpected 20% raise when he completed it. It appears that the credibility of these nontraditional programs continues to grow at about the same rate that they proliferate throughout the world.

One could look on these adults, most of whom hold adequate although not prestigious positions, with a deficiency mentality—people who have finally recognized limitations and obstacles in their work life, due to their poor decisions as young adults to drop out of college for the job at hand. Another approach is to take a more systemic view—that higher adult education is a societal way of giving these adults the illusion of future upward mobility that it will actually never grant. Or, on a personal level, a further approach is to suggest that this educational pursuit is a way of coping with boring jobs and keeping oneself productively occupied throughout the day or night when isolated from family and friends. However, I view them in a more positive light—that they have been competent, successful employees, able to move forward in meaningful careers without relying on educational credentials that now merely enhance their demonstrated competence. Truthfully, various individuals I studied could represent each of the above perspectives. However, regardless of its impact, further education should have a positive effect on their lives and those with whom they associate.

Success of This Educational System

Hawks College was not these students' first college experience. Many of them already held associate degrees from other institutions or had several years of university experience before enrolling in Hawks College. Only Francis Jershon and Lyn Vaughn had not taken prior university courses.

Five or six students mentioned difficulties they had experienced earlier in trying to attend regular classes filled with traditional

age (18- to 21-year-old) students. A passing comment, like this of
Harry's, is typical:

> I tried one course during the day at [Some College] and that
> was a mistake, I think. I was in my middle 30s, and I was in a
> classroom with people 18 years old, and it was very awkward.
> So, I learned my lesson. I take classes now at night, and I am
> very comfortable with it.

However, in Craig's case, it may stem from personal feelings of
inadequacy in a class versus successful past experiences with alternative education:

> The good thing about this is that I was never very good in a
> classroom situation. The teacher, in teaching the class, is trying
> to mold your mind and you have to be a certain way. Whereas
> in this, there is no intimidation, except maybe somebody
> responds in a way you don't like. But, there is none of that visu-
> al intimidation. . . . For instance, say you have a low self-esteem
> and you don't feel confident. On this, there is nobody looking
> at you, nobody sees you, and you can compare your respons-
> es. And that brings out a lot of confidence, I think.

Craig continued on a similar note:

> As a matter of fact, for eight months when I was in high school
> I was really sick, so I had a tutor. I was like a D student, and I
> went to a B+ student, without a classroom. The tutor would
> only see me once a week. This is when I was in high school.
> So, I was always uncomfortable in classroom situations. But,
> here I don't feel all that bad.

They told me consistently that Hawks College was working well
for them, for various reasons. Several of them chose Hawks, in part,
because they could transfer all of their previous college work and earn
credit for relevant life experiences, like Melody:

> Dan: Did you then transfer that [previous course work] in?
>
> Melody: Yes, it all transferred, and I've been able to obtain life
> experience credit for the secretarial work that I've done and my
> work with computers—word processing. So, that was nice.
> And, I also got credit for marketing skills in one of my jobs.

In fact, one student, Dennis, got experiential credit for over 72
hours, based on relevant workshops, seminars, and work experience of
the past 21 years. However, the average for these students was 9 to 12
hours, with some, like Jack, not using that option.

Besides fitting in with other adults who were pursuing degrees, and the benefits of experiential and transfer credit, students most strongly commented on Hawks College's flexibility in working around their demanding or remote work and lifestyles. To Kerry, that meant removing travel:

> Dan: Why did you choose Hawks over other [university] programs?
>
> Kerry: Basically because I do most of the work at home. I wasn't involved in any long distance traveling. Sometimes in the winter its not the best around here.

For Harry, it meant flexibility:

> Dan: So, what drew you to Hawks?
>
> Harry: The sense of freedom of it where I didn't have to be in a classroom all of the time. You are going to have balance. Now I am taking a course that starts up next week in the classroom at [Some Name] College and the other course I am taking through DEC [Distance Education Center]. I think that the freedom of it was very nice too. Its a situation that when you work all day you just can't be in a classroom.

Dennis enjoyed adjusting schooling to work demands:

> Well, I think the primary advantage of that is that you're not in any structured time schedule. I mean you can almost adapt course work to fit your own personal schedule, especially if you're working full time. I mean there are times when things come up and you can't really go every Tuesday or Thursday night from 7-10 for a classroom situation. It physically isn't possible. And some of the extra outside classroom work that may be required, oftentimes you don't have the time to do it under such a structured, regimented-type schedule. Working at a distance and working one on one, you can kind of tailor-make your own schedule. That is a great advantage. If you become overloaded at work you can put off some of your meetings, so-to-speak, to fit your own schedule.

Whereas Melody just liked being able to study at home:

> Melody: I am pregnant now. Everything is happening this year, so that is really why Hawks is good for me now, so I have the flexibility of not having to have sitters or someone take care of the child. I can be at home and do my work, which I see as a real advantage.

Dan: What does your husband think of all of this?

Melody: He thinks it is great, so he is happier than if I were in a classroom. I mean, three nights a week before I was always tired and miserable, and now I come home from work, relax and have dinner, put sweats on and then do what I want to do. If I don't want to do it on Monday, Wednesdays, and Fridays, and can do it on Tuesday, Thursday, and Sunday, or whenever I want to. So, it is nice. It doesn't interfere with our lifestyle at all. And, some weeks, maybe I don't feel like doing anything, so I don't. But, the next week I do, or whatever I want to do. So, it gives me a lot of flexibility.

Rick said he was too busy to take regular classes. His schedule allowed him to take only the individualized degree program, like Hawks College offers, with both tutored and distance courses that enable him to finish his bachelor's degree.

I was impressed with the continual praise of Hawks College, its innovative flexibility and accommodation of adult learners, and the caliber of its advisors and instructors that surfaced in my discussions with these students.

The Social Context of Distance Learning

A common stereotype of distance learners is their isolation and loneliness, given their physical separation from the academic institution with its libraries, students, and instructors. Certainly some of that image of "the loneliness of the long distance learner" is correct, as surfaced in discussions I had with Craig and Len in particular, who lead fairly solitary lives, both at home and at work. Both Kerry and Len told me of visits to their local college, 30 to 40 miles away, just to talk with professors and other students.

However, generally these students are very connected with others and have extensive social relationships with family and fellow workers. Here are some examples:

- Ralph talks often with his wife about how communications concepts from the course might apply to the field of nursing. He also advises other firefighters to take courses in order to advance in the force.
- Craig talks with others at work, especially Ted, about his course subjects, but is careful not to alienate those who have not taken college courses.
- Kerry talks with police officers, a school superintendent, several former professors, and his family about his studies.

- Dennis shares a certain camaraderie with various friends and family members who have also graduated from Hawks, but he did not share much of his school life at work.
- Rose and her daughters read each others' college writing assignments; she discusses with them their class preferences, and they study at home together.
- Betty now shares her studies with family members and co-workers to the point that they are tired of hearing about it. Yet one woman at work told her that she wanted to continue with Betty for her master's degree.
- Harry talks to select co-workers about his studies during coffee breaks, instead of the common chitchat. Several of them are also taking classes.
- Carl is always trying to apply concepts from his courses at work, telling those he supervises all about his studies and ways they all can improve the store's operation.

Others, such as Vicky, Dennis, Lyn, Kris, and Randy, hold jobs that involve a great deal of communication and social interaction. Many with more solitary occupations may find similar social exchange among close friends and family.

Fingeret (1983) discovered that illiterate adult students belong to strong social networks, characterized by reciprocal exchange. The social networks either support or inhibit these adults from involvement in literacy programs, as the exchange balance becomes upset by adults gaining new skills and competencies for which they formerly had to barter. My study supports those findings for these adult students involved in distance education. I speculate that those I talked to reflect only one type of potential adult student—the ones with support or at least few social barriers. Distance students may be more independent, self-managed, and autonomous, but their interdependence needs to be acknowledged as well.

Many networks exist to sustain these adults in their studies, and they speak of times when they dropped out as periods when important players in these networks themselves needed their support, or the network collapsed. Like literacy workers, distance educators need to view their students as engaged individuals in various social aspects of life.

However, the fact remains that no one in these peoples' immediate social world is involved in the particular course of study that these individuals are. On the surface, distance education may magnify that aspect of isolation, but most of adult education, particularly in higher education, involves the same dynamics. Adult college students rarely see their peers except in the classroom because their social interactions in work, family, and the community involve different individuals. Computer conferencing allows distance students to at last interact with their direct course mates, but it most likely will not replace an important social environment that exists in these students' worlds outside of the virtual classroom.

Family Valuing of Education

The support networks are usually strongest for this continued higher education pursuit in the immediate family. Fifteen of these students parented in a nuclear family situation; of the remaining five, three were single (two of them were living in their parents' home), one was divorced, and the other widowed. But even these nontraditional family units expressed a strong, familial ethic toward education. In only Ted Gardener's and Craig Brook's case did I find a friendship outside of the family that exerted strong pressures toward obtaining a degree—these two students work together and closely influence each other's pursuit. But both Ted and Craig have supportive families and are seeking higher education for family purposes.

Family connections, especially spousal ones, exerted strong influences on the students' educational pursuit. A typical question I put to these students was, "What does your spouse think of this?" Notice the gender dynamics that seem to surface here: Male students' wives tended to view the degree as a means of family progression and assisted with the process; female students' husbands took a more passive encouragement role, that of not being an obstacle.

The men's response: Miguel answered that his wife thinks he is crazy, but she supports him because this is the best way for him to get an education right now. Ralph said his wife was 100% behind him because he wants to do it, and it is a good investment in their future. Ted replied similarly. Craig mentioned several times his wife's support and her valuing of this degree to make them more secure as a family.

The women's response: Kris told me her family is used to her schooling, and she works it in on her own personal time; her husband likes the computer networking and views it with mild interest. Melody replied that her husband is supportive of distance education, more than if she were in class; "It doesn't interfere with our lifestyle." Vicky told me that, since she is separated from her family during weekdays, schooling fills a family void during those periods for her; she does not let it interfere with her "sacred" weekend time with the family. Betty's husband, who primarily supports the family, told her to go on for her master's, her doctorate, if she wanted to, and she could, as money and time are no longer issues. Rose responded that her former husband was not encouraging, and her parents were surprised that she would consider college, but her (now older) daughters were very supportive. With her divorce, she can pursue education without spousal hindrance.

However, family values of education often transcend gender differences—both spouses see this as a means of moving ahead. Harry's wife was taking courses for her degree along with him. Ted's wife was gearing up to do so as well. Melody's husband is in the thick of starting up his own business, otherwise, she said that he would like to be taking classes too. In Jack and Craig's case, they too (like Vicky and Betty) are schooling during their off hours to keep productively occupied while the rest of the family is gone at work or school. The men are not totally supported by their wives—they schedule their studies around their spouses' work commitments, and Ted, Craig, and Carl each told me of needing to arrange child care themselves for pressing school times.

But, on still another level, there were families that I studied who placed much of their identity around schooling and education. For example, Lyn was trying to convince her husband to go on for his doctorate, once she completed her degree. They have both a stepdaughter and daughter who are public school teachers, and she said, "education just runs in the family." Consider Rose's case—divorced and a single parent—she is taking classes with two daughters who are also in college after she found that she could get better financial aid if they all enrolled together. Francis, another single parent, spoke with pride of how each of their family graduated this year: her with an associate degree, her oldest daughter from high school, and the youngest from junior high. Also, Harry, whose wife is also working on her degree, spoke at some length about the positive example they are setting for their children, not just about the value of a college degree, but also that parents can make career changes and go to school later in life.

By far the individual (and family) who prized education the most was Betty Omgast. She married her husband, in part, because his being a college student set him apart from the electricians and plumbers she dated. Together they decided that he should go on for his law degree; it was their mutual goal on behalf of the family, and she worked to support him in that venture. She has tried to inculcate into her daughters the strong feeling that education is just "something that you do." It is part of locating oneself at the highest point possible in America's class system. She told me of continually directing her daughters' university pursuits. She counseled her daughters' friends about majors—even paying a year's tuition and dorming expenses for the first year of college for one of them (which has not yet been repaid), simply so this family friend could aspire and have that experience. Education is an integral part of the Omgast household:

One of my daughters has this one boyfriend who is a marine. He says, "Mrs. Omgast, when I come out I'm going to school. I can't wait." They'll give him money or whatever they do for education, but right now because he's in the helicopter division he does shift work and is not able to take classes now, but wants to when he comes out, first thing. And he knows, and I let all the boys know that my daughters go out with, that if they don't get an education, "don't even think about getting into the family." [we laugh] . . . But it works. Hey whatever is the driving force and makes them succeed. Whether its to win approval to get the money, whatever it is . . .

In my will it says if you go to school you get so much a year to support you, and if you get a master's you get so much, and if you get a doctorate you get that much [we laugh]. My will is all broken down into degree of education. They'll go for it. I tell them they can get an extra $10,000 a year in the trust. . . . I did that will last year before I went on a trip. About a year and a half ago we took a trip to Europe. It was a long plane flight and I said, "You know I've always thought of this. I don't have a will." And I always tell my kids this, but who is going to obey my orders when I am dead? Now I'm so happy. I won't be here but I'll still be directing. [laughter]

What becomes apparent in these students' lives is that family support networks become a two-way, synergistic process. Not only do various family members help the adult student, but the students (e.g., Betty Omgast) also support other family members in their pursuit of their shared value of education—by exemplifying it in their own actions, telling them of its value, influencing their friends, and helping them create a circle of friends who similarly prize this same ideal.

Views of Education

But why do they value education? The prevailing attitude was that education is a means of getting ahead in the world. Ralph told me that the good study habits that come from an education helped him to score high on civil service examinations, an essential element for promotion in the fire department. To Francis it is a means to a career—a way to have any impact outside of one's own family and community environment. When Craig said, "Education is everything," he meant that it provides an opportunity for people without means, correction officers (and even inmates), to advance into more productive, satisfying lives. Also, it enables people to get the skills and competencies to perform better in their positions, such as being able to communicate effectively. However, most of these students see the bachelor's degree as a necessary title one must have to get or keep a job in today's society.

Several told me how nice it was for them to be able to talk intelligently to others at work—to engage in meaningful conversations without feeling intimidated. Some, finding no such interactions in their own sphere, went to school (in part) for the intellectual stimulation. Len explained:

> That is how it is, if you are fairly bright. If you are not talking about the Super Bowl, the bowling scores, or pro wrestling, people hear you talk and they think you are kind of strange. You, [Dan], are at a university, so you probably don't notice this as much. When I went up to Nyer Lake College I fit in because they talk about other things, but you go anywhere else, and they don't.

However, there are personal reasons some look to education. Francis elaborated:

> So, I would say that it is 50% career oriented and 50% for my own self-worth—to develop. My philosophy kind of is that we have all been given certain talents to develop and then the responsibility to develop them is ours. And, I think that I carry a certain responsibility toward that. I am kind of feeling that now that the kids are bigger that it is my responsibility to develop these talents that I am born with or think I am born with [laughs].

And Betty finds education to have intrinsic worth that others respect:

> I never really took the time for myself that I should have. But it was always there in the back of my mind. So I've always respected education, but I just never took the time for myself. I was always too busy doing things; you know manual things in fixing a house and working so he could go to school. So now that I have the ability and financially can afford it, I don't need to work full time and I just think its a wonderful thing [that I can take classes]. . . . I'm doing it now just for the sake of education. It makes you feel better inside. It just makes me feel good.
>
> I like to know a little bit about everything. My daughter asked questions before, and my husband has a very good memory and just pops out with the answers. He can remember something he learned in the eighth grade. He has a good memory. And this daughter says, "Daddy I hate you. You're always so smart." [laughter] And he just blurts out this one word, and who the heck ever heard of that word. But he has a good word. He has a good memory. So we laugh because its just nice. I say that to my children, "Isn't it nice when you know a little bit about a lot of subjects?"

And I also encourage them to travel. We just came back from Tennessee. I just went to [some city]. My daughter couldn't go. Nobody was able to go so I just said, "What the heck, I'll go and if I like it I'll go back with the family." But to me its an education. I sat there and listened to Shakespeare. I just thought it was great. Like I said, I like it, only because I'm a believer in it. I know some people need to work. And I wish I had done it for myself earlier [go to school]. My job today would be different. I don't know what it would be, but I also like to be respected by other people. I think that [education] is a means of respect.

SCHOLARSHIP ABOUT DISTANCE STUDENTS

General Studies Of Distance Learners

Several scholars sought to summarize the research to date about distance learners but found it in a state of disarray (Cookson, 1989; Gibson, 1990; Mackerron, 1984; Sheets, 1992). Mackerron (1984) discovered this literature to be "expressions of individual opinions based on personal experiences, evaluation of specific distance education programs, doctoral dissertations that examined specific aspects of distance education programs, and case studies of individual distance education programs" (p. 62). Gibson (1990) found that theories of distance education differ widely on their inclusion of various personal and environmental factors in understanding student learning. Cookson (1989) similarly stated that "descriptive and prescriptive articles outnumbered reports of actual systematic inquiry" (p. 22). Coldeway (1988) suggested that the research base in distance education has only just arrived at a stage at which discussions about methodology, evaluation, and triangulation make sense. Presented next are these scholars' attempts to cluster studies and present themes.

Cookson (1989) found three types of research dealing with student outcomes (i.e., factors that lead to successful retention and completion of distance education programs): (a) studies searching for reasons for student dropout, (b) studies attempting to profile successful distance students, and (c) studies that research institutional factors affecting participation. Sheets (1992) organized the research similarly: (a) characteristics of distance students, (b) comparisons of distance and conventional learners, and (c) factors that affect persistence in distance education. Mackerron (1984) looked at: (a) factors that augment adult participation at a distance, (b) conditions that inhibit such participation, and (c) distance institutional practices that enhance participation. Gibson (1990) used personal factors and environmental factors that influence learning behavior as her framework, based on Lewin's field psychology of learning. Collapsing their categories, I summarize their major findings next.

Distance Student Profiles

Using statistics from various international open universities, Sheets (1992) found the majority of distance learners to be over 24 years old and employed. Women outnumber men in New Zealand, Canada, and Israel, but the opposite is true in Britain, Germany, and Spain, possibly representing cultural differences. Open universities, which offer major distance education programs, attracted "second chance" students initially, but now are being used by more degree holders for continuing education purposes.

However, Gibson (1990) reported that most studies that looked solely at demographic variables of age, sex, and so on, failed to find any significant difference between distance and classroom learners. She found that adults' educational background, particularly academic ability, indicated which students would succeed in a distance setting.

Differences Between Distance and Campus Students

Most of this research, according to Sheets (1992), seeks to determine motivating factors. Some research finds distance students more inclined toward structure and lacking self-esteem than regular students. Cookson (1989) concurred, citing Kennedy and Powell (1976): "While most dropouts report external or circumstantial reasons for withdrawal, they often have a demoralizing history of educational failure and bring feelings of insecurity and educational and intellectual inferiority to their studies" (p. 69). Although distance learners bring increased experience to the instructional setting, they are sometimes overly reliant on instructors (Sheets, 1992). Motives for pursuing education at a distance include physical distance from the institution, scheduling conflicts, preference for distance education modes, and easier entrance into institutions offering distance study.

Gibson (1990) found that cognitive personality and learning style differ in research done about distance students. Much research indicates that field-independent learners (i.e., those whose personalities are more autonomous and less sensitive to context) succeed in dis-

tance education, although other studies found no significant differences. Another study she cited found external degree students' learning
styles to favor competition among peers, a relationship with the
instructor, the ability to set their own objectives, the ability to deal with
ambiguity, a preference to reading (over listening, seeing, or direct
experience), and an expectancy to do average work.

Retention and Persistence of Distance Learners

Mackerron (1984) found that distance students pursuing higher education were barred from that quest in much the same way that the adult
education literature has described regular adult learners as being
obstructed. The distance education personnel he interviewed agreed
that career advancement was the greatest motivating factor for participation, whereas employment responsibility was the greatest inhibiting
factor. Student profile studies usually try to identify characteristics that
lead to successful distance education course completions. The research
Cookson (1989) cited found these factors significant in such a profile:
gender, age, previous level of educational attainment, time away from
formal schooling, high school grade point average, and previous correspondence course performance. Sheets (1992) agreed with this list, but
found gender and marital status to be insignificant. She stated that
these demographic factors only make up 10% of the variance.
Additionally, the research she summarized found that student behavior
after enrollment significantly affects completion—those who quickly
finished the first assignment studied more hours per week and more
often completed the course than their counterparts.

Institutional Practices that Promote Student Participation

Mackerron (1984) found that the flexibility the educational institution
gave distance students over the time and place of study was the chief
reason students chose this mode of study. Gibson's (1990) research
review found tutorial support, in telephone, peer, and face-to-face
means, to positively affect course completion and satisfaction. Both
Cookson (1989) and Sheets (1989) cited several successful practices
that institutions have employed to enhance student completion, such
as having pacing constraints; mailing reminders to apparent laggards;
adding counseling, tutorials, or computer conferencing; and speeding
up assignment turnaround rates. They both looked at the inconclusive
efforts to isolate student background characteristics that predict their
successful integration into college life. Rather, this literature suggests

that distance students need to integrate their work, family, and social lives into their educational commitments.

Life Influences While Pursuing Degree

Just a few studies touched on the distance students' life situation, goals, and personal factors that affected their pursuit of a formal education. Robinson (1992) looked at demographic characteristics of distance students at a Canadian university and found that the majority of them were working women, pursuing an education part time. Most of them had prior university experience. Gibson (1991) found that self-confidence impacts student success in an external degree program. Factors that enhanced self-confidence in a learning context were instructor empathy, success in completing work, progress toward a goal, and students' perceived understanding of themselves and the educational process they were undergoing. Peruniak's (1988) study examined the lives of distance learners through a mailed questionnaire to a random sample of college students. He found that these adult students were successful in their courses, self-directing and positive about life, and did not consider themselves marginal. There were larger numbers of women taking courses, and they had unique needs—a concern for inner direction, concern for others, and desire for personal development. These students worked full time, both in the professional and service sectors, and felt strong family obligations. Their ordered priorities were career, family, and education.

Another researcher investigated the rhythm and flow of a computer conference, thereby revealing how adult students fit this activity into their lifestyles. By studying the hard-copy transcripts of a computer conferencing course, Harasim (1989) plotted the participation patterns of the students. She found that the smallest group—full-time graduate students—used the system during the weekdays, but the majority of the class who worked full time Monday through Friday used the system most heavily on the weekends. Unsurprisingly, the heaviest usage on weekdays was in the evening, but participation was spread throughout the day on weekends.

Implications of These Student Descriptions

This portion of the research emphasized the individual nature of distance education—adult students bring much variety to the learning situation, which rarely is taken into account. Morgan (1984) stressed the need for qualitative research approaches to unearth these characteristics, yet proposed that the "distance" of this study mode also brings distance to most research attempts. Hence, questionnaire forms of research predominate. Research that seeks to understand distance learners must look at both the individuals with various personal characteristics (the focus of most studies) as well as the living dynamic environmental context within which they live (Gibson, 1990).

The importance of individualizing the instructional process, although a necessity with our new understanding of knowledge formation and the learning process, runs counter to the conventional distance education approach, which uses mass delivery models (Granger, 1990a). Some scholars (as summarized earlier) sought to synthesize the literature about distance learners; for example, Gibson (1990) found distance students to have autonomous, flexible, and ambiguity-tolerant personalities. The categories of student orientation I presented earlier roughly match those of Morgan (1984)—all types from his research were represented, but social orientation was missing, as expected. Roberts (1990) found that distance university students held learning- and career-oriented goals, not social and cultural ones. These students were self-confident, independent, achieving, and persistent. However, differences existed on goals and academic self-concept by gender, class, experience, and income level. Distance students were more confident and learning oriented than their conventional counterparts.

Roberts's (1990) finding that distance students had predominantly job or career development orientation (60% to 73%) fit this study's results. I mentioned surprise at the large number of Hawks students planning on further graduate education, but I have since found similar studies at the same institution (circa 1989) that found that 60% of their students had a graduate or professional degree goal. Also unusual was the gender imbalance among these students, but I have since found another study on Hawks that reports that a 60:40 male to female ratio exists in their distance education enrollments generally. Similar institutional statistics for their Distance Education Center found that 56% of the distance students were also taking tutorial, tutor group, and classroom courses, so my sample seems representative on that dimension, too.

However, an understanding of the personal characteristics of distance students is not enough. For example, the major difficulty with Granger's (1990a) learner profile approach to individualizing distance education is its entire focus on the learner's knowledge and learning experience, not the holistic context within which that is developed and supported. Indeed, Gibson (1990) exhorted distance educators to take environmental factors into greater consideration, especially in their theory building. Some research points out the importance of environmental factors. For example, Cookson's (1990) review of persistence studies found that students primarily reported both domestic and occupational reasons for dropping out, such as time demands, financial burdens, and child care issues. Granger (1990a) echoed a theme of my study when writing, "many adult students are important members of their own communities and function there quite effectively" (p. 166). Another qualitative research study mirrored some of my findings—that gender issues arise on spousal support for students taking computer conferencing courses. It found that wives tolerated their husbands' online activity, but in the reversed roles, husbands had more difficulty coping with "the resultant disturbance to domestic routine of their wives' on-line endeavors" (Grint, 1989, p. 191).

Missing from scholarship about distance students were the types of portraits I presented in this study; however, Mason (1990) did present profiles of individual students, focusing on their access and participation in a computer conferencing course as part of an evaluation report. Also absent were findings about these being first-generation students and the nature of their support networks, especially those provided by families who also value education. Small's (1986) qualitative study of Australian distance students in high school found urban and rural students to differ significantly in their current life situations and former school experiences. The urban students had poor earlier experiences and held low-level positions, versus their rural counterparts who worked in dynamic jobs and had positive earlier schooling. This rural-urban split did not occur along this dimension in my study. Those I interviewed who mentioned negative school experiences spoke of bad college experiences, especially as returning adults.

CONCLUSION

Distance education students are more than the incarnation of psychological variables, drives, and motives; they are active, engaging adult, human beings (Blumer, 1969). This chapter emphasized that point by revealing the priorities, goals, dreams, supports, values, and beliefs of this selected group of 20 students taking distance courses. Their individual circumstances and personal aspirations come directly into play as they take on a new educational challenge, such as computer conferencing, and seek to make it a part of their overall education pursuit.

Granger (1990a) advocated a distance education approach in which individual learner profiles, similar to those portrayed here, are developed and used for individualization and personalization of distance education by advisors, instructors, and support staff:

In order for distance educators to develop programs which serve individual learners most effectively, the individual learner must be understood within his or her context. By context is meant the complex of situational factors—social, economic, psychological—which can positively or negatively affect the learning experience and how the individual creates meaning. (p. 164)

He challenges instructional designers for distance education systems to come up with ways for learners to tailor their distance courses to meet their peculiar needs and build on their unique strengths. This type of course design may require greater modularization and advisor and instructor tailoring of the content and learning activities with each student to provide effective learning.

Successfully obtaining an adult college degree, especially through a distance format, involves a combination of factors such as: (a) self-confidence that one can succeed; (b) a love (or liking at least) for the process and intellectual stimulation of learning, not just the accomplishment once completed; (c) an ability to continue a project and demanding lifestyle over many years and establish such long-term goals for oneself; and (d) the steady support of a job, family, and social network to undertake such a project. The students described in this chapter each, for the most part, reflected these important characteristics.

In summary, this chapter described the 20 individuals who participated in the study. I used a typology to present them, based on the impetus for degree pursuit, within these categories: "necessity learners," "recareerers or ladder climbers," "rainy day planners," and "star gazers." Next I presented general characteristics these students share: (a) they were of the first-generation of college-degree seekers in their families; (b) as working adults, they placed education as a lower, although important, priority; and (c) these students did not appear to differ much from the "typical" Hawks student on various demographic, descriptive measures except possibly gender.

The chapter concluded with some unique outlooks, trends, and observations—not held by all of these students, but often espoused by a majority of them. First, these students could be divided into two groups of equal numbers: those who were taking all of their courses through distance means, and those who took a mixture of instructional formats—distance education, tutorials, tutored groups, and classroom courses. Second, the majority have greater dreams of pursuing graduate degrees after achieving the undergraduate degree they are working toward and/or anticipating that this degree will enable them to make important career leaps. Third, they were enthusiastic about Hawks, having earlier tried several other colleges. Fourth, most adult distance students are socially connected in meaningful relationships outside of the educational environment—they are usually not isolated or lonely as they are often portrayed. Family structures of various types uphold and sustain the value of education, of which these students' pursuit of an adult university degree is but one manifestation. Finally, education for them means developing a career, enhancing personal competence, fulfilling one's potential, and gaining the respect of others.

3

Perspectives of the Computer Conference

No matter when I put the computer on, even if no one from my class is on then, I can still see that other users are on, and I still get the feeling that they are there. It brings life to them to me. I definitely get the feeling that they are there. And when I type into the program I feel like they are hearing me. I just feel their presence —Betty Omgast (July 25, 1992)

Computer conferencing represents a new instructional delivery system for distance education, burgeoning just in the past five to seven years. Harasim (1989) argued that this medium presents a whole new educational domain, unique in its characteristics, and to which conventional classroom paradigms are not wholly applicable.

This chapter explores Hawks College student perspectives of the "online seminar" from a variety of angles. First, it examines the context within which students take these courses, both their physical setting and the course's fit within lives and relationships. Next, it investigates the pedagogical structure of the computer conference—including technical issues, course requirements, assignments, and student and moderator roles. Then it examines the nature of computer conference learning, student perceptions of involvement, textual communication, asynchronicity, pacing, interactivity, participation, collaboration, and learning through this medium. Finally, it examines the scholarship about computer conferencing that proclaims it as an appropriate medium for adult learning.

CONTEXT

It is easy to forget the surroundings of those studying online, but these factors can play a significant role in an adult's ability to maintain effective study throughout the course of a computer conference, to say nothing of the years required for a degree.

Physical Setting

Certainly, the convenience of participating in the computer conference from where one normally spends significant periods of the day—the home or the office—is a selling feature of this delivery medium. Of the 20 students involved in this study, 15 of them (75%) accessed the conference from their homes, 4 got on from work (20%), and 1 person had to commute to a Hawks College unit to access the computer conference. Of those who accessed the computer from work, Miguel also logged in at home and Kerry was thinking about buying a personal computer for added convenience and continued use of network systems after the course. A number of factors may be responsible for the preponderant computer access from home: (a) many of these people do not use computers on the job; (b) schooling is viewed by the workplace as a personal, private activity to be done away from the job; (c) workplace demands and social strains with co-workers make study difficult, even after hours; and (d) students may want to make productive use of home computer equipment they previously purchased.

Because I conducted most of my interviewing by phone, I did not directly view many of these study sites. However, I did view Craig's basement study area:

> The basement was a large carpeted area of several rooms which had a computer work station on a desk dominating one of them. It was an IBM PC clone with a printer and modem. Books and papers covered the table top and most of the side wing of the desk. He cleared materials off a stool nearby for me to sit down.

In contrast, I was able to observe Kerry working after hours on the police department's computer:

A bulletin board at the entrance to the room displayed mug shots and missing persons. The room contained two plain metal desks, at one an officer was smoking and filling out some form. Behind him against the wall was an IBM PC clone, a printer, a cheap stereo, and a radio which would blurt out police dispatch material (this went on throughout the interview). He asked Kerry if he needed the desk; Kerry replied that he did, so the man moved to the adjacent one.

When I asked Kerry if this arrangement was uncomfortable, he replied:

No, I come in late at night when there is nobody here. But, lately I've been staying after work, from 4 to 5 PM, and sometimes I'll come in the early morning. I don't get in the way. In fact, I've been in here when they were booking someone, but I just ignored them and they ignored me.

Facilities like Craig's seem conducive to study; so did the one Carl wrote me about in our email exchange:

My homework area is very simple. We have a very large bedroom. In it I have a recliner with a lamp where I do most of my reading. I have a large "office" type desk that contains my complete computer setup. There is also a bookshelf upright attached to the desk. Here I keep all of the texts and study guides that I am currently working with; as well as a dictionary and other reference manuals.

However, some students do not have dedicated or sufficient facilities and have had to cope:

Dan: And, what is your computer workstation like?

Francis: Not sufficient. Its just one of these tables that just kind of fits the computer and the monitor and the printer pulls out on a drawer under it and the keyboard pulls out on another tray. Its not expansive enough. It was sufficient for the nonuse the computer was getting when it was just here. It was just a backup for my husband to do his work from work. . . . Now that I'm using it for school I really need more space, more of a desk where I could spread out and leave things where I left off, rather than have to create this pile business. . . . I think the ideal situation for anybody to learn is to have your own space in your own room where you can have a desk or some type of quiet corner where you can be. I would probably say adult learners who are in my situation wouldn't have that, especially the mom. We're fair game.

Life and Relations Context

It was common for students to mention other people in their lives with whom they shared this educational experience. Kris, Ralph, Melody, and Rose spoke of sharing their computer conference experience and college studies with spouses and other family members. Craig, Betty, Lyn, and Carl talked more about these exchanges happening at work. Kerry and Len mentioned seeking out mentors or academically oriented friends with whom they could discuss their studies.

However, computer conferencing activities interfered with some domestic relationships. For example, Len told me he had to do his computer printing during the day so as not to disturb the slumbering household at night when he is typically online. Craig shared how his wife nagged him to get off the computer and do some house projects. And, Francis told of her daughter's resistance:

> I plug in the modem, and the whole world is mad at me. They can never get me on the phone anymore. If I could afford it, I would get another phone line put in here.

The impression we have of distance learners is that they work in quiet solitude, but often noise and commotion is going on around them, elements with which they have to also interact or contend. Distance study settings are not always isolated; they may be in public areas that are full of disturbance and activity. Also at work are the information exchanges and learning that happens as these students share course ideas with family, friends, and co-workers and report opinions, facts, or insights they receive from them back to the conference.

STRUCTURE

Technical Support and Background

How do distance education students get connected to the mainframe computer at Hawks College and learn to use the computer conferencing system? Hawks College has an 800-telephone number so students do not have to pay long distance telephone charges for modem access. The college also offers an inexpensive modem rental program so home computer owners can access the networks without making a more costly modem purchase.

Eric Watson, the college's technical support person, explained their training and support system to me. First, as soon as a student enrolls in a computer conferencing course he mails out a packet of materials—short procedural instructions that give them enough of the basics to connect to the college's VAX mainframe computer system. Once the students get onto the mainframe and can send electronic messages, Eric provides 90% of his support through e-mail. The computer system is all menu driven, so he told me they usually learn to use the various computer applications by trial and error. Most of the students' questions have to do with more advanced features, such as uploading and downloading files or using nonstandard computer hardware or software for accessing or processing the online information. Hawks College has developed specific task and equipment instructions, but has tried to encourage students to stay with the standard PC hardware and software they have chosen to support.

Because of their dispersed student population, he did not believe in-person training was feasible, and the few workshops they had given were poorly attended. Rather, he felt that people want rapid responses to their immediate questions. The Hawks advisors I spoke with told me that the college now offers a basic computer literacy course that introduces students to basic PC operations; also, the telecommunications course gave students fundamental skills in accessing and using network resources.

Eric works to get them up and going two weeks before the computer conference officially starts. Different courses require different amounts of technical expertise. For example, Alice Web's writing class required online submission of all assignments (involving file uploading), whereas David Engle's Constitution course requested that all assignments be submitted by regular postal mail. Most computer conferences were structured, Eric said, with a specific branch set aside for technical assistance issues, and he responds to all of those because support is outside of the instructor's role. However, David, being knowledgeable in all facets of the computer conference, provided his own technical support for the Constitution course. The next chapter deals more specifically with how these distance learners overcame the technical demands of the computer conference.

Course Structure and Assignments

Along with other course materials, the distance students received a syllabus that outlined course purposes, assignments, participation requirements, and the structure of the computer conference. Although these differed from class to class, I describe the requirements of the 4-credit hour, upper level undergraduate Constitution course, and then contrast that with the other ones.

The content of this course came from a 13-part videotape series and the reading of three texts. The instructor required students to turn in four topical papers of not less than four pages each and to actively participate on the computer conference. Students were expected to read widely from current newspapers, periodicals, and references that would commonly be available in local libraries or through interlibrary loan; they were to use these references in their papers and the online discussions.

The computer conference area consisted of permanent and topical discussion areas (called *branches* or *items*). Permanent areas remained active throughout the conference, and participation on them was strictly voluntary. These items included: "The Pub"—a chitchat area for students to talk about any topic (commonly known as the "electronic lounge"); "Bulletin Board"—an information branch in which students and instructor posted announcements of interest to the others; and "Introductions"—a place for students to introduce themselves and become acquainted. The bulk of the course conversation took place on graded topical discussion areas that only remained actively open to accept messages for a 3-week period but could be read anytime later (after the discussion had occurred on them). Each of these dealt with a different course topic, synchronized with the readings and videos. The instructor opened the topical items in an overlapping sequence so two or three were active at any one time; to these he required students to post at least two notes weekly.

The communications and computer ethics courses I studied had quite similar structures to that of the Constitution course. Neither of these courses, however, had an accompanying video series, but they involved reading three or four texts and submitting written assignments. The Telecommunications course was only a 1-credit hour class, so it involved much less reading. Both it and the writing course had quite different structures and assignments, but those will be adequately explained as their elements become relevant later.

Some courses required students to use computer network resources, whereas in other courses this was an optional component. Universally, students used electronic mail, primarily for discussion within the Hawks College computer network"—to advisors, other students, and instructors. In conjunction with their courses, some students joined related Bitnet electronic information exchange and discussion groups; commonly known as *listserves*;[1] these may have a membership of hundreds of users scattered around the world. Another option students

---

[1] *Listserves* is the way these discussion groups are referred to in this document. Because of an 8-character command limitation, they are commonly referenced in the computer support literature as LISTSERV.

used, especially in the Telecommunications course, was the "phone" facility—a system that facilitates two or more computer users typing onto a split-screen while on the computer at the same time.

Student Moderator Role

The instructors varied in the amount of time and attention they gave to their computer conference courses, but in all cases the environment encouraged lots of student exchange of communications. One instructor was always online, according to students, and responded immediately to every issue, concern, or question that was posed. Another one would not be on for four or five days at a time. Students seemed to favor the more attentive and available instructor.

David, the Constitution course instructor about whose instructional style I learned the most, was viewed as a referee by his students. He set up the issues in the topic under discussion or established an example scenario and then challenged class members to add their comments, based on their informed opinions from relevant experience and course content. He stepped in to "stir up the pot"—changing aspects of the scenario or challenging prevailing views that had emerged—thereby letting students know he was monitoring their discussion. He also sent private e-mail messages, encouraging silent students to "speak up" or to encourage raving or outrageous students to practice greater "civility and self-discipline."

Although participation on these computer conferences was mandatory, several students posted many more notes than the weekly requirement, and some posted far fewer. Students in the Constitution course primarily expressed their own opinions, but sometimes groups formed that took specific political views and dominated the conference for short periods. Kerry and Craig claimed to have become "teacher's helpers" later in the course, encouraging less "vocal" members to participate more and praising their contributions (though not without taking issue). The students who volunteered to help with my research were the more active participants in their respective conferences (by their own and others' reports), with some exceptions — Judy, Randy, Harry, Ted, Francis, and Jack.

THE NATURE OF LEARNING BY COMPUTER CONFERENCING

> Len: Its kind of hard to describe what this is like if you haven't experienced it yourself. Under the item you have a whole series of responses by people about the topic. It's as if you had a type-writer and everyone took turns typing on it.

I liked Len's metaphor and would like to embellish it a bit. Computer conferencing is like having a room full of typewriters, perhaps set in groups on different desks, clustered by subject area. And, each one is labeled with a specific writing topic. During the week, day and night, men and women enter the room from different doors, rarely at the same time. They spend anywhere from a half hour to two hours at a time reading what others have typed at the keyboard on each topic and adding their own ideas. Some of them will make photocopies of what they and others have said so that they can refer to it later. Then they leave, only to return in a couple of days to see who has responded to them, what they have said, and how the various topical discussions have progressed. This section examines how those I studied viewed the computer conferencing environment and how it advanced or slowed their learning.

Hype About Technology

Several of the students I talked to were attracted to their course, not just for its subject, but because it was offered through a computer technology about which they wanted to learn more. However, the glamour wore thin quite early for four or more of them who experienced technical hurdles in just getting connected and learning the ins and outs of the conference enough to participate. Others who experienced no such difficulties gradually took for granted what they had viewed as an exciting technological learning system as they became involved in the day-to-day work and tedium of the conference. But for other students the novelty of the conference never wore off. They were eager to find and take similar courses.

An Addictive Medium

Once involved in this course and other network activities, four or five of the students found "networking" and the conference discussions, particularly the "electronic lounge," to be pleasurable diversions from their studies, work, and family demands. Miguel explained how online discussions (including course conversations, e-mail, and network discussion groups) was a perfect hobby for him—he likes to stay home, be alone but meet many people, is shy, and finds it very interesting—there is "always something going on." Carl found it a recreational reprieve from his book studies and writing assignments. Kerry was planning to buy a home computer so he could participate more in network activities.

Indeed, many of those to whom I talked, both those who favored and those who disliked the medium, expressed compulsive urges or guilt to frequently monitor the relevant e-mail and computer conferencing discussions in which they were involved. Craig, for example, spoke about how he had to manage himself so he did not "waste too much time" online. Len's relentless involvement with network discussion groups was a factor in his dropping the Constitution course.

Text-Only Communications

Online discussions must consist of the alphabet, numeric, and alphanumeric symbols available on a standard computer keyboard—a characteristic which has several important implications. For instance, Jack claimed that by reading peoples' entries he and others paid more attention to what was being said and were able to remember that information much longer than if it had been spoken. Likewise, some felt that the text environment more truly conveyed ideas and aspects of peoples' personalities than an in-person setting because these communiqués were unhampered by irrelevant physical characteristics and cues. Randy explained the deliberate composition procedure involved in computer conferencing:

> Randy: You also have time to look at the screen and decide whether you really want to send it. That is a different kind of thing, too.
>
> Dan: And rework it, you can decide if you want to do that?
>
> Randy: Yeah, I definitely do rework it to see that what I say is definitely what I mean. You may temper something a little bit so as not to be so harsh or to be more general. . . . So, you tend to generalize and soften things up. Now, you won't do that if you open your mouth up and let it out. Whereas with the screen, you get to view it for awhile and then send it.

But, several other conference students disagreed—a text-only communication lacks important body language aspects that truly deliver the message. Judy best articulated this perspective:

Do you really have the ability to say things as best you can through this medium?" . . . I think of myself, when I look back over some of the things I have written, I don't have the chance to go back over the draft and see if it encompasses the thing as much as I really want to. Whereas, if I were saying this, I could read a reaction and I could understand that this person isn't understanding what I am saying, and I could clarify at those points, and I could also get a sense of whether they are really understanding what I am really trying to say. In a situation like this, that is not possible.

Judy makes a good point, and I was struck with how much body language was involved in one of my interviews (as I recorded in an observer comment at the time):

[He] seemed comfortable speaking with the tape recorder rolling, but I was quite aware that he was conscious that it was going. He sat across from me in kind of a closed posture (folded legs and crossed arms), but as the interview got flowing, his body language loosened up too. But, he was always talkative and spoke openly of topics that showed me he was not hanging back, too much. I smiled at him during the interview and looked straight at his eyes. He seemed to always be looking away, maybe from his pondering thought processes, but also, I felt he avoided eye contact. I had never noticed that about him on the other two occasions we have met. I don't make anything of it really—he is not shy, nor is there anything he is trying to hide from me, and he is not ashamed—those are usually the reasons I know of that people don't look at you. Maybe, my staring at him was making him uncomfortable, and that was why he was looking away.

However, we may make too much of the relevance of body language in face-to-face communication. As one computer conference moderator explained to me, a puzzled classroom look may mean confusion or deep thought processes. Similarly, a friend of mine told me of a job search guide she had just purchased that was so detailed it explained how you should communicate your integrity through hand motions—to which I queried whether there was a companion volume for potential employers for interpreting interviewee's hand expressions.

On the negative side of the text nature of computer conferencing, several of the students thought this means of communication was terribly inefficient—taking perhaps an hour to input the messages and read other people's notes when equivalent communication could be accomplished in a regular classroom in about seven minutes. A common comment I heard was that these courses were just more demanding in the amount of effort required. Francis explained:

> Somehow I think you feel that maybe the class will be a little bit
> light because you don't have to travel. But, I didn't find that so
> with my first experience. It was really heavy. . . . So you feel like
> instead of commuting you are going to be doing tons more
> work. I might as well just drive to class.

Perhaps more obvious or intuitive was the oft-repeated comment that the computer conference favored people who wrote well—a reason Dennis, Betty, and Melody enjoyed participating–because they considered themselves good writers. Craig may have been attracted to this medium in part to practice and improve his writing. Those were Ted's main reasons for taking the writing course.

David stated that in computer conferencing all discussants have equal, open-ended "air time." In other words, those who have much to say can write as frequent and lengthy responses as they wish. However, this feature may tend to bring out people with important ideas who may not have been willing to share them in a classroom, thereby inhibiting the real talkers—they find it simply takes too much energy and time to ramble. No one can easily monopolize this environment because (as Lyn and Jack explained) if someone becomes long-winded or verbose, you skim their note or simply do not read it. Some others expressed displeasure at some of the more "vocal" participants but read their messages anyway. Rick expressed more of a middle-of-the-road view:

> I think the variety keeps us going. If everybody was long-wind-
> ed it would become a drag. And if everybody just put down
> bullet points and answered the question with a point and that
> was the end of it, then it's not fun anymore. You know every-
> body likes to put their cents in and—just like a classroom, some
> of them can answer the question in two sentences and some
> of them are going to make a speech.

Unique Pacing Characteristics

Computer conferencing allows students and instructor to not only be geographically separated but to participate in the same conversation at different times. On the surface, these features would appear to give students ultimate flexibility and convenience in interacting with the system. But, as I was to learn from these students, the pacing features of computer conferencing present a challenge.

Computer conferences typically move forward at a fixed pace of progression from one major topic to the next every couple of weeks. For the typical classroom-based student, computer conferencing means disciplining and organizing space within time demands to "attend" and participate in the conference. But, the medium's pacing provides challenges for the correspondence course-type student as well. Whereas in the past they could attend to other concerns easily and place the course on the back burner, they soon found that computer conferencing forced them to keep a relatively fixed schedule. All too easily either type of student would fall behind. Those who had told me it was almost impossible to catch up and get back on schedule.

The Joys and Dangers of Asynchronicity

Being separated in time from other students means a delayed and halted conversation that progresses erratically on the conference. Kerry saw an advantage to this for more honest initial communication:

> You could say what you had to say. You might've offended somebody but they didn't let you know and you couldn't predicate your comments on some factor like that.

This time delay, coupled with distance, takes away the physical intimidation factor you might have felt in person, said Craig, Ted, and Lyn. Rick and Betty both said that even if no one was actually on the system at the same time they were, they felt their presence there. Miguel told how the asynchronicity and distance of a network system allowed him to present and discuss a subject with many hundreds of people online, an activity he could not perform in front of a much smaller crowd at a professional conference.

Yet, asynchronicity has its drawbacks too. Some students told me it was hard to keep up their enthusiasm, interest, and knowledge on a topic over a sustained period of time. They became frustrated at not immediately "hearing" back from those to whom they spoke, and by the time others responded, days later, they had forgotten the particulars of the original conversation and resented having to go back and reread the discussion. Judy explained:

> To me it's too far removed and when somebody writes something, you don't have the opportunity to say I don't understand what you mean. You cannot get that immediate feedback. It takes too long for me. I don't have the time and I don't want to be bothered with it. I'm the type of person that if you say I need this and this and this then I'll give you X, Y, and Z. And then if you tell me you need more, then I'll do that. But when you have to write something and it comes in the mail then it

goes back and then by that time I'm like over and done and I want to move onto the next thing.

Interactivity

One distinguishing characteristic of computer conferencing is its inter-activity—the capability for students to receive in-depth, specific feedback to their questions or about their performance. Students involved in computer conferencing can be disappointed by the buildup and anticipation of glitzy computer technology, only to find that they have to wait days for responses. However, the advantage of computer conferencing interactivity according to these students was that you could bounce ideas off of the other students as well as the instructor. Carl explained:

> With this thing there is the fun of getting an appreciation of many perspectives. It is a similar environment to what you would have if you were working in a classroom side by side with somebody. The only difference is that you are doing it electronically. To give you an example of that, one night [David] and I were having a dialogue in regards to flaming[2]— whether it is appropriate, how we can differentiate whether it is right or wrong, if someone is being argumentative, or if you are personally attacking someone. And we probably have 45 to 50 responses to each other on that issue. So, to me that is very good because I am really learning what his perspective is.

However, computer conferencing is not inherently interactive, either. Kris explained that she felt the discussion in the Constitution course read more like a series of disjointed soliloquies. Because of delayed feedback, these students went off on tangents or would submit stiff, pre-prepared responses that no longer fit the conversation at hand; it seemed to her that lots of separate speeches were going on. The conference is only interactive if students make contributions to which others can respond:

> Ted: There were four or five people that were more advanced and they dominated the conversations. And they'd come out with something way over everybody else's head, and the rest of us just sat back and waited. [laughter] . . . Sometimes you'd

---

[2]*Flaming* refers to caustic communications and name calling in computer-mediated communications. Scholars postulate that it is the text-only communications environment, in which people are somewhat anonymous and removed from one another, that causes this emotional spear hurling to go on.

> read it and say "Wow, what am I supposed to say?" In one case
> we were supposed to make comments on the discussion, and
> this one girl put in three or four pages right off the bat. It killed
> it for everybody else because she said everything. It just kind of
> ended it right there. [both laugh]

Betty explained how she had to start a conversation about an assignment of hers that the instructor posted online as an example because
no one commented on it.

Also, a computer conference lacks interactivity if the student is
not dialoguing on it frequently. Miguel told me that being on several
times a day makes it easy for him to keep up with the online conversations. Likewise, Craig told how he had to be on regularly to keep up. If
all the student does is read without responding, regardless of the other
multiple contributors, the experience can be fairly passive and didactic.
Also, the conference is not interactive unless people are committed to
talk. Rose explained that her second computer conferencing course just
"isn't generating the same volume as the writing course did," so she
was not enjoying it:

> I think what happened is that there were many times that I did
> come home and log on, and no one had sent anything for me
> to view. But that didn't happen in the other course. There was
> always something going on, so it held my interest.

However, it seems that computer conferencing will remain an
environment for discussion and comment. David told how students
rebelled against his first didactic conference:

> The very first thing I said online that was serious, after getting
> acquainted and all of that, I put out this esoteric thing five or six
> screens long. And, the very first response I got back was, "Slow
> down, David." (Those were the days before they had the 800,
> toll-free numbers, so the people had to pay to connect.) "I'm pay-
> ing for this phone call, and I don't want to read your damn lec-
> tures!" [laughs loud] And, it hit me! He is right! "He doesn't have
> to listen to you." I realized that I didn't want to read it either!

Participation and Group Dynamics

These courses required mandatory participation for attendance
purposes, to have distance students demonstrate their attention to
course tasks, and to contribute to increased interactions among students. This is how the Constitution course syllabus explained it:

The success of this way of learning depends on each of us pulling her/his weight. Therefore, as would be true in any seminar, class participation is required and an important component of your final evaluation. Participation means making a direct contribution (entering responses), not simply reading what others have to say. Generally, I'll expect each of you to average a minimum of 2 responses per topical item per week (permanent item responses are entirely voluntary). This will vary, of course, depending on the topic—sometimes you'll have a lot to say, sometimes not so much—but over the entire course, I expect everyone to be an active discussant.

Actually, participation followed a different pattern. Conversations started out slowly but reached their peak several weeks into the course, as people got caught up in the fun and novelty of learning in this new environment. Contributions died down toward course assignment due dates and holidays. During the last month it was at its lowest level because students were busy completing assignments and it no longer was as exciting for many of them. I would often ask how important computer conference participation was toward their overall grade and received a variety of answers—from 25% to 50% in the Constitution course (the syllabus did not say).

Many spoke of being reluctant at first to "talk" to a conference of complete strangers:

> Miguel: At the beginning I am much more of a listener or reader than a person who says much. You don't feel secure about who is listening to you. So, you try to get a feel for the environment first.
>
> Dan: And how do you get to have confidence in them?
>
> Miguel: Oh, reading about them and realizing that they are people just like me.

But, Betty explained how these "online biographies" can also be intimidating, especially if they do not portray you in the best light:

> There was a new student, and I looked to see if they put their name in, and I see that they made the same mistakes as some of the others, i.e., taking three or four screens to do it because they didn't know how to do it. One guy put his information on two or three times because he didn't know he had already saved it. He went from weighing 220 pounds to 215 by the third time he wrote it. I laughed about that one. Its almost as if someone had stood up in class and told a joke.

However, most people seemed to settle down into steady, confident patterns of participation before long. In fact, some people found that computer conferencing overcame the shyness they typically feel in class settings:

> Melody: I find that when I am in a regular, traditional classroom, I don't speak up as much. I'm more on the quiet side, but through the computer I don't mind saying whatever is on my mind, so that is why it works for me. You can say what you want to say, and you don't have to feel shy, or whatever.

Yet, because there was so much student participation, several of these individuals thought the conversation was out of control. Ted told how the instructor tried to steer comments in the writing course back from impassioned discussions about social causes, but the students just kept the same conversational topics rolling. Rose saw the value of off-topic conversation and humor but had difficulty deciding when it had gone too far—when it dominated the discussion—and she expressed her difficulty as an uncomfortable "listener" in steering the conversation back to a course content focus.

Many initial attempts at computer conferencing will replicate patterns of the traditional classroom, as teachers and students cling to their socialized role patterns:

> Betty: But I noticed that the people are most stimulated when the teacher gives a statement. I notice when the students give statements, some people will respond too. For instance, if I say something, somebody will respond to me. But what I find is that I'll say something and a couple other students will say something closely related but not directly related to what I just said—unless I've insulted somebody or somebody strongly disagrees. We are each talking but not necessarily responding to each other. But when the teacher says something, then everybody gives a direct statement to what he said. So I notice that he'll start the conversation and everybody has a comment directly on what he said. Its to show him that "I'm listening. I'm paying attention." [laughter]

And instructor involvement likely plays a direct role in how actively students participate. Miguel told me that the instructor for his course, Bob, was so diligent in communicating that the conference thrived, even with a handful of participants. Bob would respond to his messages, posted several times daily, within an hour. Miguel said, "He is tricky . . . believe me, he knows when I am breathing on the computer!" In contrast, Betty said that when her instructor went away for a vacation (it was unannounced, yet she could check the system to see that he had not been on for a week), students just ceased speaking altogether. However, these students do not feel the moderator's involvement needs to be overbearing to be effective. Students of the Constitution course felt comfortable with David's part in the conference—beginning a topic, setting up a scenario, and then monitoring and refereeing the ensuing online conversation, stepping in only to stimulate further thought or bring the discussion back on course. However, having his continual presence there was important.

Collaboration Or Competition?

Many of the students told me of pressures they felt to be actively engaged in the discussion—wanting to get in the first and the last word. Craig, particularly, spoke of the thrill of competition with other learners on the system, and I became convinced that his whole involvement in this degree program was his way of competing with his brother's triathlon feats. Harry stated that everyone seemed to want to outdo each other in sounding scholarly, using big words and academic phrases. Kerry told me that his online work had to be sharp and well thought out because he would have to defend it against the others.

Indeed, David (a course instructor) explained that this educational system is geared to judge people by their "ability to compete and represent themselves"; not that they "read well or are good people, but that [they] are strong in [their] viewpoints." He believed that computer conferencing fosters "controlled aggression" and brings out shyer types (particularly women). Also, he said that the conferencing milieu suppresses those who typically dominate a classroom because everyone has unlimited, equal "air time."

However, many of these students I spoke with saw the pompous, competitive exchanges going on and chose not to become involved. Harry told me he admired them for being able to put so much thought, time, and effort into their communications, but he was just too busy to imitate them. Judy told how intimidated she was by these "constitution addicts" who seemed like lawyers already; she waited until they started just "going off" with their own opinions before expressing her own.

However, ideal collaborative learning associations seemed to emerge online as well. Vicky, for example, told of the wonderful group learning experience in which she was engaged while taking the "Telecommunications" course—mutual posing of problems and discoveries; giving and receiving from other students; and advice, tips, and instructions through computer conferencing messaging and "phone" exchanges. Miguel and Carl both told of how delighted they were at the detailed, cooperative exploration in which they were fully engaged with a dedicated course instructor, as they hoped to understand and resolve efforts surrounding the ethical use of computers. Also, Rose (described in Chapter 5) explained the wonderful group learning that occurred in her writing course. Vicky explained how the conference invited you to get to know others:

> In the conference there is what they call the "electric lounge." Different people call it different things, but basically its where you can talk about anything. You can kid, you can joke, you can tell about your family, your weekend, what you do, and that sort of thing. So it's a free exchange of lighthearted informal conversation outside of the learning process. In that way I have come to know the students. I've learned a lot about them. You know you find out about their families, their kids, where they live, and start finding commonalties. And as I said, you become very close to them, and so when you get into a problem and you want to telephone somebody on the system or send a note and ask for help or go back into the conference and say, "Gee I tried this and it didn't work," everybody just kind of jumps in and helps. I'll have to tell you that I've been a manager for 13 years in a manufacturing environment, and at first I thought this talk was a total waste of time. Really, that was my first reaction. We are using valuable CPU time to talk about [insignificant stuff]. But as I got more involved in it I started to understand the long-term value of doing that.

Vicky also mentioned how working with others at a distance had changed her:

> I think as a result of interacting with all of the students, I've learned to be a little bit more intuitive. I'm the kind of person— I've got to have all the data in front of me. And I've got to read it and absorb it and I need more data before I make a decision, instead of cutting the cord sometimes and just going with the flow. And I think that exchanging ideas with others has enabled me to think more intuitively; to go on my intuition more, as opposed to seeking out more data. And it has made me a little more relaxed in the learning process I think.

Perhaps there are dangers with either extreme. Competition can draw out aggressive players and surface the contradictions, discrepancies, and difficulties that usually accompany extreme positions. However, many students have more cooperative learning styles which seek win-win approaches to learning. The hazard here, though, is that a sort of "group think" sets in in which absurd ideas and positions go unchallenged in mutual efforts to maintain harmony at all costs. Suffice it to say that computer conferencing seems to inherently enjoin discussion and conversation. Unlike the classroom, in which seating arrangements establish either didactic or mutually shared discussion expectations, the online classroom has no such focal point—conversations will be diffused and participatory. However, design factors and instructor style play a greater role in determining collaborative or competitive patterns than the medium itself.

Computer Conferencing Learning

Morgan (1984) found that distance students' views of learning paralleled those of Säljö's (1979) studies in Sweden—that learners have five different conceptions of what it means to learn. The first three conceptions view learning as a passive information and skill acquisition and reproducing endeavor. However, those learners with the other two conceptions define learning as an active, interpretive process reorganization of their position and worldview based on new perspectives and opinions. Olgren (1991) looked at the learning strategies adult students use in correspondence study. Interviewing 20 adult students taking a correspondence course in marketing for their baccalaureate degree she found three types of learning groups, roughly in equal number, distinguished by their goal orientation to learning. These goals affected the learning strategies they employed and their ability to remember later what they learned. Two groups exhibited a surface orientation to learning: the "reproducers" and "comprehenders." Both of these were extrinsically motivated and had poor recall of course content several months after the course. Her third group—the "appliers"—learned through deep cognitive processes, sought to fit the content into their lives, and were able to later recall and integrate that content into their daily lives. Perry (1970) found university students to develop in a similar hierarchical progression from absolutist intellectual positions to relativist ones that embraced personal commitment. In a similar fashion, I found that these distance students who "attended class" by computer conference varied in their perceptions of the medium's effectiveness, based on their conception of learning.

For those who viewed learning as primarily the acquisition of new information, computer conferencing was not seen as vital or necessary for learning:

> Dan: How important is this computer conferencing portion of the course to your overall learning?
>
> Randy: It is important because it takes the place of the class-

room communication—pulling everybody along and keeping
everything jelled together at the same pace. . . . But, in terms
of learning, it is really not that important. I haven't learned anything new on the computer conference, really. There is no new
information.

Dennis held similar views:

I would say that as far as David using it as part of a grade, [the
computer conference] may be half. But as far as the knowledge
that you gain from it, it would be considerably less. Only
because as in any conversation, you get off of the beaten path.
We kind of stray away from the original subjects and then he
has to pull us back to his original question.

Both of these opinions lend credence to Moore's (1989) position
that a multimedia approach to distance education provides the greatest
interactivity, and hence learning. It would hold that texts and video components provide the learners' interaction with the content, whereas the
online experience provides for learner interaction with the instructor and
other learners. Eastmond and Ziegahn (1993) suggest how online course
design can incorporate a wide variety of offline experiences and resources
through learning contract study for a wider range of interactivity.

However, there were some who wondered if any learning was
going on during the computer conference. For example, both Ted and
Craig found the online conversations, even in the "electronic lounge"
areas, as pompous academic posturing. They intentionally tried to
"lighten" things up a bit or bring the conversation down to "people
level" by making continual references to passing drinks and food
around, asking other students' favorite beer or seafood smorgasbord, or
trying to organize an online football team. One student appreciated
their outrageous comments, but a couple of others thought it was pretty "goofy," not seeing how their comments related to learning and feeling it was wasting their time. Judy questioned the value of even some of
the topic-centered discussion:

I'm wondering about how much [of what] we are doing on
the conference is real learning versus just everybody venting
their opinions. And that is something I was not going to be a
part of initially. I was going to stay within the parameters of
what we were talking about. But, when everybody started to
go off and give their opinions on various things, I said, "Well
shoot, I have some things to say about this, too." . . . When I
was writing [my opinions] I was sitting there going [loud voice
in rhythm] bang, bang, bang, bang, bang, bang, bang.
[laughs]. [In the same cadence] "How can you think that if

> Clarence Thomas was a blah, blah, blah, blah, and she didn't
> leak it to the press and she didn't blah, blah, blah." And I'm sit-
> ting there, and I'm getting very just like livid. I'm livid! I'm totally
> angry. But we tried to keep it within. . . . Every once in a while
> we would try to throw in a word like "First Amendment" or
> "Fourteenth Amendment." I mean, I don't want to say that the
> whole course is like that. But, if you want to know what I
> remember about it, that is what I would remember, rather than
> the War Powers Act.

Other complaints these students had about learning by computer conferencing surfaced in our discussions. Several felt the classroom
offered the advantage of personal contact, which this lacked, but they
had traded that luxury for the convenience of learning from their location at their own schedule. Also, there was little enthusiastic lecturing
and charismatic presentation, like one might find in a classroom course,
according to Judy, to make her want to delve deeply into the content.

For the many who viewed learning as a change of personal perspective about contextual knowledge, or as a means of applying knowledge by finding its relevance in one's life, computer conferencing was
vital for that process:

> Kerry: In a way, [computer conferencing] is the thing that is
> tying everything together. You have to read up for the discus-
> sion. If we didn't have to come on, putting ourselves in center
> stage, then some of us may not see the relevance in what we
> are doing. The papers in the course are more directed toward
> the reading, but the conference is more a place to give our
> opinions and impressions. . . . The discussion has changed. At
> first, people would cite Gerald Ford or Orin Hatch when they
> gave their opinions, but now they speak their opinion as their
> own. It is good for us to realize we have opinions—to speak
> them; it sharpens our minds.

Carl spoke of the deeper mental processes involved when working
online with the content:

> I think by far [the computer conference] is a much better learning
> experience. . . . There is no doubt in my mind that working with
> the other students in CONFER just sticks to you better. But when
> you are reading it out of a textbook there's a certain level of com-
> prehension, and a certain level of understanding, and a certain
> level of retention enabling you to use the information. I think
> those areas I do much better with after I've gone through the
> CONFER conference and worked with a group of guys one on
> one. It just forces you to use your mental facilities or to have bet-
> ter concentration on the material as you are going through it.

The Telecommunications course, focused as it was on student development of network computer skills, brought opportunities for collaboration, discovery, and experiential learning:

> Vicky: What I have found is this form of education online gets you into the experiential learning more than any other delivery methods that I have taken.
>
> Dan: In what sense?
>
> Vicky: Well, he gives you objectives for the course, a set of objectives for the course that you are to achieve. He gives you a guidebook on how to get into the system and then all the mentoring help that you need through the CONFER and himself, and then it's up to you.
>
> Dan: So you go out and kind of discover it all.
>
> Vicky: Yes, discover. What a way to learn! When I got into this telecommunications I began to see myself how well we learn from doing. Well in this telecommunications course, and if others are made like this, the opportunity to network is absolutely phenomenal. I mean, you can carry on an online telephone conversation with someone, that you are having a problem doing certain things. They can walk you through it because they've been through it. Or Bob, I can call him anytime, send him a note, and he'll walk you through it or try and help you do certain things. Again, I don't know if all telecommunications courses are like this, but it's extremely interesting because of the wonderful support you get and the experiential learning, the actual discovering and learning as you're discovering.

A common remark by those students who had taken predominantly distance education courses in the past was that this medium opened up their study world where they found other classmates or peers, making them feel more a part of Hawks College. Rose said:

> It was exciting to get to know them through the written word. The whole learning experience for me, I think, was much nicer than sitting here night after night just doing my work by myself. It is nice to have that input.

Craig told of this medium's advantage over correspondence study:

> [The correspondence course he was taking] doesn't have a modem with it so there isn't interaction with other students. There is none of the competition factor. You don't get insight into what the professor thinks. You get one letter from the professor, and then he corrects your work.

David, the instructor I interviewed, told why he thought computer conferencing created a superior learning situation over individualized study, the mainstay of Hawks College's instructional system:

> Adult students are able to bring relevant experience to the conference, which makes it easy to conduct a seminar in the participatory fashion that I do. And, that is the problem with just independent study. These adults have relevant experience, and so they just tailor the content to their own experience, and it becomes reified. It is not like in the computer conference where they are challenged to think differently.

Other important aspects of student learning by computer conferencing, which often goes unnoticed, are the unintentional, incidental skills, knowledge, and attitudes picked up during the course. First, there are usually a whole set of computer conference and networking skills that students pick up as they connect to the conference, learn to interact with others on it, and (perhaps) extend their online information gathering to reach online databases, libraries, and discussion groups. Also, there are a whole set of learning-how-to-learn skills that these individuals develop in order to succeed in a new instructional environment. (These skills are the focus of the next chapter.) Another area, a topic addressed in Chapter 5, is the formation and maintenance of social relationships and online alliances or friendships. Additionally, there are a whole set of communication protocols, habits, etiquette, and role patterns that come into play in this environment—taken from other instructional settings and many of which are socially constructed as the group faces new online circumstances and produces thoughtful, trial-and-error responses.

ADULT LEARNING IMPLICATIONS FOR COMPUTER CONFERENCING

Contemporary scholarship on adult learning shows the complete shift in the goals, content, activities, and evaluation of learning, as Candy (1991) wrote:

> In the past, self-direction was seen essentially as a personal quality or attribute; knowledge as a fixed and enduring set of "facts" to be mastered; learning as a process of acquiring attitudes, skills, and knowledge from outside of the self; and individuals as substantially asocial atoms, independent of their social and cultural environments. In the new view, though, self-direction is acknowledged as a product of the interaction between the person and the environment;

knowledge is recognized as tentative, evanescent, and socially constructed; learning is defined as a qualitative shift in how phenomena are viewed; and individuals are seen in the complex and mutually interdependent relationship with their environment." (p. 246)

Although academics have written numerous volumes on various
dimensions of adult learning, I just touch on the scholarship that is
most relevant for establishing the context of adult distance study
through computer conferencing. These aspects are: self-directed learning, experiential learning, reflection in learning, interactivity, and collaborative learning.

Self-Directed Learning

The principle of Andragogy to which scholars have attended the most is
self-directed learning—"the view that the individual learner is capable of
assuming considerable responsibility for and control of learning activities when such opportunities are provided" (Hiemstra & Sisco, 1990, p.
238). This tenet could rightfully be promoted as the major aim of adult
education, claimed Brookfield (1986), but he also cautioned scholars in
claiming that it exists naturally among adults; rather, self-directedness
is culture and class bound, exists in children's learning, and may be
socially dysfunctional. Despite the fact that the concept of self-education has a long history going back to the ancient Greeks and Romans
(Candy, 1991), adult educators only began to embrace the phenomena
wholly in the last 40 years with Knowles's Andragogy and Tough's learning project research, as they used it to determine instructional strategies, policy, and research directions (Hiemstra & Sisco, 1990).

Much of the literature surrounding self-directed learning is concerned with conceptual definitions and distinctions. Brookfield (1986)
contrasted self-education—the external processes of design, resource
selection, strategies, goals, and evaluation—with (his notion of) self-
directed learning: "an internal change of consciousness" (p. 47). Rather
than developmental tasks providing the impetus for learning,
Brookfield posited that self-directed learners "emphasize instead the
pleasure and joy that resulted from the act of learning" (p. 45). He
found "the most fully adult form of self-directed learning, however, is
one in which the critical reflection on the contingent aspects of reality,
the exploration of alternative perspectives and meaning systems, and
the alteration of personal and social circumstances are all present" (pp.
58-59).

Candy (1991) divided self-directed learning into the following
four areas:

- personal autonomy—referring to self-directedness as a personal characteristic in all aspects of life.
- self-management—the willingness and capacity to conduct one's own education.
- learner control—a mode of organizing instruction in formal settings
- autodidaxy—the individual, noninstitutional pursuit of learning opportunities in the "natural societal setting" (p. 23).

Hiemstra and Brockett's (1991) Personal Responsibility Orientation (PRO) model of self-direction in adult learning contains similar elements. The distinction they make is between the learner's internal characteristics to take control ("learner self-direction") and the external demands of the instructional transaction for learner control ("self-directed learning").

Both Candy (1991) and Brookfield (1983, 1986) challenge adult educators to reexamine the self-directed learning research findings and practice injunctions that fill much current adult education literature. First, they challenge whether adults are self-directing in all aspects of their life or learning; rather, they assume more control over learning with which they have more knowledge and mastery. Learners often begin their studies without clear goals and strategies; these evolve during their studies. The concept of "self-direction" implies individual activity, but most learning occurs within groups.

How do educators assist adult learners in becoming more self-directing, if this is their aim? Brookfield (1986) stated that complete self-directed learning, in which the learner exercises full control, contradicts expectations of the institutional setting, but the highest forms of learning rarely occur without facilitation. He recommends that learning be a transaction process, using the learning contract as the mechanism to mediate between the learner's and the institution's position. Hiemstra and Sisco's (1990) six-step individualizing instructional process model also uses the learning contract as its core element. However, Candy (1991) revealed that no research backs up adult educators' claims that facilitation approaches with learning contracts necessarily enhance learning self-directedness outside of institutional settings. In fact, several scholars note how resistant adult students and institutions are to these approaches (Brookfield, 1986; Candy, 1991; Hiemstra & Sisco, 1990).

Individuals in a distance course taught through computer conferencing exhibit some degree of self-direction: They decide to take the course, usually on a voluntary basis. Also, they must decide when and where they will study, within the constraints of their life situation. Given the many-to-many interactivity of computer conferencing (Harasim, 1990b), these courses become more flexible in content and activities. The emerging discussion often is guided by the interests and initiatives of the participants. But true self-direction, such as expressed by Brookfield (1986), is not possible; what self-direction happens rests on the facilitator, sponsoring institution, and the adult learners themselves.

Experiential Learning

Andragogy suggests that adults bring a wealth of experience to the learning setting on which educators can capitalize. The notion of experiential learning is somewhat different; rather, it proposes that adults effectively learn from experiences. The emphasis is on present and future activity. Brookfield (1983) distinguished between two types of experiential learning: (a) the direct interaction of the student with the phenomena being studied (usually arranged by an institution), and (b) incidental learning through active engagement in everyday events— work, family, media, and community affairs. Experiential learning, he argued, involves both experiences (not inherently educative in and of themselves) and learning—the positive growth response that individuals may take through reflection and action in a novel situation (like being unemployed).

The amount of conscious involvement, learning focus, and action orientation are the defining characteristics between formal, informal, and incidental learning (Marsick & Watkins, 1990). Formal instruction, which typically has little experiential or action component, is very conscious and learning focused. In contrast, incidental learning, the "byproduct of some other activity, such as task accomplishment, interpersonal interaction, sensing the organizational culture, or trial-and-error activity"(p. 4), is highly experiential or action oriented, but lacks both learning intent and conscious reflection to learn. Informal learning, that loosely structured learning activity undertaken by individuals without institutional direction, is both reflective and active.

Adult educators become involved with experiential learning as they assist learners in their own self-directed pursuits, usually in an informal learning mode. Brookfield (1983) discussed how some higher education institutions have awarded credit for experience when adults demonstrate that learning through portfolio preparation or test completion. *Experiential learning cycle* (1990) provided a five-step model of experiencing, publishing, processing, generalizing, and applying for facilitating structured experiential learning.

However, adult educators even have important roles to play in incidental learning. Marsick and Watkins (1990) demonstrated how much incidental learning can be dysfunctional to both individuals and organizations, and they proposed several facilitation strategies to assist incidental learning, primarily to set up situations that require learners to deeply reflect on their assumptions and induce learnings from them.

The discussion nature of computer conferencing allows for some incorporation of experiential learning, in providing structured and challenging experiences to knowledge developed from prior incidental learning. For the many many students who are unfamiliar with computer communication technology, simply being a part of a computer conference provides experiential learning, although the learning is not in the content area of the course. However, much of the potential for experiential learning must be incorporated into offline activities, perhaps through the use of a learning contract.

Reflection In Learning

Whatever adults encounter in their world—ideas, experiences, emotions—does not happen in a total vacuum. Through reflection they examine these stimuli and determine what meaning to give them and whether the inputs fit comfortably within their current belief system or challenge it. This process "of reflecting back on prior learning to determine whether what we have learned is justified under present circumstances" (p. 5) is central to adult learning, although ignored by learning theorists (Mezirow, 1990a). Reflection in learning stems back to John Dewey and other philosophers and has wider scholarship by contemporary theorists in women's studies, social construction, and critical thinking.

Reflection means examining why or how one has come to make judgments, assumptions, or to hold ideas, according to Mezirow (1990a); simply acting based on what worked best in the past is only "thoughtful action without reflection" (p. 7).

Two of Cross's (1981) types of learning—self-understanding and stage progression—which invite humanism and developmental theory respectively, rely on reflection. Gibbon's (1990) model of learning-how-to-learn incorporates reflection in several of its components, notably the developmental domain that requires critical reflection. Nor does he confine this activity to adults:

> Children are natural, autonomous learners. To progress beyond reaction to reflection, they must develop an inner dialogue in which the child as reflective learner mediates—with reason, intuition, and creativity—between the influences of the environment and collective experience in order to generate insight, decision, and invention. (p. 75)

Mezirow (1990b) gives three purposes for reflection: "to guide action, to give coherence to the unfamiliar, and to reassess the justification for what is already known" (p. xvi).

There is nothing inherent in computer conferencing to cause reflection or critical reflection. Yet, it presents many of the necessary elements: a group inquiry environment that invites analysis and synthesis of readings, opinions, and experience, without limits to the amount of feedback the learner can give or receive. Given skillful moderation toward facilitating reflection, it will likely occur.

Interactivity

Research strongly suggests that heightened involvement with instructional materials and feedback about that activity increases accurate and sustained learning (Fleming & Levie, 1978). But, is all interactivity the same? Moore (1989) found the hypothetical construct of interactivity problematic, and, to more accurately define it, he divided it into three types: First, there is the interaction that the learner has with the content (Learner-Content); second is the interaction between the student and teacher (Learner-Instructor); and finally, is the interactivity that involves the exchange students have among themselves (Learner-Learner).

Moore (1989) argued that the various distance education media should be evaluated based on their capability to facilitate each type of interactivity because each is desirable (if not essential) for learning. He found that texts, video, computer-assisted instruction, and interactive video strongly promote Learner-Content interactions but not the other types. Correspondence study provides both Learner-Content and Learner-Instruction interactivity but is deficient in its Learner-Learner capability. Moore submitted that audio/video conferencing maintains strong Learner-Instructor and Learner-Learner interactivity but is not particularly effective in promoting Learner-Content interactions. This probably also holds true for computer conferencing interactivity.

In order to glean maximum interactivity benefits, Moore (1989) suggested that distance education efforts involve multimedia. This allows one medium's strength to compensate for another's limitations. Indeed, this often is the case when conferencing media involve outside reading assignments—a means of capturing the Learner-Content interactivity in which conferencing media are limited.

Collaborative Learning

Fundamental to collaborative learning is the mutual, cooperative investigation of knowledge, exhibited in this formal definition:

> Collaboration . . . is a pedagogical style that emphasizes coopera-
> tive efforts among students, faculty, and administrators. Rooted in
> the belief that learning is inherently social in nature, it stresses
> common inquiry as the basic learning process. Although academi-
> cally and culturally challenging, it benefits participants by making
> them more active as learners, more interactive as teachers, more
> balanced as researchers, more effective as leaders, and more
> humane as individuals. (Whipple, 1987, p. 3)

Smith (1982) proposed four conditions on which a collaborative
learning group should be formed: (a) all participants take responsibility
for developing and evaluating the program, (b) the learning climate fosters freedom of expression, (c) all participants are skilled in joint
inquiry and problem solving; and (d) participants continually diagnose
and improve their mutual learning process. In reality, this means that
participants view knowledge acquisition differently; they believe it is
created collaboratively, not just transferred from the teacher to the student. Adults must come to see knowledge as being held communally,
rather than individually—the synergistic whole being greater than the
views of any single individual (and individuals are encouraged to hold
differing views; Whipple, 1987). This epistemological position is similar
to that upheld by social construction and feminist theorists
(MacGregor, 1990).

Collaboration calls on new roles for adult students. MacGregor
(1990) described the student role, one that is very adult in character:

> (1) from listener, observer, and note taker to active problem solver,
> contributor, and discussant; (2) from low to moderate expectations
> of preparation for class to high expectations, frequently having to
> do with reading and preparing questions or other assigned work in
> advance; (3) from a private presence in the classroom to a public
> one; (4) from attendance dictated by personal choice to that having
> to do with community expectation; (5) from competition with peers
> to collaborative work with them; (6) from responsibilities and self-
> definition associated with learning independently to those associ-
> ated with learning interdependently; and (7) from seeing teachers
> and texts as the sole distributors of authority and knowledge to
> seeing peers, oneself, and the thinking of the community as addi-
> tional and important sources of information. (p. 26)

MacGregor also alerts us to ways the teacher's role changes with collaborative learning. The instructor gives up being the sole source of authority, control, and power (while still retaining it for institutional purposes, such as grading) and shifts the burden of "covering" the content to one that is mutually shared.

If collaborative learning is a distinctly adult mode of inquiry, then this has strong implications for the distant student participating in a computer conference course. Harasim (1989) called computer conferencing an "augmented environment for collaborative learning and teaching" (p. 60) because it gives learners more flexible options over their learning; it removes the prejudicial biases of face-to-face contact; it eliminates time and space boundaries, and it promotes group work.

Harasim (1990b) submitted that computer conferencing can amplify intellectual development through collaborative learning. Five characteristics of computer conferencing—many-to-many communication, place-independent group communication, time-independent communication, text-based communication, and computer-mediated learning—promote active learning, which requires both engagement and construction of meaning. She argued that it supports divergent thinking through idea-generating activities.

Other Assumptions About Computer Conference Students

Several other characteristics may distinguish distance students' learning through computer conference courses from other adults. First, they must have high levels of independence and self-direction to undertake the elaborate learning project such a course represents (even if delivered under the auspices of an institution). As Knapper (1988) stated: "Distance learners are generally highly motivated and, out of necessity, placed in a situation where they must take responsibility for guiding their own studies with only minimal help from an educational institution" (p. 70).

Second, participating on a computer conference presupposes a level of knowledge and skill with computer telecommunications that not all adults share. Typically these students must be familiar with the operation of a personal computer, a word processing program, a modem, communications software, mainframe access, and computer conferencing software—all of which are "end-user" computer skills, but they become a formidable learning requirement if sought all at once. So, it seems plausible that computer conferencing attracts those adults who have some of these proficiencies already.

Finally, computer conferencing participation may have class and gender dimensions. Personal "home" computers are still owned by members of the educated, financially secure middle or upper-middle classes. Access to the upper-division undergraduate or graduate university courses typically offered in this format attracts these same constituents. Several research studies suggest that women have been socialized to avoid computer usage because of its math and science connotation (Hawkins, 1985).

Scholarship on the Nature of Computer Conferencing

Perhaps more has been written about the nature of the computer conferencing environment—its implications for learning and teaching—than any other aspect of this technology. Harasim (1989, 1990b) claimed this is a wholly new educational domain with its own characteristics, advantages, and limitations, which I have already discussed. Kaye (1989) finds computer conferencing to be a new type of education, having properties that place it somewhere between distance education and the traditional classroom. Most of these writings laud and promote the medium. However, the way these adult students perceived computer conferencing is perhaps more in line with Mason's (1990) view:

> Computer conferencing suffers badly from the unrealistic expectations of its users and promoters. The motor car was only expected to be as good as the horse; computer conferencing is expected to provide the intellectual, social, and information requirements of an entire university without one ever leaving the confines of one's own island. (p. 23)

Several researchers explored student perceptions of the online communications medium generally, not just computer conferencing. Grabowski, Suciati, and Pusch (1990) found that graduate students felt e-mail was effective for exchanging social and academic information with their peers and professors. Those who chose not to use it did so because they felt no need for it, found access to the computer network inconvenient or unavailable, or simply had not learned the necessary skills for using the technology. Grint (1989) found that students thought it difficult to carry out conversations in asynchronous time and felt they were overloaded with trivial information before being able to contribute. They were inhibited by their impression of a large, "lurking," anonymous audience who would read their contributions. Students perceived that unless they contributed facts, which was difficult in the new subject matter area they were studying, their contributions to the conference were unimportant. Therefore, they disliked reading the opinions of other students online. Status and gender also affected participation among those he studied.

Harasim's (1987) research on two graduate courses taught through computer conferencing is probably the most telling about how students perceive this medium of any study done to date. Using both quantitative and qualitative approaches she found that students spent longer online than they were required by the course, and they felt that this medium was effective. Some of the advantages students listed computer conferencing included: increased interaction, access to a group, the democratic environment it fostered, convenience of access, control over the instructional process, motivation to participate, and the textual nature of the computer conferencing medium. The disadvantages they mentioned were information overload, the medium's asynchronicity which caused delayed responses, difficulty following online discussions, loss of visual cues with this communication, increased access inconvenience, and health concerns about computer radiation.

Other studies support Harasim's conclusions as well as add some additional insights. Hiltz (1986) found that students commented among themselves and valued computer conferencing more when it was a supplemental activity of the course and not the main medium of instruction. Students said that convenience was the greatest advantage of computer conferencing, but the awkwardness they felt in communicating with unknown persons was its greatest liability. Robinson (1992) found that convenience of access at the student's own time schedule was more important than the separation in proximity of distance learners. Rice (1982) found that having specific tasks increases peoples' use of a computer conferencing system and that much shifting occurs from conference topic to topic as participants become familiar with the software. McCreary and Van Duren (1987) found that those of higher or lower status submit written contributions less frequently to computer conferences. Graduate students' participation was more active and horizontal (among fellow students) than was the online activity of undergraduates. Differences in content areas did not affect participation. Scollon (1981) found that the Native Alaskan students she studied were easily confused by the excessive and scattered communication online. Instructors could not attend to the many students in the course (60 people), and the volume of communication was particularly difficult for everyone to process. The students welcomed a return to the audio cues of teleconferencing.

According to Feenberg (1989), group dynamics of social constraint and approval are missing in computer-mediated communications. However, my study indicates that social norms operate within the conference, many of them the same ones that affect face-to-face communication. Graddol (1989) suggested instead that different sorts of communication conventions are created online: Turn taking is not in sequence, rather it is replaced with being the first to make a conversational point as the norm; turns are scattered throughout the conversation, shaping topics of discussion differently; computer conferencing supports those who join the discussion late or who simply want to lurk. He stated that "computer-mediated communications represents a new cultural context for which |students| need to develop a new communication competence" (p. 241).

Asynchronicity is usually mentioned in a positive manner in the literature—a means of promoting reflective, well-written exchanges (Kaye et al., 1989). The students involved in my study found these aspects as well as the negative ones previously mentioned. Grint (1989) also found asynchronicity to be a major participation barrier; it caused disjointed conversations when more continuity was desired. People would not initiate a topic unless they could see themselves having the time to respond later. However, this disjointed conversation remarkably improved feedback patterns for those I studied who had primarily used correspondence study in the past. Cookson's (1990) review of persistence studies found that completion rates rose dramatically when correspondence course turnaround was reduced by several days. The low attrition rates in computer conferencing courses (less than 10% in OISE's graduate courses; Kaye et al., 1989) may be due to this factor.

Just as this study found, researchers at the British Open University noted that much online conversation seems trivial. Mason (1990) suggests this is so because participation is primarily optional, and student inclination in a new instructional environment is to engage in informal pleasantries. Grint (1989) argued along the lines I propose:

> |Being delivered by computer| the majority of students perceived CMC to be a mode of communication configured to transmit technical expertise. It wasn't just that too much information existed within the conferences or that most of this was trivia, but the criteria for assessing triviality itself reflected unquestioned assumptions about technology. Thus, technical information was usually defined as objective, valid, and usually accurate; sociologically informed information was normally perceived as biased, subjective, and irrelevant—it was trivia. (p. 192)

Graddol (1989) argued that even such informal communication is socially structured and educationally significant. Few of the students in my study complained of excessive triviality because an explicit norm, seemingly adhered to, was that such chitchat should only take place in the "electronic lounge" area.

Like several of the courses I studied, Mason (1988) suggested that those participants with dominant personalities who write well can take over a conference. However, studies of the Ontario Institute for

Studies in Education's conferencing suggest that fewer students domi-nate online conversation (Harasim, 1989; Kaye et al., 1989). There is almost universal agreement that teachers do not monopolize the dis-cussion as they do in a typical classroom, nor are similar conventions in place that give them the same capability to manipulate who con-tributes and what they say (Graddol, 1989).

Grint (1989) argued that conferencing does not flatten the sta-tus hierarchies—rather students, particularly those who chose not to participate, searched them out. However, other writers claim that com-puter conferencing levels the hierarchies and makes status appear-ances unknown; therefore, homebound, disabled, and those working unsociable hours can mix, regardless of their appearance and attire (Kaye et al., 1989). Manninen (1991) found class differences to affect participation in courses taught using computer conferencing. Middle-class students found it easier to access the computer network, and they discussed actively on the system. In contrast, working-class students contributed less, in reactive responses, but their participation increased over time. Studies indicate fairly equal contribution rates to conferences among participants (Harasim, 1989; Siegel, Dubrovsky, Kiesler, & McGuire, 1986). My research revealed aspects of both per-spectives—participants valued not being able to see what others were like, but in fact, if they so desired, they could know quite a bit about each other. More significant was the finding that computer conferenc-ing fostered sharing among those from diverse backgrounds, whether these characteristics were known or not.

Grint (1989) found that invisibility or relative anonymity acted as a barrier to many—writing to strangers in words that seemed final and fixed once sent. However, my informants spoke of this barrier infre-quently and of gradually overcoming it—possibly because they were the more active participants in conferences in which involvement was required.

Mason (1988) claimed the "medium fosters co-operation rather than competition between students" (p. 29) because it is written, inter-active discourse (Kaye et al., 1989). But this assertion remains unsup-ported by my research; rather, many factors determine whether the computer conference will be collaborative or competitive or a passive or interactive experience. Several students reported that they needed to keep up with the conference flow or be left behind as Mason (1988) had written.

What I described in this study as a negatively addictive, com-pulsive medium (to some such as Ted or Francis) was an environment of fun to many others (Betty, Carl, Miguel, or Vicky)—as Mason (1988) wrote:

|The computer conference| is great fun! It is exciting to log into a continuing flow, to give and take, to experience the growth of the group creation. The element of surprise, suspense and curiosity is roused. . . . Conferencing is unpredictable; it is unpackaged; it is serendipitous. This element of fun is, I believe, the real ace in the conferencing pack of cards. (p. 40)

As my study indicated, computer conferencing offers some unique advantages for distance education that merit its continued, expanded use. As advocated by Granger (1990a) and noted by Mason and Kaye (1989), computer conferencing individualizes distance education as no other medium can. Also, as advocated by Granger (1990a), computer-mediated communication (CMC) allows distance instructors to take a more active role than the passive one of correspondence study. Mason and Kaye (1990) argued that the best role of computer conferencing is as one component of a multimedia distance delivery system—one in which learners have the option to choose the medium that best suits their learning style, the nature of the content, and their preferences of the moment. Limiting media to just computer conferencing would impoverish the learning environment. The literature speaks of collaboration, reflectivity, and interactivity as being important characteristics of this medium (Harasim, 1989, 1990b; Kaye, 1989; Kaye et al., 1989; Moore, 1991), but this study questions whether those elements are always present with computer conferencing instruction. Perhaps one of the most significant contributions of this research is corroboration of an earlier scholarly observation: "Any or all of the media with 'educational potential'—books, television, lectures, cassettes—can be used well or badly. It is the application of a medium which defines the outcome for students, not its inherent characteristics" (Mason, 1988, p. 38).

CONCLUSION

This chapter served three purposes: First, it described the context and structure within which the distance computer conferencing courses took place; second, it explained the views students held about the nature of this learning environment; and third, it examined scholarship about the characteristics of computer conferencing that enable adult learning. Most of these students participated in the computer conference from their homes. Both at home or at work they often interacted with others, sometimes discussing their schooling; their online studies impacted others, who may or may not have been supportive of these activities. Some of their study areas were not conducive to distance work, having neither work space nor quiet seclusion.

These courses involved reading textbooks, writing assignments, and participating in the computer conference each week. The online structure included both general and voluntary discussion items as well as topical and mandatory ones. Students often used local libraries and computer network resources, such as listserves, electronic mail, and the "phone" facility, as part of this experience. Instructors varied in the amount of attention they gave to the conference—some monitored students throughout the day, whereas others were absent for days at a time. The coach or referee-type role David played in the Constitution course was typical of many such online courses. Student participation varied; the active, "vocal" students were more engaged in this research (with exceptions). Students formed alliances online and helped the instructor in encouraging more silent classmates to participate.

The bulk of the chapter dealt with students' perceptions of computer conferencing as a learning environment. The novelty of learning with computer technology often gave way to demanding involvement in meeting course requirements. Many of these students seemed compulsively attracted to continually monitor online notes and conversations—considered by some as a time-consuming necessity that interfered with home life—whereas others found these activities to be a recreational respite from work and study tedium. These students saw the text-only communication aspect of the conference as a means for relaying human personality and meaning in a different way than could be done in person; it favored good writers and provided for more equal participation, but was seen by some as an overly time-consuming and inefficient way of communicating. Primarily both distance or campus students who took these courses found themselves having to adjust their schedules to the microflexibility and macroregimentation of online pacing requirements. Asynchronicity was thought to enable people to initially express their viewpoints and speak to large groups; yet some students had trouble sustaining disjointed communication on a topic over several weeks.

A hallmark of computer conferencing—interactivity—can be heightened or diminished entirely by the way students craft their notes and stay ahead or behind the discussion, as determined by their online frequency. The chapter discussed how students overcame initial intimidation at "talking" with strangers, how they patterned their own involvement on the instructor's participation patterns, and how message volume ebbed and flowed during the semester as they were affected by other assignment due dates. Collaboration, although a proclaimed feature of computer conferencing, was most apparent in the writing and telecommunications courses; competition seemed to dominate the Constitution course, perhaps reflecting the instructor's teaching style.

Whether students felt the computer conference enabled learning was strongly related to their conceptions of learning. One group found they picked up no new information online, and the conference became a "soapbox" for everyone to vent their opinions. Others, however, found these discussions useful for formulating personal positions, applying ideas to new situations, exploring alternative interpretations, and reinforcing the content they learned from texts or videos. Elements of discovery and experiential learning came out strongly in the telecommunications course. Those students who primarily took correspondence study found that this medium gave them deeper glimpses into their instructor's thinking as well as the opportunity to "hear" other students' opinions on course content. Also, these adults learned several things unintentionally: computer networking skills, learning-how-to-learn skills, the building and maintenance of online relationships, and electronic communication protocols and student role taking.

Several general conclusions are also in order, supported by the examples given throughout the chapter. First, this study found that the online environment represents a different instructional world with its own set of advantages, limitations, and challenges. Also, instructional philosophy, student-teacher relationships, attitudes, and roles often replicate themselves in this environment. Finally, several aspects of this research, particularly surrounding collaboration, reflection, and interactivity, call into question whether these characteristics are somehow inherent within this instructional delivery system.

4

Learning Approaches to Electronic Study

> So, with these classes, you have a lot of assignments and papers to write. But, they [the instructors] don't talk to you very much. You read instead. Aristotle is your mentor. You've got to think that way. Karl Marx is your mentor or Locke. . . . You see the problem with [the college] is that it is easy to get discouraged; you are all alone. So you have to put yourself in the frame of mind that you have many teachers. Once you've got a hold on that, then you start to get some insight into what you are learning—Craig Brooks (October 1991)

I was excited to hear Craig's learning approach during one of my first interviews. Later, when I sought for other examples of this perspective among Hawks students, I became disappointed—this was not a shared perspective of all students. In a follow-up interview with Craig, I was even disappointed to hear him say that he had made it up on his own because I was looking for socially constructed views of learning.

Later I realized that I initially missed the proverbial "forest for the trees." Craig's statement simply represented a fascinating example of someone who took an ambivalent, difficult learning situation and created his own workable approach for dealing with it. This confirms Blumer's (1969) view—that people are actors who determine how they will handle and shape the events of their lives, although constraining conditions within situations impinge on them. Like Craig, adults develop and apply their own learning approach based on their individual learning preferences, philosophy, and style. These will be confined to the instructional milieu; such as a computer conference, within which they find themselves and the learning approaches they have found effective in other settings.

This position is in contrast to that of most distance education research, which focuses on the objective reality of student characteristics (Cookson, 1989; Gibson, 1990; Sheets, 1992). Their approach is that because adult students possess certain attributes, they will have successful distance learning experiences. The primary role of research is to discover those variables and determine what those characteristics are, aiding the institution in recruiting that clientele or setting up appropriate institutional responses. In contrast, this investigation indicates that students are free agents who work out their own actions toward successful learning outcomes as they view them. Given adequate levels of interesting content and instructional presence, they will compensate for difficulties in their environment and put out the necessary effort and strategy reformulation to make this new, online experience successful.

Some of the strategies these students employed were socially worked out or came from guidelines and suggestions they had been given by the instructor. But, more typically, these students borrowed from their "bag of learning tricks" the approaches, strategies, and tactics that had worked for them in other situations—either instructional, familial, or vocational contexts. They experimented with these, accepting, discarding, borrowing, and so forth, until they came up with patterns that fit them. The result was an eclectic, idiosyncratic learning approach.

REVIEW OF RELATED LITERATURE

Fundamental to the self-directedness, reflection, experiential learning, collaboration, discovery, and other properties of adult learning is the notion of learning-how-to-learn (LHTL). Smith (1982) defined LHTL as "possessing, or acquiring, the knowledge and skill to learn effectively in whatever learning situation one encounters" (p. 19) and noted that it encompasses these concepts:

> (1) increasing the individual's self-awareness and capacity for self-monitoring and reflection when engaged in educational activity; (2) helping people to become more active learners and to assume an

appropriate amount of control of learning-related activity; (3) broadening the individual's repertoire of learning strategies; (4) preparing people to accommodate the requirements of different delivery systems, methods, and subject areas; (5) enhancing learner confidence and motivation; (6) compensating for metacognitive deficiencies . . . ; (7) improving group inquiry and problem-solving skills; (8) helping people to make sound choices among the educational programs and resources available to them; and (9) fostering organizational learning. (p. 4)

Characteristics of LHTL

Gibbons (1990) submitted that LHTL are higher order skills than the content being taught. LHTL are a set of skills that draw more learning from life's experiences and to a greater depth than that which any simple content presentation can achieve. He argued that learning and LHTL are similar and overlapping processes, but learning is an operational function (i.e., to "do learning"), whereas LHTL is an executive function (i.e., learning "how to do" something). "The criteria of appropriate and successful LHTL are generalizability, control, and autonomy" (p. 67). In other words, better LHTL skills allow skills to be transferred from one setting to another, give learners more control over an instructional situation, and allow them to exercise autonomy (or self-directedness) in carrying their learnings forward. Simons (1992) revealed how either teachers or students can activate the learning process. Ignoring short-term learning gains, instructors should encourage adult students to gradually take more responsibility through applying LHTL. This approach meets lifelong learning ideals and reaps long-term benefits.

LHTL scholars note that context is the greatest determinant of which LHTL skills will be employed, and a majority of LHTL skills are context specific (Candy, 1990; Gibbons, 1990; Smith, 1990, 1992). Learning skills vary significantly from setting to setting, as differences are perceived by students in the tasks they must perform and what they see as teaching and evaluation in those settings. Smith (1990) identified various types of contexts: institutional settings, subject matter, personal learning, and culture. Institutions set forth policy and norms that circumscribe what learning can be sought and by whom. "Each [subject matter] has its characteristic modes of analysis and discourse" (p. 16). Art values creativity; economics values analysis; and science values problem solving. Even models of teaching create the type of learner response a particular subject values. Candy (1990) questioned the efficacy of teaching generic LHTL skills devoid of the specific content and problem setting that the learning addresses. The context of personal learning refers to the unique set of individual characteristics that each person brings to the learning situation, such as goals, modality preferences, learning styles, emotions, and repertoire of known LHTL strategies (Smith, 1990). Finally, the cultural context of language, gender, race, ethnicity, and values affect LHTL strategies as well (Smith, 1990).

LHTL With Computer Conferencing

Harasim (1989. 1990b) claimed that computer conferencing, increasingly being used for teaching distance education courses, represents a unique medium with characteristics for increased collaboration and intellectual development. She outlined some of its features, such as the creation of an active, collaborative, and interactive learning environment, which is text-based, fosters many-to-many communication, and is independent of time and place. Harasim claimed these demonstrate that this medium is like no other distance education one, nor is it like the classroom to which it is constantly being compared. Other adult learning ideals it appears to foster are experiential learning, reflection, and self-direction. It also represents unique challenges to adults who have not encountered the difficulties also associated with this medium, such as accessibility, small window problem, keeping track of the online discussion, disjointed transactions, problematic metaphors, procedural decisions, socioemotional issues, participation, and typing ability (Davie, 1989).

Gooler (1990) argued that the technological changes that now engulf us are of such a kind and speed, and fundamental enough so as to have profound effects in all aspects of our lives. He wrote that the emergent information technologies, those that integrate computers, telecommunications, and video, have changed the learning process by allowing learners to use multiple modalities, interact with the technology, and have greater opportunities to learn cooperatively with others. LHTL in the information age means skills of "(1) locating and accessing information resources, (2) organizing information, (3) self-diagnosis and assessments, and (4) greater skills in collaboration" (pp. 322-324). Computer networking facilitates each of these.

Learning-how-to-learn (LHTL) theorists posit that being able to effectively process and use information represents a more important skill set than concentrating instruction on the acquisition of knowledge (Gibbons, 1990; Smith, 1982). But relatively little of this scholarship deals with study techniques outside of conventional settings. Candy (1990) explained that along with learning content, we constantly form learning strategies and develop concepts about ourselves as learners. These views can be both enabling and inhibiting. Candy said that "when |learners| approach a new learning task, they cast around for some analogous situation from the past to give guidance as to how to approach this new situation" (p. 41).

Despite its uniqueness, students trying out computer conferencing for the first time receive little guidance about how to participate, organize their lives, interact with offline materials, reflect, express themselves online, and use the online experience for successful completion of the course. Yet, those who had successful experiences with computer conferencing courses had to have made these decisions and brought about the necessary changes in their study habits and lifestyles.

Exemplars

Craig Brooks and Carl Winer, two of my key informants, act as examples throughout this chapter. I contrast their learning approaches with the other 18 distance learners involved in similar courses offered through computer conferencing. Craig, who just turned 40 years old, works as a security officer at a psychiatric hospital in a nearby city. Married, he has three children and owns a home on a country road on the outskirts of town. While his wife worked during the day and the children were in day care or at school, he worked at his distance education courses in the study area that dominates the basement of their home. I observed Craig there interacting on the computer conference one afternoon, but most of our interviews were held over the phone.

Carl was also in his early 40s. He manages a grocery store, which is part of a large, regional chain. He commuted an hour each way to the store, where he worked the day shift. When he worked evenings, he went to the store later the next day. He worked at his distance courses in the evenings, on the mornings of his "late" day schedule, and on his days off. He studied at a desk in his large bedroom. We talked a couple of times on the phone, and he answered a series of my questions by e-mail.

GENERAL LEARNING STRATEGIES

Many of the learning approaches students use in other situations work well in this type of distance study. These students told me about such things as study patterns, scheduling, working with others, establishing attitudes or a learning climate, seeking task information, getting feedback, and using one's own learning style preferences.

Study Patterns

Craig studied during the day. He worked the night shift and pursuing a degree may have been his way of keeping productively occupied when his free time did not coincide with the rest of the family's time at home. He found he could handle the work load of two classes a semester and was sometimes able to dovetail the assignments of both that way. He seemed able and willing to devote more time to the courses than most other students. Craig studied better now that his young daughter was in day care while his wife worked during the day—it was just too hectic before when he tried to tend her while studying.

        Carl told how he was finally glad to have found some time in his adult life to pursue education after decades of entire dedication to his job and family life. He still had to occasionally arrange child care for his youngest child and adjusted his study schedule around parenting and work responsibilities. When he first started at Hawks he took reading and writing brush-up courses, which he felt helped in his distance education work. He told me that when he studies, he establishes a set agenda with specific tasks and time allotments for each study session—but he tries to keep these realistic so as not to overstress himself.

        A common theme that emerged from our discussions of study patterns was the ability to fit that valued activity into an adult lifestyle of constant demands, thus making productive use of time and space. For instance, Lyn fit in two distance courses a semester, along with family time, a full-time job, PTA activities, and being a Cub Scout leader.

Scheduling

Craig described the study period of his day as follows. He gets up at about 9:00, goes down to the basement, and gets onto the computer first thing to check his e-mail, the computer conference, and any electronic discussion groups to which he belongs. Then he shifts the computer screen to WordPerfect—it waits patiently to accept any notes, ideas, outlines, or assignments on which he feels like working. He may have reading to do, yet he still works with the computer on. He rarely takes notes on his textbook reading; to keep moving productively through it he uses a highlighter to "circle stuff," making his books impossible to resell later. He interrupts these study sessions several times to go get a cup of tea and expects to have good days and bad days for pushing out his assignments. He will do this until just after noon. Then he will quit, unless he has assignments pressing up against deadlines. Until his work starts later that afternoon, he will eat lunch, work around the house, or go canoeing. He does a lot of the reading for his courses at his security job at night between making rounds and has considered getting a laptop computer so he can do his writing assignments there too.

Carl explained that his retail work schedule fluctuates weekly, if not daily, making distance education courses the only possibility he has to obtain a degree. He calls Monday, Thursday, and Saturday his "going to class" nights, studying from 7:00 to 11:30 PM. On Tuesdays and Fridays, because he goes in later for work, he can do written assignments in the mornings. He calls Wednesday his day off, the "big paper day." He has tried to keep Sunday (his other day off) as a family day but has had to use it for school because of his heavy study load. Carl likes to schedule tasks in advance on his calendar and now has the flexibility to take time off work if he is too far behind and needs to catch up on assignments.

Study schedules can be defined as a daily ritual such as Craig's, a weekly pattern such as Carl's, or a semester or year-long arrangement. As an example of these longer patterns, Francis used the time between contract (semester) periods to catch up on housework and chores she put off during periods of heavy schoolwork. Each of the students told me that they have planned their studies into their lifestyle in some way. Some, like Vicky, study for a couple of hours most days—in her case it is in the evenings after work; she has a light supper on weekdays when her work separates her from her family. She places all study assignments and due dates into her schedule in order to meet them. But, for others, such as Melody, their learning is pleasurable enough that they do not have to firmly schedule time around "to do" tasks—it is just something they want to do, and they are engaged in it often enough that the work gets done. Others, like Ralph and Randy, find that their study schedule is subordinate to a hectic and variable work schedule, so they cannot be overly detailed in their planning; instead, they squeeze their studies in when they can. Morning people use that time, and night people likewise. Some students, like Kris, study at both ends of the day and even work reading assignments into their lunch breaks at work. Most of these students devote their days off to studying.

Working With Others

Craig likes to think of his instructor as a coach directing him, rather than as a teacher giving him information. That relationship is more important than those with the other students, but computer conferencing opened his distance courses up so he weighed and responded to their opinions also. When he first returned to school, his advisor told him his writing was atrocious, so he took a course to improve it and constantly works at improving it in his other classes. He tries to figure out the instructor's position—political as well as personal preferences—so he can tailor his assignments accordingly. Sometimes he goes to his advisor, as he would a counselor, for moral support.

Carl's studying affects and is facilitated by family, educational personnel, his "classmates," and those with whom he works. When Carl decided to return to school, he got his family to commit their support, and he explained to them his study needs. The semester I interviewed him, he was working closely with his instructors and advisor to negotiate a study load within familiar subjects to match the effort he could expend. Carl wanted to share his 20-year background in retailing with the other students online, and he wanted to learn the other students' backgrounds so they could all know where each one "was coming from." Finally, he tried to apply all of his learning in school to work situations—telling his subordinates about concepts and ideas, asking them to apply them, and applying them himself; this is how he thinks he actually learns.

Being active in distance learning is much more of a social enterprise than it would appear. First, many of these students told me how they negotiated with their spouses, families, and friends for support in working on a distance degree. Second, these students have contact with their advisor and the professor teaching the course—more or less depending on the individual—in working through the assignments for the course. Third, fellow workers, friends, and extended family members are often involved with these students as they discuss course concepts and seek application of them in their lives. Fourth, several students related how important it was to them to be able to obtain feedback from other students about course assignments and activities—a new dimension added to their distance education through the implementation of computer conferencing.

However, those who have been primarily distance students are often used to studying without close instructional support from the teacher or other students. As Francis, who had a negative experience, put it:

> I cannot say that it [the computer conference] was an enjoyable experience. It was a harrowing experience. [both laugh] I wanted to quit that course more times than I could say. I guess I made it work by keeping in touch with the other students. [Some student] really helped me out. I've never met the man, but he's a very patient guy and I think he's like a natural teacher because I'd ask him questions and he'd give me all this information about how to handle this machine so I could do what I needed to do.

Judy, another student whose difficulties eventually caused her to drop the course late in the semester, expressed similar social learning needs. She said she could not find out, in the online environment, whether the other students were having the same problems she was facing and that was very frustrating to her. Contrast, however, the attitude of a seasoned distance student, Lyn:

> Most people I talk with, like Betty in the office, say "I can't see how you can work that way; I don't have the self-discipline." People think they can't. They need the class structure, need to be told that this assignment needs to be in by this date, need the test scores, [etc.], but, I don't need that. Some people do; they need to know exactly what they have to do to get an A.

Establishing Attitudes or Learning Climate

> Dan: You certainly don't need to go very far to start your class, right? I mean you just go down in your basement.
>
> Craig: Yeah. [He smiles] That's right. It is great, isn't it. It is wonderful. . . . What more could a man ask for? And to be able to put insights in and be guided by a referee. This is great enjoyment for me.
>
> I like it better than going out canoe racing really. My brothers and I started out two years ago. We trained hard. My brother quit smoking altogether, and he's running and he's pretty good. And, I veered; I started college. So now my brother enters triathlons and comes in second place to somebody who is very good. This is my triathlon. I've veered away from the canoe racing, but this is just as hard as running 20 miles every day. Reading books—book after book—like this, then putting out a paper the professor will like. That's my triathlon.

Craig told me that he had to put himself in a certain frame of mind to keep studying at home alone, day after day—by imagining that he has multiple teachers, the famous scholars he reads in his courses, and by comparing what he is doing to a triathlon, grueling through the papers and assignments as he would the daily practice runs. And he expects to have "on" and "off" days for ideas and enthusiasm, so he can sustain a "long haul" educational effort. He is part of a political electronic discussion group, which he checks daily, to take the monotony out of his distance study. Craig told me that turning his computer on first thing, that constant humming, ready in WordPerfect to accept his ideas and thoughts, signals to him that it is schoolwork time.

When I asked Carl over electronic mail how he establishes an attitude or study mindset to study at a distance, he responded:

> I don't want to sound corny, but I don't have to work at get-
> ting "excited" about learning at a distance. Completing my
> degree work has always been one of my goals. Being able to
> finally achieve this is very exciting for me. I truly enjoy the chal-
> lenge and the feelings of accomplishment I receive by complet-
> ing quality work.

Only three other students—Vicky, Len, and Harry—mentioned setting up any kind of attitude for studying. Vicky reminded herself that getting this degree was a priority in her life, when she did not feel like studying. Both Len and Harry expressed their need to maintain a feeling of excitement and interest about a course throughout its duration.

Seeking Task Information and Feedback

When Craig first started at Hawks State, he asked for feedback on his writing. His advisor told him it was so bad that perhaps he wanted to stay with an occupation like roofing. Discouraged but undaunted, Craig took special tutoring with a writing instructor. He said, "I just wrote and wrote, and she was awfully critical. I tried and tried, and it helped. It helped, and that was good."

Craig used both negative and positive feedback instructors gave him in molding future assignments. When he felt he was not improving through the computer conference like the participants were, he sought out his advisor for encouragement. Perhaps this sensitivity about his own feelings prompted him to give many of the other, shy participants notes of encouragement behind the scenes. In one course in which he did not receive a response from the professor about his written work, he sent in the evaluation form asking if the instructor was even alive. He heard back then.

Carl uses his advisor as a director or supervisor of his instruction, he but personally assumes the burden for defining his individual degree program and completing the work to fulfill it. Carl, too, likes to have the instructor provide him with answers and correct his thinking about a subject.

These distance students like to know exactly what tasks they need to perform and what the instructor expects. Eight of these students mentioned their preference for structure and specific task information, and three told me of difficulties they had experienced when taking their own prerogative to develop an assignment or project, usually resulting in having to do much more work.

But more than task information, these students expect and become aggravated when they do not receive timely feedback on their course work. Receiving feedback from the instructor helps break up the loneliness and isolation of distance learning (Melody), lets them know how effective the approach they have taken was (Randy), and helps them know how to tailor future assignments (Betty). Craig (mentioned earlier), Miguel, and Jack each told me how angry they were to be given a passing grade in a course without receiving specific responses back from the instructor about their assignments—they doubted that their assignments were ever read.

Craig, Betty, Kerry, and Judy mentioned their concern that they constantly demonstrate what they are doing to the instructor. Betty explained:

> Dan: [Speaking of the lack of instructor presence online] It makes you feel like maybe it's not that important then.
>
> Betty: Right. Well if he's not reading it anyway, if I don't write anything today, it makes no difference because he's not really paying attention to me. The bottom line is that everybody wants to impress the teacher.

If others generally operated under this premise, it did not surface in our conversations.

Using One's Own Learning Style

Craig liked a strong sense of competition while learning; he enjoyed the pressure to produce and tried to achieve excellence in his work. He needed time to reflect on the academic conversation he read online, printing it out for reference, wandering about the room, and smoking a cigarette while he thought about how he would respond. He recognized that different subjects need to be learned in different ways. In contrast with the academic learning cited previously, he approached computer-related learning differently, believing that only by trial and error with occasional referencing of the manual can people learn to use software applications. Craig's thinking that he had many teachers and mentors helped him overcome his isolation.

Carl considered himself and other successful Hawks students as being highly motivated, self-disciplined, and answer seeking. But he liked to be told exactly what to do in his education. This pattern typifies the adult distance students whom I interviewed. Ralph, Melody, Vicky, Francis, Harry, Lyn, Dennis, and Rose all expressed similar views. This study reflects the learning style of the students who preferred distance education as being one of strong self-discipline, motivation, time management, results orientation, and preference for structure. They felt different from co-workers, friends, and family members in that they could carry out class assignments and tasks by juggling their own time and activities in relative isolation, without the social pressure of a classroom, other students, and the instructor to push them forward. However, they wanted to be given concrete specifics about precisely what needed to be done, what the instructor expected, and when the assignments had to be completed.

Contrast these learning preferences with those who disliked the computer conferencing medium and either dropped their distance course or endured it. Judy said she tends to cram and push tasks to completion, rather than budgeting that effort over a longer time span. She had difficulty feeling a sense of urgency, especially in this first distance education experience. Although she saw the assignments and completion dates, she did not internalize that need to produce on schedule—there was no sense of urgency for her. Judy wanted immediate feedback on her questions and could not tolerate waiting a day or two for an electronic response; by then she had moved on to other concerns. She desired a close working relationship and plenty of feedback from her instructor, which she did not get in this experience. Also, Judy disliked the competition and detailed, reference-filled notes of others (like Craig) in the conference. This indicates that learning styles can sometimes be in conflict. Kris simply found the online component too time-consuming for her demanding schedule and discovered that she enjoyed learning by watching videos and taking notes better than through conferencing. Len found the structure oppressive—he preferred to be engaged elsewhere in online network discussion, even if he could not get course credit for it. Ted told me he got behind early in the course and never fully did caught up to where he could meaningfully participate online.

Those who were typically distance students (using correspondence study) found that computer conferencing provided too much structure for their lifestyles; whereas those "regular classroom" students found that there was not enough structure to this experience, such as the constant schedule and social support of a class to prod them onward. It appears that structure and control pervade the macro-computer conferencing experience, and students need to take constant self-control over the microtasks—contingencies to which both types of students needed to adjust.

The faculty I interviewed at Hawks State agreed that the distance courses provided more structure than the other formats their institution offered. They felt that it fostered aggressiveness in shy people (often women), whereas it pulled back others who dominated in other instructional settings. They felt that distance students who use computer conferencing tend to be more "technophiles" to begin with, and there is no longer any gender basis to influence who will enjoy or learn effectively with this medium.

ONLINE STRATEGIES

> Dan: *When you talk about pressure, do you feel pressure to get in on the conference real quick?*
>
> Craig: *There is competition here. You want to be good. You know he is grading you on this. And uh, pressure? Yeah, a lot of pressure. Sometimes I feel like standing up, scratching my head, and throwing a book. But that's good. How else can you learn?*

Computer conferencing represents an entirely new learning environment with which learners have to deal. The following are some of the areas I discussed with them about their online learning strategies: becoming comfortable with the technology, deciding participation frequency, dealing with asynchronous multiple discussions, overcoming information overload, avoiding silence or being ignored, communicating in an ambiguous text-only environment, deciding one's own contributions, and processing the online information.

Learning Technology

One of the first hurdles distance students face when taking a course through computer conferencing is learning the computer telecommunications procedures. Craig had not had any difficulty in getting the modem and software working for this course, even though this was a first experience for him. He had already used a PC and word processor for his writing assignments for other distance courses, so this network activity was mainly an extension of that. When I visited his home, a month after the course started, he was able to quickly move around from one topic to the next, using commands that he had memorized to avoid the time involved in accessing and reading menus. However, Craig's use of the computer was not particularly advanced—with all of the online correspondence he had done by February, he was just getting around to learning to upload and download files because he was finding his current information processing habits just too time-consuming. He also had not yet learned to skip ahead on various topics to start with just the unread messages. Craig's co-worker friend, Ted, is also working on a distance degree from Hawks and uses a similar computer system. They often support each other in learning to use various computer features.

Carl, too, found it easy to connect to the college mainframe, but took the 1-credit Telecom course to learn how to use the online system—an online course from which he learned about the technology from the instructor, the manual, and the other students. He learned enough technical skills for taking a computer conferencing course, but no more—just enough that he feels comfortable and can get his studies done.

Two factors that strongly influenced whether students had a successful experience learning by computer conferencing were: (a) prior computer and networking background and/or (b) the existence of a support person to ease them through initial technical hurdles of signing on with their own computer and learning the rudiments of the computer conferencing system. All 12 of the students who reported a successful experience had this in their favor. Of the six who had bad experiences with the medium, four reported these factors as a root cause of difficulty with the course. Of those, three thought they could attempt the medium again, given the proper technical understanding they had now acquired (although it was too late for current success). Of the two who gave it mixed reviews, one complained of initial technical problems that left him behind the rest.

What were the technical difficulties these students complained of? Several of them reported that they had gotten off to a late start because of initial computer problems and then found it nearly impossible to catch up and feel ahead of the game. Francis said initially she got lots of e-mail documents from her instructor, felt overloaded, and did not know how to process them. Also, she could not get off of a listserve once she joined and was suffocated in its e-mail. Len experienced a similar situation and could not get Hawks Support personnel to increase his machine's memory/storage. Jack, who went to the Hawks Center to access the conference, became frustrated as they shifted him from machine to machine, each having different keyboard emulation. Indeed, the distance course I took required me to learn new networking and conferencing skills—obstacles I was only able to surmount by getting offline support from a friend, coming to the experience with an adequate level of technical competence, and lots of effort (practice and procedure follows). Had I not captured the extreme frustration of those experiences in my fieldnotes, I would have forgotten that aspect of the course. Those whose experience remained negative kept those memories.

However, even for those with earlier technical experience or support networks in place, they still had to learn a computer conferencing system and how to use it in a way that worked effectively for them. Here are some learning strategies they employed. Ted switched communications software to upload or download files more easily. Vicky experimented on the network, and once she discovered how something worked, she reflected on and tried to document those procedures, jotting down notes on a "cheat sheet" which she kept handy by her computer for later reference. Francis created a card file in a similar fashion, a technique she learned from another student; indeed, when she ran into a snag online, she would check to see if her instructor or a fellow student was currently connected and tried to engage them in a "phone" conversation (online) to resolve the issue. Betty followed the instructions in the support manuals to learn advanced features, such as uploading and downloading files.

Several patterns emerged from the students' learning of the technical features of the computer conferencing environment. First, students only learn enough about the system to get by with the skills that are required. In several cases I observed students rotely using commands and procedures they had memorized and sidestepping functions they knew would make them more productive online, but had not yet discovered how to perform. Perhaps *discover* is a good word to describe the kind of computer learning going on—it is task specific, not formally undertaken, involves trial and error, occasional conversing with others, and reference glances at the manual (if all else fails).

This self-directed approach to learning the technology may keep people from becoming aware of their ignorance about key functions or mastering crucial skills that would make them more productive. The various computer conferencing courses require different levels of skill; students rise to the level of minimum competence expected by each situation and rarely higher, unless they are very technically oriented and enamored by computer conferencing. However, just because some of the technically advanced students had learned more ways of processing the online information, it did not mean that they would necessarily use more complex or sophisticated procedures; it simply gave them more options. Others who found they could get by with rudimentary skills generally stayed limited to those.

These technical competencies are truly metalearning skills, so they are of low priority to the majority of students. They are so set on gaining the content of the course and achieving its outcomes, they rarely attend directly to mastering these "process" skills—competencies for which they receive no credit or grade. Eric Watson, the college's technical support person, told me that attendance at any "in-person" session for gaining these competencies was low. He interpreted that response as students not needing such instruction. I have also seen low attendance and interest at these types of events I have conducted but believe, instead, that it is because of students' perception of these being less important than the "ends" of their course. One advantage this distance medium has over some other ones is that students can network with each other in gaining technical skills necessary to work in this environment; that they need to do so indicates the height of this technical learning hurdle.

Deciding Frequency

Craig realized that the system was sluggish in the late morning when he usually signed on, but this was when he usually had to use it. On his days off, he worked late at night when the computer "really flies." He felt pressure to be on frequently, almost daily, to compete with the others. But, later on in the course, he dropped back so that he could add more details and statistics to his notes. When I interviewed him six months after the online Constitution course was completed, he was still signing onto the network every morning, but he had to discipline himself to stay on for only a half hour or less. He said, "I could sit in front of it all day, but it takes a little thinking, you know. I can't sit there all day. I've got to cut the grass and do my homework!"

Carl is online everyday, and it seems like there is a "two-week catch-up" if he is off the system for even two days, as he "misses the flow" of what is being said.

That students log on, based on their life and family schedules, is almost a given, but it is interesting to see how their attendance spreads throughout the day. Rick, Lyn, and Dennis are on before 8:00 AM while the system is fast, before their work begins. Francis was on after 9:30 AM, after her first bus run. But most of the students appear to use the system in the evening hours when they usually study, such as Kris, Ralph, Rick (again), Vicky, Randy, and Kerry. Betty and Ted were the only late niters, but Miguel was on the system four or five times from early morning to late at night.

Not surprisingly, those who enjoyed the system the most were on it most often, usually daily or every other day: Ralph, Craig, Vicky, Kerry, Miguel, Betty, Lyn, Dennis, and Rick. They had few problems with information overload, multiple discussions, asynchronicity, and being ignored, simply because of their frequent involvement. Those who had less successful experiences logged on two times a week or less and curtailed their online time for each session. Kris had planned on only being involved online Saturday mornings and resented having to be present four times a week to keep up.

There can be strong feelings associated with one's access frequency. Compare Ted's guilt . . .

> Ted: And I know that if I get behind I'll stay behind because it's awful tough to catch up in a computer course.
>
> Dan: What is it like to be behind?
>
> Ted: You always feel like you are under the gun. You walk in the house and look at your computer and say "Gees, I should go over there and sit down and work on that computer."
>
> Dan: So you walk to the refrigerator, instead. [both laugh]

. . . with Miguel's feelings of anticipation:

> Dan: It sounds like minding that several times a day really keeps you on top of things.
>
> Miguel: Fortunately, I can get on at work, so that is a big help.
>
> Dan: I assume that it makes the conference more interesting that way.
>
> Miguel: Yeah, I am waiting for something to happen.

It seemed that some students (Miguel, Rose, and Betty) seemed compulsively addicted to the medium—logging on frequently and constantly concerned that they might be missing out on something. They (along with Dennis) complained that there was not enough being said on the conference because others were on less frequently. Several mentioned that online frequency ebbed and flowed with assignment due dates or the instructor's online schedule. Kerry found that his (and others') notes were lengthier if they had been absent for some time. Indeed, the interactivity—an applauded characteristic of this medium—is only present to the extent that learners keep up with the online conversation and contribute frequently. Otherwise, the environment becomes one way, didactic, and passive. So, it appears that the individual's learning approach here is to find a frequency that maximizes interactivity, yet still fits within his or her lifestyle.

Overcoming Information Overload

Craig experienced information overload more with his several electronic network discussion groups (listserves) than with the conference itself. He found it hard to interact with others when there was so much to read. And he did not feel that he could be gone from the system for more than three days at a time without being overloaded.

   Carl's approach for dealing with information overload was simply to organize his time better and to establish study goals for each
time period. A common strategy was to ignore the conversations going
on in the optional, chit-chat areas of the course and to concentrate
attention on the assigned topics. Ted stayed up all night long once, just
catching up on his computer conference. I did the same for the online
course I took. Vicky forced herself to sign off after she had been
"immersed" in online information for several hours; she found at that
point she needed to reinforce what she had learned online through
reviewing her texts and notes.

   The computer course conversations were generally not a problem for these students to process; it was the Bitnet discussion groups
that they joined—often as an assignment in the computer conferencing
course—that caused this problem. For instance, here is what happened
to Miguel, a person who is about as electronically connected as
humanly possible, after just a four-day hiatus:

> Miguel: It was hard [to catch up]; I haven't even finished. My
> mailbox was totally packed with mail and it was of course a
> thousand blocks over my quota. And I have to try to read and
> read and read and read. This was of course just my university
> mailbox. In my personal mailbox . . . when I opened it, it said
> around five megabytes. Impossible to read. So that one I
> couldn't even open, couldn't even read it.
>
> Dan: So when did you get back?
>
> Miguel: Last Monday and I'm still catching up. . . . It's hard to
> go on vacation and come back.

Avoiding Silence or Being Ignored

   As I interviewed several other participants, I sensed that they did
not always respond or feel favorable about Craig's online remarks, so I
asked Craig if he felt his contributions were ever ignored:

> If my stuff is ignored then I know that it is not as good as it
> should be. I think I must have done something wrong. But I
> shouldn't feel that way, since lots of people's stuff does get
> ignored. Well, mine doesn't get ignored that much because I
> am a radical, a different sort of guy. I like to pick on people.
> Then they can't ignore you; they have to answer back. I like the
> debate and the conflict because I've got to keep interested in
> this stuff.

Carl felt that he was never ignored. When I asked him about possible frustration with "silence" or inactivity in the conference, he explained that there was always something happening online, and he would find that "a welcome surprise." Yet, he noticed less activity when assignments were due.

There are two types of silence in this online conversational world: (a) the feeling of exclusion when no one responds to a contribution you have made, yet the conversation goes forward; and (b) a total lack of participation by others on the network as frequently as you would desire. Ted, like Craig, experienced silence of this first type. He said he felt uncomfortable throughout his course—the "odd man out"— because everyone else was so formal and ignored his humor. Betty, Miguel, and Rose exemplify the other type—frequent conversationalists who became frustrated at the lack of timely response by others.

Betty, feeling disappointed when no one else had responded, checked a special computer conferencing feature to figure out when the other participants were last on the system and how much of the conversation they had read. She waited for a day or two for others to take the lead, but if they did not, she jumped in and started the discussion herself. She led with an extreme position (but a perspective that she could honestly espouse) to stimulate others to contribute. Also, she concluded her notes with a question to invite further responses. However, Rose told me she just stopped signing onto the computer very often because not much was being said. This lack of activity made the course less interesting for her than the very active online writing class she took the semester before.

Dealing With Textual Ambiguity

Craig always wondered if others were composing directly online or putting their responses together offline. He told me he could tell a novice conference communicator by the flaws, typos, and disjointed lines or if the notes were all in capital letters. Carl said that the textual nature of the medium forces you to be more clear, concise, and selective, so it sharpens your writing skills. However, if he read someone else's contribution that he could not understand, he sent follow-up notes, just as he would follow up with someone if he did not understand them in a regular conversation.

The text-only world of computer conference communications influences the discussion but never seemed to become such an obstacle that students could not cope with it. Ralph said he could not tell if others were "chucking a bluff" because he could not see them. But Len intentionally liked to play with the online text ambiguity to observe how others would respond. He tried to diffuse "flaming" by interjecting humor. Rick also tried to add levity as his typical "class clown" self but found it harder and missed hearing peoples' laughs at his ploys. Lyn remarked that informal conventions became established because of this text environment, such as using capital letters only to indicate shouting and strong words or exclamation marks to suggest emphasis. I sensed that much of the polite conference tone on which several participants commented was the result of not wanting one's comments misread as offensive online.

Deciding on Contributions

Craig had elaborate strategies for preparing contributions to the conference. He composed all of his responses in WordPerfect, edited and spell-checked them, and then printed them out. Then he signed onto the conference and located himself where he wanted to post his note. He then retyped in the whole message because he had not learned to upload files or cut and paste them into the mainframe from his word processing package. When he composed his note, he tried to make it fairly generic to cover the issues and to fit it anywhere in the discussion sequence. Before he typed it in though, he read the note immediately preceding his own and tailored the first sentence or two of his own note to address those issues (composing this online).

Craig liked to change and add to the scenario the instructor had set up—to use his creativity, to add humor, and for conflict. Whenever the conversation got tense, and he thought people were just posturing, he would try to tell a joke, make a witty remark, or say, "Let's have a beer." This lightened the conversation up for him and made it more human; otherwise, he said, "I can hardly stand it." For example, near the end of the course, he decided to organize a football team online in the "pub," asking other class members to sign up to play various positions. This also kept it interesting for him—to see how others would react. (Randy said he thought a lot of this was pretty goofy.)

Sometimes he sent private e-mail notes to other class members to smooth over his public, negative comments. To Kerry, he sent a note saying (paraphrase), "Us conservatives need to stay together against all of the liberals I sense are in this class!" Later in the course, possibly based on instructor feedback, he would go to great lengths to fill his notes with obscure references and details that he got from library books, which he thought were required; some students saw them as ridiculously beyond their efforts and the course expectations.

Dan: So, checking out the books isn't a problem?

Craig: No, in fact I've had up to 30 books here at once. I had to take two loads of them in my Volkswagen [Van] just to get them in.

Dan: [laughs] Just for this course?

Craig: Well, just about. Once you get them home, though, most of them turn out to be useless. But, the parking at the library is $1 an hour for the first hour and $2.50 thereafter. So, you run in and get all the books that you can and take them home.

He told me that sometimes he would search through related conversation on a network discussion group, trying to find relevant arguments or ideas he could use in his computer conferencing messages, without letting anyone know where he had gotten the information. He found it hard to put together responses for the conference and wished this were a lower level course so he could feel free to practice and "know what to look for." He explained, "A lot of this is just experimentation. There is no book out there about it."

Carl usually wrote directly online for the regular conversations, preparing just one response per branch. Within the note he reacted to all of the unread messages posted there, separating his ideas with paragraphs. If he had a lengthy contribution or assignment, he composed it offline in his word processor and then uploaded it.

Carl responded to his personal e-mail first, then any personal notes he received in CONFER, and finally posted notes in the various branches of the conference—the same sequence in which he read his mail. He responded only to some of the notes, especially those in which he wanted someone to get back to him, always trying to stay with the conversation flow of the topic. He would not respond to an item if he had nothing to say, but he realized that some of his peers responded to every item. He tried to keep the dialogue going on an issue until the group reached consensus. When he prepared to post a note on a medical listserve about computer ethics, he felt intimidated by the educational background of the people on that network, so he carefully composed his request beforehand before uploading and posting it.

These students were divided on their strategies of responding to the online conversations. Nine of them would type their responses in spontaneously, whereas eight of them composed their contributions offline on a word processor and uploaded them. Three people did it both ways, depending on the length and formality of what they wished to communicate. Certainly those who composed their responses offline tended to be more technically competent, but this was not always the case—some who could easily compose offline simply found it cumbersome, so they "shot from the hip" instead. These "spontaneous" students for the most part worked carefully on their responses, too—preparing a short outline from which to write, composing their responses in the VAX editor, and reworking their notes for clarity, additional ideas, tone, spelling, and grammar, in much the same way that those offline were doing it. So it appeared that most online contributions were quite thoroughly crafted pieces of writing, regardless of the participants' technical procedures for developing them.

Judy, one of those who dropped the course, criticized this deliberate, reflective approach to composing work online:

> Dan: And I get the impression that you write spontaneously.
>
> Judy: Oh yes, oh yes, and that is why I wonder if anyone is getting any idea of what I am really trying to say. Because I go from pretty much a free association in there, as I would in a classroom, you know. But, at least in the classroom I can see everyone with puzzled looks and know, "They are not following me at all!" Or, "they are following me" or "I'm making myself clear" or "I'm not making myself clear." But, you don't have that here at all. And, I don't have the time to construct something beautifully beforehand—I don't have the time and I'm not going to do it.

Betty, in contrast, explained why she prefers being able to thoughtfully compose her responses offline:

> I'll put it in my word processing. I'll get very relaxed. I'll use spell checking and then I'll go back and add a line or take out a line, or move something down here or add it up there. I like that. It gives me the freedom. . . . I just feel better. Maybe it goes back to the proper student days. You know, where it's like the teacher is calling on me and I was very shy in public. Remember my father was very shy and that's my background. So when the teacher called on me I was like suffering even though I might have known the answer. But to get it to come out of my mouth was another thing.

This sense of shyness in communicating around strangers is not unique—two potential students in our distance education initiative at Syracuse University last spring confided to me that they rarely spoke out in class and thus feared a participation requirement that would require them to regularly express their views.

Miguel, Judy, Rose, and Ted said they often felt intimidated by the intellectual level of the communication going on, so they did not immediately want to join in. They would hold off contributing until they had read many of the other students' contributions, thereby getting acquainted with them first. Rose said she overcame her shyness by asking for other class members' help with solving technical problems; their subsequent communication broke the ice for her.

Several of the students expressed unique contribution strategies. Betty logged on late at night (at 10:00 or 11:00 PM) so she could read everyone's comments and put in the final word for the day. She tried to respond directly to the last note posted, thereby maintaining the continuity of the discussion, but she was not overly concerned whether others had taken equal "air time," as she explained:

> I would contribute frequently. Sometimes I'll say something and somebody else will say something. If it's enough of a stimulation for me to add to it, then I'll go back in because I realize that if you're sitting in a class you don't take turns. If you want to say something you just jump in and say it! That's pretty much the way my personality is in my family. Say it. Just jump in. Don't wait. In my house, and I have an Italian background, nobody sits quietly waiting for you to talk. If you're going to talk you've got to jump in and talk while you've got the opportunity because everybody will just go on and on and no offense, but sometimes you'll have two and three speaking at the same time and we all hear each other. So I find on the conference that it's not difficult for me to go right back and be the very next person speaking. But normally there are a few people between, only because we all come in at different hours of the day.

Kerry, mentioned by the professor as the ideal student, had some peculiar contribution strategies. For instance, when he worked alone at the police station composing his messages directly online, he talked to himself, working through his arguments fully before entering them online. He tried to express his own views, referring to the readings, but was careful not to summarize them in his notes. He limited his notes to one idea (as suggested by the instructor) and sought to support his position with examples in short notes. Even when he had nothing to add or was not prepared to respond directly, he would "say something," just to let the others know he was following along. To encourage others' participation, he followed up on their notes, especially those who did not contribute as much.

Yet, not all of the contribution strategies were unique—attitudes or actions were borrowed from other roles as students. For example, Betty and Rick, as well as others, directed their comments directly to whatever the teacher said online and felt that the other students did as well—contributing more whenever the teacher "spoke." Francis, Betty, and Harry wanted the conversations to focus directly on course content and task information; they felt uncomfortable reading or contributing to social conversations or those in which people expressed their feelings. They tried to steer the discussion back toward course objectives.

The contribution strategies of these online students represents a mixture of factors. First, there are idiosyncratic ways of determining when and how to join the discussion—individuals figure out what best fits their technical abilities, comfort levels, and so forth. Second, there are social conventions that shape contributions—taking turns, recognizing others, socially trying to fit in, and so forth. Finally, these students carry with them techniques and attitudes learned in other instructional settings—to pay closest attention and respond to teachers, to portray a task-content orientation, and to demonstrate unique, cogent thinking. Even severe shyness in classroom settings may carry over to this environment.

Processing Online Information

How did Craig deal with all the messages he received in the computer conference? As he read through the other peoples' responses to discussion items, he used the "print screen" key to dump them to his printer. He avoided reading the other students' responses to the conversation until he had done his own reading of the texts and formulated his own position because he did not want to be swayed too early by their perspective. After the work of the course and deadlines set in, he stopped reading and contributing to the optional, off-topic, "pub" item. Once he had read through the discussion on an item, he signed off the computer system and again read through all of the notes that he printed out, highlighting important points and deciding to which of them he would respond.

Because Carl considered himself busy, he got right to task online. He did not seek to get to know the others, being rather driven toward assignment-oriented conversation. He usually read the branches in the sequence in which the system displayed them. He made sure to read all of the messages in a branch before posting any response. Carl rarely downloaded notes to assist him in composing responses, but sometimes he downloaded a discussion to refer to when he prepared a paper. He preferred to process CONFER directly online so that he could be over and done with it when he turned off the machine; that way he was being "more efficient."

As was the case with contributing strategies, these students can be divided between those who strictly dealt with their discussion messages online versus those who read and worked with them offline. A common strategy, used by five of the students, was to read the discussion online, possibly printing the screen of any message to which they wanted to respond directly. Then they would develop responses to those selected items and post them in the appropriate conferencing areas. An equal number of students printed out the whole conversation to read it offline. (These were also usually the more technically advanced students who also composed their responses offline.) It was common for this second group of students to refer more directly to texts and other readings in their notes as well. Only Dennis appeared to have formally organized the online discussions into a tabbed notebook for easy reference.

The computer network and conferencing system itself placed constraints on the ways students could process the online information. For instance, without exception, students mentioned their sequence of processing online communications as: (a) reading and responding to personal mail, (b) processing any listserve messages, and (c) reading through various conference branches and responding as desired. However, this strategy is the sequence presented by the system. Also, students told me that they never responded to notes on an item unless they had read all of the unread notes posted there first. This strategy makes sense because someone else may have already made the point you were planning to make in the conversation. However, one student revealed to me the computer constraints of operating otherwise. If you responded immediately, the computer would skip you to the end of that topic area automatically, and it was difficult to reread the messages you had missed. As another example, in the online course I took, which had a threading[1] capability, you needed to determine whether your note should be used by the system as a comment on another note, or if you were expressing an independent, new idea. But neither CONFER nor the conferencing software I used at Syracuse University had that feature, so these students were not required to take that aspect of their communications into consideration.

Also, those with formal data processing experience tended to process their computer conferencing information offline, hoping not to tie up system resources. Rick explained:

---

[1]*Threading* is a feature whereby the computer conferencing software keeps track of all notes that referred to an original note. In the software we used, the "COMMENT" command indicated to the system that the note about to be posted referred to the one on which you were positioned. When reading notes, you could issue the "REF" command, and the system would list all of the notes that were based on the note on which you were currently positioned, regardless of how much further along in the conversation they had appeared.

> I print the responses then go sit down and read them. I don't
> stay on the system. That would tie it up for no reason. I read
> them, digest them, take notes, then formulate a response. Then
> I sign back on another time and put the responses in.

However, there were also some idiosyncratic ways of dealing
with conference messages that were not system related. Both Ted and
Dennis described their strategies of first skimming through the messages and printing them out before work (in Dennis's case) or before
bedtime (in Ted's case) and then thoroughly reading them for further
understanding and response preparation 8 or 12 hours later during
their primary study time. Ted also found himself just reading to stay
afloat in the course, given the volume of messages and being behind,
so he was not getting into the conversations.

Betty would monitor the system earlier in the evening, as she
was interested in how the discussion was taking shape, but waited until
the late, off hours to actually process it in any structured manner. Kerry,
someone who primarily responded online, would always read through
the conversation to date to refresh himself on what others had said so
he could once again establish the conversation's context. Unlike Craig
(described earlier) who avoided reading others' remarks before becoming involved, Vicky (taking a course about computer networking) read
through all of the others' questions and answers before attempting any
computer task so she could learn all the pitfalls and mistakes others
had encountered.

Lyn would not read through the lengthy responses that some
long-winded participants made; neither would Jack. Rick would read all
of the responses because he felt they all added variety to the conversation and might contain ideas to which he could respond.

In summary, the processing strategies these students employed
were influenced by a number of factors. First, the computer software
itself dictated some of these strategies. Second, peoples' technical ability and data processing background inclined them to deal with the
information on- or offline. Finally, they borrowed or invented strategies
that became unconsciously habitual—ones that uniquely fit them, their
learning preferences. and lifestyle.

DISCUSSION AND CONCLUSION

This research corroborates much of what the LHTL theorists have
said—that although there are generic LHTL skills, much of learning and
learning approaches are unique to specific contexts (Candy, 1990). It

used specific examples from the computer conference experience of distance students to substantiate this. This study also agrees with the theory that adults personally and idiosyncratically approach a learning endeavor based on their own set of personal learning characteristics (Smith, 1990). Likewise, Small (1986) found that distance students who had formerly had positive school experiences employed a wider variety of LHTL strategies in their correspondence studies than their counterparts with previous poor experiences. Mason (1990) argued that student passivity is a major hurdle for effective implementation of computer conferencing; other distance modes have spoon-fed learners so that they are unaccustomed to taking charge of their own learning. However, this study posits that individuals become active and self-directed when they produce their own LHTL strategies.

This study indicates that media represent a whole other context within which learners apply LHTL skills and, depending on the students' familiarity with the characteristics of that medium, may play as big or greater role in determining LHTL strategies than content itself does. This study dealt with learners' approaches to the unique characteristics of computer conferencing—technical access, asynchronicity, multiple conversations, information overload, interactivity, text-only environment, and so forth. In contrast, most LHTL models have dealt with generic LHTL strategies that are best applied in conventional classroom situations. This study's contribution is its illumination of what strategies are evoked when adults approach an unfamiliar instructional medium, such as computer conferencing. Certainly, all media create unique conditions within which the learner must cope; these conditions partially dictate LHTL strategies learners actually use and learn in that instructional setting.

This study also corroborates other research findings about what distance learners think makes instruction effective. They want explicit directions and resist being self-directing; they seek to apply their experience, look for practical knowledge, and are intrinsically motivated (Robinson, 1992). They prefer instructional strategies that build confidence and relevance. They want clear details on the amount of work required and its usefulness to them, as well as timely feedback. Least important concerns were opportunities to work with others, seeing role models, achieving personal goals, actively participating, and being entertained by unusual teaching techniques (Burnham & Walcott, 1991).

An important aspect of taking courses by computer conferencing is acquiring the technical skills to perform online. Evaluations of computer conferencing at the British Open University found that only a third of new users learned to use their system enough for active participation throughout the course (when online activity was only a minor course requirement; Mason, 1990). Many of those who learned skills had family or friends to help them out, as did those in my study. Reports of the University of Toronto's conferences indicate that initial technical difficulties are a major problem and "have a negative impact on learning interactions" (Kaye et al., 1989, p. 30). Wells (1992) reported that estimates of mastering computer conferencing systems vary from two hours to a week, depending on the system and the level of proficiency required.

Another important finding was that picking up learning strategies is primarily an incidental learning process. It was first in our interviews, possibly, that these students reflected and articulated their strategies. Marsick and Watkins (1990) showed how incidental learning occurs as individuals pick up information and skills along the way, as they perform some task (their real objective). Because LHTL strategies are a means of learning and rarely an end in and of themselves, students learn them incidentally. Learning strategies are rarely the focus of students' efforts to acquire new skills and information (i.e., the content of instruction). So they are rarely consciously aware of their strategies, unless asked to reflect on them, as in the research process. They underplay the value of their learning approaches, disregarding the need for acquiring more efficient information processing habits, in their quest for learning outcomes or mastery of content. Many of these skills are picked up incidentally, in a "hit and miss," "trial and error" fashion, but once learned, they sink below consciousness to an habitual performance level. The institution engenders this same preoccupational focus. Candy (1990) suggested that superior learners are fully aware and consciously choose their LHTL strategies. This research calls for further investigation of this issue, as it seems that these processes are quite removed from most of our consciousness.

5

The Dynamics of Online Relations

The characteristic that sets computer conferencing apart from other distance media is its almost inherent capability of group discussion. This increased group involvement, although characteristic of newer telecommunications technologies (Barker et al., 1989), is perhaps most pronounced in computer conferencing. Although audio and video conferencing allow for group interactivity, in practice these media are more one-way instructional systems, given their synchronous delivery with limited "air time." But not so for computer conferencing. Harasim (1987) discovered that students contributed 90% of the discussion and generally liked this arrangement. Also, the interactivity among group members compliments that of the student and the course content and interactions with the professor for enhanced engagement and learning (Moore, 1989). This group-oriented, highly participatory and distributed communications environment has been hailed as democratic (Harasim, 1987) and collaborative (Harasim, 1989, 1990b; Kaye, 1992a).

This chapter begins by examining the strong views students held about the dynamics and polarities involved in the conference—when people come together online with different political, ethnic, age, gender, and social attitudes—and how computer conferencing facilitates the expression and examination of those. Then it reports the social relations that form in the computer conferencing environment—how these influence learning, and their strength, purpose, and permanence.

DYNAMICS AND POLARITIES

Just before Kerry got out of my car—I gave him a lift from the police station back to his home, he told me that he used to get excited about all of these people, separated by wide distances, being on the computer conference and chatting daily about the same esoteric topics. But, it did not fascinate him anymore; he just took it for granted. Perhaps it is the same for most participants.

It is easy to think of this separation in terms of geographic distance between the student and the instructor, but even more so the computer conference bridges a larger relationship—that of each student with his or her peers—and it spans time as well. More subtly, I saw other chasms beginning to be crossed with this medium—cultural, social, racial, ability, and age-related gulfs that often separate us from others. Sometimes these crossings are more hostile and threatening, as the conference reaches out and places participants who normally would not associate with each other in the same virtual space. Judy explained:

> I would call myself "not conservative." . . . It is just what I call "Mid-America Syndrome," which being in a metropolitan area people tend to be much more pro-choice than the pro-life people you find in the rural areas—the nature of the beast in a more cosmopolitan situation. And most of the people in the conference are from like [Rural City], and one person is in Minnesota [I think]—from a wide section of the country (the East coast), but from all over—from wide distances. . . . And I don't know if being down here in lower [State] is different. I've been to upper [State] and it is beautiful; I loved it, but the people seem to be much more conservative. And, I am obviously not.

Geographic Political Dynamics

Ted, one of these rural conservatives, told me that when he took the writing course, he thought they would be examining sentence structure, passive voice, and the use of metaphor; instead, the writing all revolved around women's and multicultural issues—topics to which he had little affinity.

> Ted: You know I was just trying to jazz 'em up a little bit. One of the first things is that one of the women just started running down white guys. White guys are terrible. They are the problem of all the world. And I came back with "Sure, blame it all on the white guys." Wow, I swatted a hornets nest!

Dan: And what would people say in response to that kind of thing? Would they just agree or ignore it?

Ted: They'd say "well some people take it too personal." But if you're a white guy and they're always slamming white guys, of course the white guy is going to take it personal.

It was curious to see how those with liberal views, such as Judy and Randy, thought the conference was highly conservative; whereas those with conservative positions (Kerry, Dennis, and Craig) thought it to be very liberal in nature. Each group interpreted the nature of the group based on her or his individual position. However, Dennis explained that people expressed their opinions freely:

Dan: Do you think that if there are pro-life members that they will be intimidated that [the instructor] was so frank in stating his position?

Dennis: No. No I don't think so at all. As a matter of fact, in talking about free speech and the right to assembly and all that, he indicated that he was a draft card burner. Well I don't have a lot of respect for those who went around burning draft cards, but it doesn't inhibit my thoughts or anything. As a matter of fact, then we got on the Kent State thing and I kind of defended the soldiers. Some people took issue to that, but that's just part of general discussion you know. They have a right to their opinion, even if it's in opposition. I enjoy those little confrontations we get into.

Lyn (among others) said she felt they could express themselves in this environment:

Once you get into it, it's great. You no longer feel that there are 250 people out there. Instead, you can just be yourself and just say what you think. No one is watching you. At least, you can't hear them laughing, or get hit with their projectiles.

Kris thought that by living in a different state than the other participants, she was able to broaden their consideration of Constitutional effects on issues in other parts of the country.

A positive effect of these conversations was to invite individuals with firm stances to consider and debate the positions of others.

Dan: Did you find that you grew a lot through the conference?

Craig: If I have to judge myself, I would be a conservative. But, I can see why some people have some liberal views and [I see] a little more the problems people face. But, I will always be somewhat conservative. But, I have found that there are different approaches to handle every problem. To realize that, that is important.

Carl spoke similarly:

> What is interesting is that when we first sit down in the discussions, speaking for myself now, I'm usually adamant in my opinion. Usually everything is black and white to me. Then I find out that maybe its not so black and white and maybe there is a little bit of gray area.

Concerns of Ethnicity, Age, and Disability

The distinctions among participants by race, age, disability, and sometimes gender were imperceptible, or if known, were more easily forgotten in the computer conferencing medium. Several participants told me they thought this brought about more honest communications:

> Dan: You probably don't know or might not know the race or ethnicity of any of the participants. I don't know if that matters or not.
>
> Kris: You know I've never thought about it. I guess going from the names, they could be just about anything. . . . I think it might be easier to say the things you really feel, particularly because you aren't in a classroom or sitting across the table from someone. And the responses are delayed. You don't immediately have to defend what you've just stated.

Craig spoke similarly:

> I've kind of wondered [about ethnicity], but I don't want to ask, since it might color my thinking. It's colored enough just by their responses. I'd hate to say, "Are you black?" I'm the type who would, too. I don't mind saying that. But, I think that would color my responses. I mean, I would think, "That guy's a black," and I wouldn't want to do that. . . . You could be any color and respond any way you wanted with free thinking. You know, black people sometimes push themselves into thinking, being like the other black guys. I've seen that.
>
> Dan: Yeah!
>
> Craig: Like they are brothers, you know. And, maybe they have a little different viewpoint. And, this way. . . . Like, [say] I'm in law enforcement. I don't really want people to know that because people will think, "Oh that's the cop."

There is a contradiction here—that people would want to disguise themselves or view others shrouded (in part a dishonest act) in order that more honest, truthful, complete communications might emerge. These incidents speak to our inability to be open, honest, and completely forthright to others different than ourselves, especially when they are strangers.

Age surfaces as a case in point. Kerry, one of the most "vocal" participants in the Constitution course's computer conference, describes himself as "the baby of the group" at age 23. He talked about the age dynamics of the conference:

> Being younger, I may not have gone through some of the 1960s. Whereas some of the older people had been involved in the civil rights movement or had seen it. I remember at one point there was a discussion on the Cuban missile crisis, which was something that happened even before I was born. So to me it's words on paper. Whereas a couple of other people could write their firsthand experiences.

However, Kris told me that the participants in that course had a lot in common, as they were all in their 40s and 50s; growing up in the same era enabled them to better share information because "we are all in the same boat." Without the constant physical reminder of age being present (as might be in a classroom situation), individuals forget this aspect of other students, and it ceases to consciously influence their participation.

I often wondered what the composition of the conference was—beyond the male-female makeup that was fairly apparent. I assumed that most participants were European-Americans (except Miguel), with no physical disabilities, because those elements never came up in my discussion with these students about themselves. I became aware, however, of how difficult it is to directly ask these questions—a cultural taboo:

> Miguel: How do you ask that? You can't just send them a note asking, "Are you really a boy?" It is difficult, and it is not something you can easily do. . . .This same thing happened to me on the [Some Name] conference I am a part of—I started to work with a woman from Teheran. Her name was spelled O-I-D-A. I had no idea if that name was a man's or a woman's. And, I wrote to her for over two months, hoping that I could find that out while I was working with her to get something together. . . . He or she said that they were coming to Mega City and I thought, "Oh my god, what am I going to do?" I don't know who I'm looking for—a man? I tried to ask that person a little bit more about what they do for a living or about their hobbies, but I couldn't determine their sex.

A friend of mine postulated that we all assume that the unknown participants on a conference are just like ourselves. Important learning goes on when the online conversation reveals that we do not cherish the same values and beliefs or take the same positions. I thought how in the summer courses I studied, especially, that among the participants who chose not to be interviewed may have been someone who was "passing" (Goffman, 1963) and who may not have wanted a disability, affiliation, ethnic origin, or some other element known. However, Rose convinced me that computer conferencing does make these outward physical features insignificant—possibly a reason for self-selection not to join a computer conferencing course:

> Dan: I just wonder if [not knowing peoples' physical appearance] allows for some communications to occur that might not otherwise.
>
> Rose: I'm sure it does. I'm sure that there is a certain freedom to that as well. Especially someone perhaps who doesn't have a great deal of self-esteem. They may feel less inhibited by being viewed through a screen and not by being actually seen.
>
> Dan: Of course, it might work the other way around. If you are extremely attractive and articulate and have a nice voice presence or a charismatic person, you might find this really lacking? [chuckles]
>
> Rose: [serious] Yeah, I think it is such an individual thing. I think someone who felt that their physical beauty was their best asset might not even be interested in this kind of thing. If they felt like they got what they needed by being physically seen, they might not put themselves in the position to study with a group they can't be in front of.

And What About Gender?

Gender issues surfaced early on in my study of the Constitution course as an aspect of computer conferencing that had been ignored. Consider Kerry's comments:

> Dan: Do women participate in the Pub?
>
> Kerry: No, I think they've come to believe that it is only for guys in the Pub, so they don't talk in there anymore, but they do in the regular topics quite a bit.

He then added later:

I guess Len, Craig, and I go back and forth with all of the discussions. We have pretty much left all of the others behind. . . .
It's just that, the three of us have sort of taken over the conference. We let the others participate, but we kind of have control. It is sort of chauvinistic, I guess.

Also, he responded to another question quite insensitively to gender:

Dan: These notes by the women are fairly short.

Kerry: Yeah, I think Lyn and Kris seem to hold back these days.
Maybe they've been shoved back too many times.

So, I became alarmed at Craig's house to read the disparaging
comments these men had made about Lyn's job as bursar of a small
college, and her responses back seemed to me to show someone who
had been quite offended. These gender issues seemed so strong that I
arranged to drive two hours to interview Lyn in person, rather than conduct a telephone interview, when she told me she had just dropped the
course. I asked her about these comments in the interview:

Dan: I saw that when you introduced yourself as a bursar,
some people came back.

Lyn: Oh, I got beat up on that something terrible. . . . I laughed
when I read that because that is just normal. When you get
your financial aid, people are giving you money. When you go
to admissions, you get the paperwork that lets you in. But, we
don't do anything for you. The bursar just takes your money,
and you have to stand in long lines for that to boot. We get
beat up a lot.

Dan: Weren't you offended? . . .

Lyn: No, we laughed. You can't take it seriously because you
know they are just joking.

So, I dropped gender as a prevalent theme, but it surfaced again
later in the conference when Judy responded to Craig's sexist remarks:

There is this one guy who pissed me off big time, who said
something about, "Oh yeah, I used to work at the state prison
in [Somewhere] . . . and I found out that I was being transferred to the women's division, so I thought, "Wow! all of these
women are going to want me." This is in the middle of a conference, the middle of a Constitution class!

So, I wrote back, and I was so pissed off, and so I pulled all
of the stops out. I said, "What kind of a sexist remark is that!"
And, he said a couple of other things like that that were really

sexist, and I got totally offended. Then he came back saying, "Of course I didn't mean them; of course I was joking." And I said, "Maybe I took it a little harder than it was meant." I said, "You may be joking about this stuff, but there is some truth that seems to come through when people make comments like that!"

Other interview discussions led me to believe that the online environment was not dominated by men.

Dan: I was just wondering if they were talking online about just the kind of things that men are interested in and maybe you didn't feel as much a part of the discussion.

Francis: Oh no. Everybody just talked about course stuff, even in the "electric lounge" part.

Dan: You mean they weren't talking about car repair, boxing, hunting, and that sort of stuff.

Francis: No. Not really. They were very inclusive actually. Two of them are from the same area and sometimes they'd get off on a subject like that, but even if they did, they'd include others. Like one gal loved to shop and they'd say "Come to this area to shop. We have malls and we can use your shopping. Come improve our economic condition."

Gender issues did not just surface as content remarks in courses; they also were connected with the use of technology itself. I mentioned how my sample, which was as wide as I could obtain, included a relatively greater percentage of males than that represented in the overall Hawks student body. And I observed at my visit to the local Macintosh users' group during this study, the overwhelming preponderance of white, middle-class males; what women I saw there seemed to be wives accompanying their husband enthusiasts. Francis spoke most candidly about these gender differences:

I think women are much more afraid of mechanical things. It's basically a societal thing. . . . It is not so much that women are not talented in fixing this or that or handling this or that piece of machinery, it's just by society (and this might be a generational thing too) they're not guided in that direction. The guy does that. I think women deal more in concepts and less in technicalities just by way of thinking. . . . A woman is thinking about a technical area if she is apprehensive about it, lets say. He [the guy] is too. He's thinking about how to solve the problem and what to do and not so much what the effect is going to be on the machine. If the machine blows up then we'll handle that too. And the woman is thinking oh my gosh what if I blow up this machine. If I blow up this machine this someone's *going to yell at me . . . and I mean it just goes on and on. We complicate it so in our minds. I think it's just a difference in thought processes.*

However, the majority of women in these courses did not mention any insecurity they felt with the technology, having already used computers in work settings (Kris, Vicky, Melody, and Lyn) or through home and personal interest (Betty and Rose). Vicky possessed as technical a computer background as any of the men. Judy (vocally feminist) was the only woman besides Francis who seemed hampered by the technology (as were two of the men). But Francis was using the course for just that purpose:

I think it was encouraging to me because the other gals who were on were no longer afraid of this and I said, "Hey, if they did it then I can." And also I just came to the point, and you have to, of knowing that if something happens to the machine you get the machine fixed. Big deal. It's not going to be that traumatic. It might be expensive but. . . . If you try it and it doesn't work, then you find a way to fix it. You just have to reset your mind I think.

My conclusions about the gender dynamics of computer conferencing are quite similar to Laura Bunks's, a Hawks advisor I interviewed. Although gender issues are involved here, they are becoming much weaker as women continually become proficient with using personal computers, electronic mail, and networks at work. Or, as Francis has done, women will make a conscious effort to successfully overcome inhibitions they feel about the technology through "hands on" exposure and use.

Computer Conferencing—A Leveler

A computer conference may bring together people from all walks of life who might never interact with one another. Those I studied ranged from an executive in a major corporation, to the wife of an affluent lawyer, to a bus driver, and night security guards. Most of these individuals held what I would classify as responsible middle-class management or professional positions: computer department manager, retail store manager and buyer, manager of a grocery store, manufacturing equipment designer, personnel specialist in some state's family services unit, deputy fire chief in a major city, and the superintendent of a waste water plant. Others held support positions with hopes of moving ahead as a result of this education: paralegal, secretary, bookkeeper, and accounting clerk. I asked the corporate manager, Vicky, if she would associate with such diverse people in normal life:

Oh yes. I do. Not socially probably because my husband and I have very busy schedules and when we are together it's he and I and close friends and the children, but we have grown up with people, with friends that, you know are gas station owners or auto repair people or milkmen or something like that. But I guess it is probably safe to say that I wouldn't. You wouldn't believe this but I'm a solitary person and when I'm in a classroom I don't mingle very well at all. But on the computer system I seem to have made many more friends. And that's very strange and don't ask me to explain it. I can't.

I have just mentioned vocation as one dimension of diversity; the students also range in age from early 20s to their 50s; they vary in residence from small town to urban dwellers in a major city; and their family situation ranges from unmarried singles, married with multiple children, to grandparents.

Arguably, this variety of occupational mix might occur in a typical classroom, but that likelihood seems dim for a number of reasons. First, physical proximity of adult students to the university they attend predicts that campuses in cities will only draw urbanites, with suburban and rural college settings drawing respective clientele. Second, classroom meeting times in the evening or at regular fixed times exclude night workers (Craig, Betty, Ted, and Len) or those with erratic schedules (Vicky, Carl, Randy, and Ralph). This would also be true of audio or video conference classrooms in distance education. Finally, computer conferencing has the potential for becoming a great mixing instructional system because it does more than just bring diverse people together—it fosters greater interaction among them as well.

Computer Conferencing: Potentiality versus Actuality

A theme of this chapter is that computer conferencing *can* provide an atmosphere for these important discussion dynamics to take place, which seems to have been the case with the Constitution course, But there is nothing inherent in the medium that makes that happen. Whether a course challenges polar thinking and asks participants to critically examine their positions and assumptions depends on a variety of factors: the subject matter, the course design, and the instructor style. The Constitution course examined contemporary controversial issues, such as abortion, sexual harassment, freedom of the press, speech, and religion. And the moderator invited controlled debate and confrontation, as Craig explained:

> He didn't put a lot into it; you didn't hear from him a lot. He was more like a referee. One thing that he did do as the conference went on—he enjoyed hearing the debates that people had. And, if somebody disagreed, he would endorse that, that was okay. In fact, for each topic he would have a beginning statement. And the last thing he would say is, "Speak your mind!"

However, the Communications course presented quite a different learning environment:

> Dan: Well, I had heard from one source that this was rather a formal conference.
>
> Ralph: Yes, I would think so. . . . It's structured. It's not as freewheeling as some of the other conferences that are out there. I think because 30% of our grade is based on our activity on the conference. I think that adds to the formality of it. And it's controlled. . . .
>
> Dan: What did you mean by that; can you explain it further?
>
> Ralph: Nobody has really challenged, including myself, nobody else's thoughts on anything there. There's a lot of "I agree," or "I disagree," "but only a little bit, or just on this." There's nothing like "Hey listen, you're an out and out boob!" Or, "Where did you get this wild idea from?" And it just seems not to digress very much from whatever the current topic is. So that's what I mean by self-limiting. Nobody's really "pushing the envelope."

Course design, teaching style, and student makeup determine to a great extent the atmosphere of the conference—whether it is competitive, collaborative, and intellectually challenging. These are not inherent attributes of the medium itself, but only possibilities.

SOCIAL RELATIONS

Working With Others Online

These students, particularly those who primarily took distance courses (about half of them), remarked how this new medium suddenly increased the perspectives and relationships they could have during their studies. Dennis remarked:

> I think it's the fact that you can easily converse with the other people. I can talk just one on one with just one other person if I want, by leaving private messages so that no one else sees them if I want to. . . . I think it's the opportunity to talk to the other class members as if you are in an actual classroom situation having a group discussion. That's a big advantage.

Influences of others online may provide the impetus for greater inquiry. For example, Craig determined after his confrontation with Judy over fair employment practices for women to do a research paper for his labor relations class around those issues. However, collaborative learning may not work for everyone in every setting and with all people.

It is hard to believe that students in the same course can have such opposite learning experiences, based primarily on their social acceptance in the collaborative ventures set up in the course design. Contrast the experience of Rose, who thoroughly enjoyed the spring writing seminar with Ted—a student in the same course who could not wait to mail his modem back as soon as it was over. The instructor, Alice Web, set the students up in four groups of five persons each to engage in collaborative learning exercises. Most of the work involved reading articles and then writing a thematic essay of about 1,000 words and posting it online for other members of the group to read and then critique in a 500 word response. Each person wrote 4 or 5 of the essays and 8 to 10 critiques—a fair amount of writing.

Rose described why this format worked particularly well for her:

> After we read something we'd put it on the computer and the people in our group would critique it. And as each of the other members of my group put their work on, I was able to critique their work. It was just incredible. Everybody was kind, generous with their time, and enthusiastic about the program. We had some wonderful, wonderful writers so we all felt that we learned a great deal from the styles they used. I just loved it.

She remembers most those students who conscientiously assisted her in improving her writing:

> I remember this one man who had done a lot of computer conferencing and he was a talented writer. He took the time to respond to everybody's writing, not just in his small group. He was very supportive and encouraging. . . . There was another person, a woman in my group, who lives 40 minutes away from me. I hope to meet her someday. She also sent in a great deal. I remember most those people who had a lot of time to put into it.

In a foreign learning environment with a group of strangers, Rose explained why the experience was not intimidating:

> Very subtle things people would pick up on. I was talking about how very difficult it would be for me to stand in front of a crowd and give a presentation, and one girl e-mailed in some information about where I could get tapes about learning how to do this. It was a very caring group. So we learned about different writing skills, but we learned so much more.
>
> Dan: Was it intimidating posting something to this group of unknowns?
>
> Rose: Definitely, especially knowing that your peers were going to critique it. And then as we got into it, myself in particular, as I saw the quality of the writing of the other people, it was even more intimidating, and yet they were so encouraging that you also wanted to just keep improving on your work. It was delightful.

It is no wonder that Rose felt intense enthusiasm to participate in the course:

> I would find myself coming home from work anxiously sitting down to the computer every day, dying to read what was new. It was like a newfound friend really.

She felt it had been a positive experience all around, and it was difficult to end it:

> It was very hard to say good-bye. Each small group in particular formed attachments. And I think everyone really enjoyed reading each other's writing, and reading the responses. . . . But I know at the time we had an opportunity to all say good-bye and leave messages for each other and so forth. There was one woman who did not finish the course because of a death of a loved one. But we all had an opportunity to get in touch with her and wish her well.

In contrast, Ted shared his difficulty at being continually involved in the conference, which stemmed from his inability to socially fit into the group:

> Ted: As far as relationships I felt like kind of the odd man out because everyone seemed so stupid and formal and nobody could relax or let off a wisecrack once in a while.
>
> Dan: Not even in . . . you must have had a lounge area.

Ted: Oh yeah. I don't know. It was very formal or something. I felt like I was in the wrong group. [laughter] I put that in one of my responses. I said "beer drinkers, phone in with a [particular type of beer]" and nobody said anything. They just kept plodding along.

However, he seemed to have made a major faux pas, which resulted in his ostracism by the group:

Ted: Just before this course started I went to a bachelor's party at a strip joint and one of the topics was how education has changed us, so I wrote a little thing about how I went to this. And how I went to this thinking, "Gee, do these girls have a day job or what are they going to do when their body wears out? How do other women feel about these women? Is this degrading to all women?" So I wrote that and people were kind of irritated. . . . I was supposed to get responses from I think it was two women in my group and neither one responded. Two guys from a completely different group responded.

Dan: Really? Did the instructor talk with you about that at all, in a private e-mail?

Ted: No. She just mentioned something about the subjunctive mood. That's all she said.

Dan: I don't even know what the subjunctive mood is! [chuckles]

Ted: Me neither. I looked it up and I still don't know.

Also, Ted had trouble collaborating with the student partner with whom he was matched up:

Ted: One person in my group had worked at a newspaper for 20 years. Here I am a novice at writing and was supposed to tell her how to write. I couldn't understand that.

Dan: So, what would you say when you commented on her writing?

Ted: I'd just look at it, and to my eyes I couldn't see anything wrong with the sentence structure, so I just did what the other people did—"Oh your mother sounds like such a nice person!" and that kind of stuff. That's all they were writing.

He really did not think he learned much out of the whole course:

Dan: And, do you feel like your writing improved?

Ted: A little bit. Some of the comments from the other students indicated I have a little bit of a problem with following theme *and I have a little bit of a problem with sentence structure. The one that pointed that out to me was the newspaper writer. All I got from the teacher was the subjunctive mood, which like I said, I don't know what that is. [laughter]*

Beyond his not fitting into the group, Ted's major difficulty with the course was that it dealt primarily with gender and multicultural issues—forcing him to write on topics about which he had little background (coming from a white, rural area) or held unpopular beliefs (conservative and chauvinistic). Compounding this difficulty was being paired with other learners who clearly had a much better command of writing and receiving no useful feedback from the instructor, whom he expected to exert more didactic leadership. This experience, although educationally useful, calls into question the andragogical principle of always using prior experience for learning (Knowles, 1984) and whether peer-oriented collaboration always works. Certainly both of these elements helped create a wonderful learning experience for Rose.

Online Relationships

The perennial question arose in each of the conferences I studied: Could it be possible to get together and meet in person sometime? Kris said:

There are a few of them there that I would certainly like to meet. [laughs] In fact they talked about that in a joking sort of way—something about a reunion or something. And I said, "If you can spring for airfare, I would certainly love to go." [both laugh]

This fact, coupled with the common interest students had about what the other students I had spoken with had said, or interest in what they were *really* like, helped spark my interest in this area. Also, I felt a need to study online social relations from a fear I had that this technology was dehumanizing. David, a course instructor, told me, however, that he felt you could get to know students online better than in person:

In its own way you get to know people better than you will anywhere else . . . and disembodied, yet. You know them in terms of their minds and personalities. You get a true sense of what that core individual is. There is no body language. A lot of what we initially use as something positive or negative in judging people is missing. I would argue that, contrary to some of the things I have said, personality comes through online more so than in person. Not the casual connections through which people ambiguously reveal their personalities through physical sensations. Whereas online, when you deal with someone for 15 weeks during a course, you get to know them, he or she—who they really are.

Nowhere in my research did an online relationship surface as strongly as that between Craig and Kerry. Both of them told me how much they liked the other person when I first interviewed them in person. They told me that they shared many of the same conservative political views, that they admired how the other person could argue his position forcibly online, and that they perceived the other as one of the main contributors to the online discussion. Both of them mentioned a string of private e-mail exchanges between them, in addition to the public postings in the computer conference. Kerry wondered if their relationship would have developed in person:

> You know there were a few times we joked about age. . . . But most of the time I never thought about it. I never thought "Oh wow, this person I'm responding to is 20 years older than me," or something like that. That's another thing that came out with Craig. You know he's older than I am and we had a question that if we had met physically at first, would we have struck up the relationship? Or would we have thought that there was too much difference in age? Whereas this way it didn't matter.

Kerry told me of their plans to get together with some of the other members of the conference:

> Kerry: Yeah. There's this group of people now that I've gone through this experience with, and we all shared the experience. A couple of us are already making plans to get together.
>
> Dan: Who is getting together, just offhand?
>
> Kerry: I'm starting out with Craig Brooks. We are starting to make plans, and then we may expand. There were a couple others who said, "Well we may be interested in the future." Dan: It would be kind of fun to see how everyone approaches each other.
>
> Kerry: Because Craig and I really hit it off in the conference. So it would be interesting to see each other and wonder if we had run into each other first, whether we would have, you know, because sometimes when you see a person, something about that person may turn you off and you wouldn't get as close as we've been able to like this.

Craig also expressed real enthusiasm about this get-together, and unlike many of these distance relations, the two of them only lived three hours apart, so a reunion might have been possible. But somehow the plans never materialized. Craig told me he had corresponded with Kerry over e-mail for several months after the conference. Kerry and he both agreed that their relationship had been stronger than I had portrayed it in the "preliminary findings" document I shared with all of the Constitution course members, just after their conference, but otherwise it was "right on the money." However, six months after the conference, Craig received no response to his e-mail queries to Kerry. Craig explained his disappointment eight months after the conference:

> Dan: I did sense that you and Kerry had formed more of a relationship than some of the other folks in the course.
>
> Craig: We haven't kept it up though. I wished we did.
>
> Dan: I thought you guys were going to get together sometime.
>
> Craig: Yes. That's what I wanted to do because especially last week, I was up that way. We hadn't kept the relationship up so I didn't get in contact. I was nervous and said [to myself], well maybe I'd better not call.

Craig did tell me that he and Dennis were still trading e-mail several times a month, but that was the only person he still was in touch with from the course. Dennis confirmed this but said of the conference participants that "we're all different and we all lead different lifestyles, have different occupations" so not keeping in touch was no different here than with any adult classroom situation.

However, there were other attempts to get together. Rose said she had received a telephone call from another conferencing student, and there is a good possibility that she might come visit her—a 40-minute drive away. Vicky told of expecting to drop in on some of the members of her conference if she ever got into their communities. Rose was surprised to meet in the "electric lounge" of her course a student from a tutored group course she had recently been in. Finally, Vicky reported that two of the students in her course actually met in person at a social function they discovered they were both going to. When they reported back on their meeting to the conference, they said that they were not surprised by the other person, having looked forward to meeting that individual from the relationship they had developed on the computer conference. However, I have concluded that most discussions of actual meetings are fantasies—distance rarely makes these situations possible within the "window of opportunity" for the comfortable meetings of mutual interest.

Many of the students seemed surprised at me asking about forming online friendships—*friend* was too strong a word, they said; perhaps *ally* or *acquaintance* was better. It surprised me to find out that three members of the Constitution course had been on the road in prior careers in music and theater—a commonalty that none of them realized about the others. Carl mentioned that Miguel (actually from Argentina) was from Chile during one interview and Portugal during the next one.

But several collaborative, nonrequired tasks indicated stronger online relationships among some of the members. For instance, in Melody's group, they circulated an online Easter card and presented it to the instructor on that holiday. During the online course I took, I discovered a Briton who watercolored and arranged a couple of e-mail exchanges between him and my wife, who shares the same avocation. Also, at my online request, a fellow student voluntarily sent me a postcard from her vacation to Italy during the conference. In this research, Betty used her online relationship with Ralph and Rose to invite them to contact me and volunteer to be interviewed, a task I was unable to do because of subject consent agreements I had made with the instructor earlier. And Carl answered some online questions I sent him with a response that covered more than three pages of printout—no trivial task for this busy grocery manager/student.

Perhaps online relations were not meant to last, but to fulfill important needs of the moment. As Vicky described:

> I got into a conversation with a fellow from [some place]. He was helping me out of a technical problem and come to find out he was very frustrated with the university system and he was venting that frustration by typing and typing and typing, and I just kind of sensed that this wasn't the time to interject. I just let him type, type, type, because he was just getting it off of his chest. He must have gone on for about 10 minutes. I'm not exaggerating. And then when we were ready to go, sign off, he said, "Thank you so much for listening to me. I feel so much better." [laughter]

Having greater online relationships may be important to more isolated learners who have the time, energy, and personal need to create and nourish them. However, many of these adults are so engaged in other life demands or have sufficient other relationships that they do not have the interest or inclination to cultivate them. Francis summed up this view of online relationships:

> Dan: And what is going to happen to these online relationships that you have formed?

Francis: I don't know. I really haven't heard from anybody since the course has been over, but neither have I contacted anybody. I guess what happens mostly with any of the classes at HSC [Hawks College], when you have a group course, seldom do you see any of these faces again. It's unusual that you do.

SCHOLARSHIP ON RELATIONSHIPS AND LEARNING

Lately, more attention is being paid in distance education to aspects that remove the instructor from the student other than just physical separation in space or time. Moore (1992) defined this gap as "a distance of understandings and perception, caused in part by the geographical distance, that has to be overcome by teachers, learners and educational organizations if effective, deliberate, planned learning is to occur" (p. 2). He used the term *transactional distance* to indicate this psychological and communications gap, exacerbated by the geographic distancing of instructor and learner from each other, with media whose fidelity does not match that of in-person interaction and makes it more difficult to view the other's perspective. Hodgkinson (1991) outlined the various aspects of "distance": (a) physical distance—separation in time or geography; (b) social distance—separation by affinity, closeness, and support; (c) intellectual distance—the degree of gap in the shared knowledge; and (d) cultural distance—factors of language, class, religion, age, sex, and ethnicity that affect the communication process.

Two factors affect the intensity of transactional distance, Moore (1992) argued: (a) the degree and nature of the dialogue possible between the teacher and student, and (b) the amount of structure in the educational program. Distance education programs that primarily accommodate one-way dialogue and are highly structured are much more distant (transactionally) than those, like computer conference-based programs, that allow more dialogue and less structure.

The material in this chapter highlights the various forms of transactional distance at work in computer conferencing. But instead of measuring that distance as solely between the instructor and the students (as a monolithic group), the transactional distance occurs among all of the participants in the conference. The support of dialogue among conference members alleviates this distance in perhaps more ways than would even occur in a traditional classroom setting. Moore seemed to agree:

> The areas of student interaction and creating knowledge promise
> to be |computer conferencing's| main contribution to distance
> education. . . . It is the dialogue by teleconference between stu-
> dents that is making possible the creation of knowledge by stu-
> dents and |a| high level analysis, synthesis and critique of knowl-
> edge. (Moore, 1991, p. 6)

This research was not the first to point out the unique type of
learning possible by group interaction in an "on-line class." Enhanced
dialogue among learners is made possible in computer conferencing by
its characteristics of asynchronicity and individuality because students
interact with others' ideas at their own pace; "the slow and reflective
learner will be able to contribute as well as the quicker and more extro-
verted student" (Moore, 1991, p. 6). Moore argued that adult students
"appreciate the relative and problematic nature of knowledge" (p. 7)—
they are ready to deal with issues of uncertainty, disillusion, and con-
troversy that have not yet been resolved. This is the type of atmosphere
computer conferencing fosters. However, none of the research I looked
at suggested why computer conferencing invites polar positions to surface, and much of this literature speaks of collaboration, instead of
hostile disagreement. As an exception, Siegel et al. (1986) found that
groups involved in computer-mediated communications were less
inhibited than face-to-face groups, "using strong or inflammatory
expressions, in their interpersonal interactions" (p. 157).

This literature only discussed the dynamics of gender online,
not those aspects of geography, political persuasion, ethnicity, class,
and so forth. Grint (1989) reported gender stereotypes existing in conferences, for example, females asking for help and males providing
technical assistance. He reported that female students expressed inhibitions about using the technology, as if they were inviting male
strangers into their homes, albeit in a disembodied form. Such expressions may be cultural, as these concerns did not surface in my research.
Graddol (1989) pointed out that in the conversational norms of computer conferencing, women can point out the sexist remarks and
assumptions of male participants without fear of interrupting the flow
of discussion or "speaking" out of turn. He pointed out, as did one
instructor I interviewed, that males cannot dominate the computer conferencing discussion like they often do in face-to-face conversations.

Kaye et al. (1989) noted that computer conferencing is a very
social medium; people like it because humans are social beings, the
medium is fun, and some people find hidden talents they possess by
using it. They see four social roles computer conferencing plays: (a)
overcoming isolation, (b) extending professional networks, (c) promoting serendipitous encounters, and (d) providing socializing opportuni-

ties. Moore (1991) submitted that because adults are usually participating in education voluntarily, they appreciate a learning environment that is less formal and more social in nature.

Few studies directly addressed online relationships. Boshier's (1988) investigation of computer conferences on listserves found that friendly relationships developed in spite of reduced cues, that participants became more casual and humorous over time, and that this medium invites more equitable participation. Phillips (1990) found that students who participated in an electronic "student lounge" maintained their attitudes of positive potential for this medium after direct experience with it. They enjoyed chatting, making friends and professional contacts, and felt less isolated. In studying group structures over time in a computer conference, Rice (1982) found that reciprocal exchange was necessary for group stability. However, I found no studies that discussed the role of online relationships to learning, nor their evolution during and after a computer conference—contributions that this research makes.

CONCLUSION

Perhaps more than any other distance medium, computer conferencing makes it possible for learners to interact among themselves as well as with the instructor. This chapter explored two aspects of group interaction for learning: (a) the dynamics involved when students from diverse backgrounds meet online, and (b) the formation of personal relationships as part of this electronic schooling.

When students from dispersed geographical areas "talk" together in a computer conference, they encounter greater arrays of opinion than would be found in a typical classroom. Such things as rural conservatism versus urban liberalism and in-state versus out-of-state aspects emerged. Several students felt that sharing opinions among themselves brought their black and white polar positions toward a more comfortable gray area. Participants felt positive about their ignorance of the physical characteristics of other class members—visible aspects of age, ethnicity, or disability that are continually apparent in a classroom setting. This allowed more honest communications to emerge and relationships to form that may not have otherwise.

Gender dynamics surfaced in this research as well: Sexist exchanges occurred on the computer conference. There were more male participants than female, and some women thought their socialization kept them from having learned computer technology earlier. However, other elements of this study indicate that the computer conferencing environment was inclusive and that most women students were comfortable, competent, and capable in using this technology—a trend that will continue, dissolving this issue. The research suggested that adults from various social and occupational roles and status were brought together who probably would not have conversed in a normal classroom because of different timing of work schedules or geographical separation. Computer conferencing encouraged exchanges among individuals from diverse backgrounds, but only if these elements were incorporated into course design, instructor style, and the atmosphere of the online environment.

The chapter's last section examined the social and personal relationships that are a part of this instructional system. First, the joyful learning experience of Rose was contrasted with Ted's endurance of the same writing course from which he derived little value. What to her was a collaborative venture with caring, helpful, and skillful peers was one in which Ted felt like an outcast and uncomfortable for his coarse, unpopular expression of opinions about gender and multicultural issues for which he had little interest or background. Being matched with students whose writing ability and experience so excelled his own seemed farcical. This contrasting experience stresses the need for social acceptance within the online course and questions the applicability of collaboration and use of adult prior experience with all distance students.

Finally, the study explored the formation, expression, and permanence of personal relationships, probing into the online friendship of Craig and Kerry, two students who "hit it off" in the Constitution course. Plans to keep in touch and arrange an in-person meeting gradually faded by the time of my last interview, eight months after the course. Conference participants did provide support for each other, often of a personal, caring nature, during the computer conferences. However, these relationships dissolved after the courses ended, not unlike most adult course situations.

6

Learning and Living in an Information Age

Dan: I am just thinking, does this technology fit into your view of an ideal future, or might there be negatives?

Francis: I'm really apprehensive about the negatives. I think its stressing the economy to a certain extent because we don't need people to do a lot of . . . things that have become computerized. And I don't think that anyone has figured out what to do with our economy in this type of scenario. But what do we do with all these unemployed people? What are we supposed to do now that machines are doing these things? Socially too, I don't know, you're sitting there with your computer and people that are just online, it is kind of isolating in a way. It is more expansive because you can reach people who are not living where you are living and talk to them, but it's also kind of an isolated socialization.

These adults are taking a course through distance education, as part of their degree program, and it involves computer conference discussions. So far this study has focused on that experience alone. However, this distance learning activity represents only one aspect of continuing technological changes that impact these students' lives, so I sought to discover their views about how computer technology fits into their personal future and the society they envision.

Part of the challenge of qualitative research is to generalize findings from the study to other settings. If this were a quantitative study, I would examine to what extent the findings from this computer conference hold for similar settings, students, instructors, content areas, institutions, and so forth. Qualitative researchers, in contrast, believe that their research is generalizable to many contexts. It captures the human experience, and because humans are social creatures, sharing more in common than holding unique differences, the question changes. Rather than asking whether these findings are generalizable, I ask: "To whom or what group do these patterns of behavior or outlook about the social world apply?" The qualitative researcher looks for dynamics from the interactions, perspectives, and viewpoints, as presented here, that will also be found in other contexts that embody similar sociocultural characteristics (Bogdan & Biklen, 1992; Eisner, 1991).

The purpose of this chapter, then, is to exercise the sociological imagination as to what implications computer network experiences have on our future society. These speculations come from student opinions and observations I gathered from a variety of contexts during my fieldwork. They reflect my own outlook as someone inextricably engaged, like others, in a technological future. This chapter asks more questions than it offers answers. It first investigates the forms adult learning may take both inside and outside of educational institutions as communication technologies further impinge on our acquiring useful information. Then it examines the impact of other communications and convenience devices and their effect on our lives.

LEARNING IN AN INFORMATION AGE

Learning takes place in several contexts: within the framework of an educational institution, within the workplace, within community organizations, or from individual initiative in undertaking learning projects. Technology increasingly affects the learning process in each of these settings, both as a means and as an end. Particularly in distance learning, delivery media increasingly involves more complex technology, usually incorporating telephone, video, and computing devices.

Learning In Schools With Technology

> The new interactive capacity of telecommunications technology possesses a transforming character which has the potential to alter dramatically the structure of the university, providing flexibility, convenience, and individual feedback and evaluation of both residential and off-campus students.(Hall, 1991, p. 106)

However, Hall admitted that higher education must determine how to effectively service students, restructure institutions, involve faculty, assure quality, and shoulder costs if colleges and universities are "to move beyond the current piecemeal, small-scale, highly expensive, and marginal efforts" (p. 107).

Those I interviewed agreed that this type of computer network communication would continue to flourish:

> Kris: I'm sure that [computer conferencing] is going to be the wave of the future. Between FAX machines and computer conferences that is the way it is going to be eventually for exchanging information.
>
> Melody: It is a good way to get a lot of information and meet a lot of people.
>
> Dan: As a society, what do you think this technology means?
>
> Rose: I would hope that it would develop into a much more used way of teaching. It has its advantages and I think that people are only going to get busier. And it does fit into anyone's schedule. There's that flexibility. I think it's a very effective way of learning as well; having that written word there.

However, there are also obstacles in implementing this kind of instructional technology:

> Francis: In higher education [this technology] would probably cut down on the cost by computer linking students. You can cover a lot more students. I know it would be a lot more work for the teacher though too because some of this work has to go to an individual. So I don't know. You don't have to have 50 people in your classroom but you still have to have somebody to go over all the work they are doing. [both laugh]
>
> Dan: Yeah, and talk to them online.
>
> Francis: Maybe with a professor and a lot of assistants. . . . In our schools now they are leaning toward computers with the budget issue this year to replace some machinery. But I think the teachers have to be taught how to use the tools and many of the teachers we have in the school districts really don't know much about computers and there's no mandating for them to learn.

Implementation at Hawks

Because a majority of the students were enthusiastic about using computer conferencing to take courses, I looked at how this technology was implemented and future plans for it at Hawks College.

Beginning with one pilot course five years ago, the Distance Education Center offered nine courses through computer conferencing during Fall semester 1993. The viability of the college's computer network depends on two factors: (a) providing a host of useful resources that attract faculty and student use, and (b) connecting enough individuals who use the system regularly to provide a critical user mass.

Students mentioned computer conferencing courses as just one aspect of the online environment that they found useful. Initially they were attracted to other services on the network: electronic mail, discussion groups, library access services, and degree planning tools. Most of these students exchanged e-mail with their advisor, other instructors, and (to a lesser extent) other students—and found it useful. Second, many of them participated in public discussion forums on CONFER or listserve discussion groups on BITNET; usually these electronic conversations were beyond course requirements. Third, Hawks sold them a library search program at nominal cost that would allow their modem to phone preprogrammed numbers of dozens of in-state online library catalogs. Finally, these students enjoyed using an online database that enabled them to examine various degrees in constructing their own individualized degree program. Additionally, they mentioned bulletin boards with events, games, and classified ads on the network. The usefulness of these services combine in influencing computer network vitality.

Computer network communication prospers to the extent that it provides wide coverage and is used by the important people in one's professional and study world. The computer support person told me the goal of getting Hawks personnel universally connected had been largely successful (95%), although not all of them were using the system. Administrators, faculty, and staff use the system primarily for e-mail exchanges. Student use, encouraged and on the upswing, still was at most 500 users, roughly 8% of the student body. Although it does not affect the majority of students, one advisor explained, it has great "individual impact" on those who use it, allowing them to develop their degree programs, keep in better contact with their advisor and instructors, and even upload and submit assignments online. He typified his e-mail discussions with students as sporadic; they would engage in active exchanges with him for several days around specific issues, and then he would not hear from them for weeks until another concern surfaced.

Beyond computer conference discussions, several students hoped that the computer would provide the connectedness to Hawks that they found missing. This hope extended from feelings of affiliation (Kris) to involvement (Kerry, Ralph, Melody) to career and graduate school networking (Len, Craig). A faculty member used the electronic network to invite Kerry to present a paper and Ralph to join a campus committee—both were favorably accepted. Craig and Len both spoke of developing online relations with faculty members for advice on graduate schools. Melody queried faculty across the state about career opportunities in social work, receiving favorable responses. Steve and Laura (faculty members) agreed that computer networking represented a possible means to link them together as a campus in some ways, but Laura explained its limited potential:

> I think it could provide a connectedness to students feeling that "Oh there are other students out there," if we had a mechanism for lifting them up, besides the fact that they were in the same institution of study. That would give them a reason to link.

This mirrors the perspective Dennis expressed of finding students in his courses coming from such different backgrounds, holding such different jobs, and expressing such different interests from his own that he felt little desire for continued contact. However, administratively the campus could be interconnected by electronic networks. Yet, Steve explained how his involvement diminished over time:

> When we first put this electronic system up, we had a bulletin board, electronic mail, and computer conferencing. I stopped participating in computer conferencing deliberately after the first year because I found that I was being consumed in endless discussions that seemed not to move anywhere. They were interesting. They were fun to participate in, but they were chomping away at about two and a half hours of my day. . . . And the committees that were meeting via computer conferencing I just didn't log to them anymore. I did use the electronic mail. I found that very very helpful. And I stopped accessing the bulletin board because I never found anything posted there that was of value.

As mentioned before, these students appreciated electronic mail links to their advisors. Francis spoke of keeping in contact with hers during the advisor's summer vacation in Cape Cod. Dennis was able to avoid frequent trips to the Hawks unit, over an hour's drive from his home, through e-mail dialogue. Melody explained the convenience of this communication system:

> For me, [Hawks faculty members are easier to reach] because it is hard for me to use the phone at work. Usually, if you have a phone, they are there, and they will get back to you right away. But, I really can't take calls at work, so it is easier for me to just use the computer.

And Miguel explained his frustration with those instructors who are not connected:

> I can't understand how there can be a tutor in a nontraditional school who doesn't know how to use a computer. That's something that I just never understand. How would you get in touch with your students if you don't use email?. . . All the professors that I've had that weren't using the computer, really had a lack of follow-up, in terms of asking me how I'm doing, do I have any problems, etc.

However, from the faculty member's perspective, the issues are somewhat different:

> Laura: I think it [email] has provided instant accessibility to me and it's harder to ignore it. [laughter] For the students I think that it's a wonderful tool. . . . You're right, a student may call and not be able to get a hold of their mentor or tutor during the day, so to dash off an e-mail message is easier. But a mentor who handles 40 students, and if all of the students are asking small questions, it could certainly increase a mentor's work load. Before all this electronic mail came about certainly there were students who were pretty independent. They didn't call a lot between appointments. And you may only see them a few times for tutoring, but I think there is potential with e-mail, for more of the follow-up to go on.
>
> Steve: [Students] seek guidance or [they] seek information. And I find that often if I want to talk to somebody about a problem and if I'm delayed in getting to them, I often have the solution by the time I can make contact. [we laugh]

These faculty members, who were not involved in computer conferencing courses, explained the increased workload electronic communications placed on them. Because some 5% of Hawks personnel were not connected to e-mail, many of the administrative e-mail messages they got were duplicated in the regular mail—perhaps a day later—and they got 20 to 40 pieces of paper mail a day. Plus, when it came electronically, they felt an added expectation to immediately respond or place more priority on it. Craig explained his e-mail relationship with his advisor:

> Craig: I can leave her a message anytime and I've done that.
>
> Dan: And she gets back with you pretty much?

Craig: Oh yes. In three or four days. But when I see her she says don't leave her too many messages because she doesn't like using it. [Dan laughs] As a matter of fact, one of my other teachers says he doesn't like it either but he's trying to get used to it. But my mentor told me the problem she has is that it's easier to talk to somebody, she thought. But I don't think so. I like to have something in writing.

It seems that faculty use of this technology is as idiosyncratic as student preference. I talked primarily to student advocates, but in reality, relatively few of the students with whom these faculty members work on a daily basis place much importance on this activity. As an outside observer, I concluded that the vision for computer network communications to link all members of Hawks College—a uniquely dispersed institution—to provide information, affiliation, and greater productivity, has been tempered by finding that not everyone has or desires access.

Workplace Training

Another area in which learning experiences are structured under the direction of an organization is the training setting of corporate business and industry. Just as computer networks allow "distance" to be a moveable point in both time and space for the instructor and student, this same technology can traverse the partition that typically separates the workplace from the academy. Vicky, manager of training in a major corporation, explained:

I think that in industry (and that's another reason why I'm looking at it), to tie it into the university and to be able to bring it into the workplace, would be very motivating for a student who's got to get a degree to certify in something. And of course it benefits the college. It gives them some funding. And yet it draws on all of the experience out there that is available via satellite or telecommunications that you couldn't ordinarily get.

The link she describes is not just one way (from business to the university), nor is it entirely credit oriented. She told me of a video conferencing system her company was piloting with several high schools and a university. Particularly in math and science courses, they encouraged the high school class to spontaneously video conference into the corporation and/or they encouraged the university's engineers or technical specialists to discuss solutions to the problems they encounter or to ask how concepts are applied in the "real world."

Corporations now use a wide variety of telecommunications technologies in providing instruction to their employees. Vicky explained that her corporation uses computer conferencing extensively for information exchange, but not for training. Shortly after beginning the computer conferencing course at Hawks College, she joined an electronic conference at work with personnel from around the country in designing the specifications for a database. Because the database she is developing services "internal customers" who give her feedback through the conference, she said, "it has been very helpful to me because it has given me insights into how the end user perceives the system and what they feel needs to be done."

Besides this computer conferencing system, they have an extensive bulletin board system. Again, Vicky commented:

> We have an electronic bulletin board that any ABCer can just put in a word, and they can look at over 101 different bulletin boards that are in their specific area of interest—about things that are happening, classes that are coming up, or new announcements, new developments, activities going on in that particular industry sector. It is a bulletin board that keeps you up to date, right at your work station.

Another instructional system available at the employees' computer work station is computer-based training (CBT), run over the same computer network that provides the conferencing and bulletin board system. She explained how employees can almost instantly have access to over 100 courses by typing a command and selecting them off a menu. This system offers several advantages: first, it provides the convenience of distance availability; second, it pretests students and recommends that they study only in those areas in which they have deficiencies; third, it allows employees to enter and exit a course at will—the system keeps track of where they left off and restarts them right at that point the next time they sign back on; and fourth, CBT provides a limited interactivity. As Vicky explained: "We are still finding that if you still keep the conversation informal and question them every so many screens, keep them engaged, and put in some reinforcement . . . they kind of like it." Vicky told me that some recent telephone training courses they offered by CBT got very high ratings, higher than some classroom courses.

Furthermore, Vicky explained new technologies they are experimenting with—also delivered to the employees' PC work station—such as video conferencing or an integrated system that provides computer, audio, and video conferencing, as well as lets users exchange graphics and PC files. Besides the variety of telecommunication technologies, her company also used more conventional distance delivery media (text, videotape, audio cassette) and classroom training.

Eventually the situation with technologies for learning becomes one of over-choice. At Vicky's corporation they have developed some procedures to determine when to provide training and which medium to use for its development and delivery. First, they have developed large databases of competencies and determined which of these the person who fills any position in the company needs to possess. By next assessing employees' competencies, they determine how fit employees are for their current positions and for other positions to which they may aspire as their careers develop. They match the behavioral objectives of their courses to this competency set to determine the training courses employees should take. This procedure ensures that competency needs will determine instruction, not media characteristics.

Second, the company relegates the teaching of lower level learning skills—rote memorization, fact and concept acquisition—to the more passive media of text, audiocassettes, videocassettes, CBT, and interactive videodiscs. Classroom courses and satellite video conferencing are reserved for higher level learning skills, such as application, synthesis, and evaluation. Third, they developed "mentoring" systems that encourage employees to make the transfer of skills taught in their courses to the worksite. Working with an assigned mentor in person and through a variety of distance technologies—telephone, FAX, e-mail exchange, and (in the future) video conferencing—workers get answers to concerns and issues and learn the specifics of applying a particular skill to their own situation.

The workplace demands increasingly more training, much of it associated with the emergence of new technology. Dirr (1990) claimed that by the year 2000 information service industry jobs will be filled by 80% of workers who must continually upgrade their skills because of changing work demands. He observed business and industry spends $210 billion on training yearly, more than either the K-12 or higher education budgets (of $144 billion and $94 billion, respectively).

Gundry (1992) discussed how Digital Equipment Corporation extends a network of 30,000 nodes in 33 countries to 100,000 employees—the largest network in the world. He claimed that this network provides ample opportunity for people to learn collaboratively from each other as they go about performing their jobs. IBM's formal strategic planning for its future training system recommends that telecommunications take such a role:

> In the year 2000, education will primarily be distributed and take place in the workstation. Students will be involved in "classes;" however, these classes meet electronically by way of video/comput-

er conferences. Assignments will be given and completed using electronic mail, and information resources include the many databases available through the network. Guest instructors (both internal and external) are easily "patched" into the network to provide lectures or participate in student projects. Automatic translation tools facilitate the interaction of students and instructors speaking different languages. Electronic classmates develop the same shared memories, allegiances, and friendships as students in physical classrooms. (Vision of IBM human resource performance in the year 2000, 1990, p. v)

Because of a more diverse, global employee base with a wide range of skills, who work flexibly with changing technologies and lifestyles, IBM seeks to develop a new type of instructional system. They envision this system to be distributed, modular, multisensory, nonlinear, transferable, and responsive. Although their official plan states that workplace learning will be "self-directed and provided in an 'on-demand' environment" (p. iv), an integral component of it is an elaborate database of "employee skills profiles." This system keeps constant track of current competencies, deficiencies, and progress toward improvement. The system is idealized to deliver appropriate instruction based on individual learning styles, culture, and language, as desired. However, it embodies a certain Orwellian intrusion into employees' competencies by constantly monitoring and prescribing training and skill areas for promotion and job performance, areas that have formerly been more private and personal.

A new trend to hit the workplace this decade has been telecommuting. According to ASTD's *National Report On Human Resources* (1992), over 6.6 million Americans work from their homes by computer and modem, usually for two days out of a five-day work week. And, the number increases by 20% annually. It reports that the reasons companies encourage telecommuting are to avoid facility and operation costs, avoid traffic congestion, help local environments, and for to gain productivity. However, issues remain, such as finding practical business reasons for telecommuting, deciding which jobs might be transportable, finding home work space, gaining family and roommate support, learning to manage employees by measuring outcomes—not observing attention to task—and legitimately assuaging telecommuters' concern over lost visibility and its effect on their promotion.

In summary, workplace training uses a wide variety of instructional media for delivery and information sharing; computer networked ones include computer conferencing, e-mail, bulletin board systems, and CBT. Vicky's corporation uses a competency development model, learning skill hierarchy, and mentoring programs to decide how to use the various technologies for learning. Corporations are continuing to spend more on training through and about technology as it changes working and learning locations.

Learning Informally With Technologies

Networks—A 21st Century Lyceum

Over the past decade, informal, online discussion groups have boomed both on the public networks, such as the Internet and Bitnet, as well as on the commercial networks, such as Genie, Compuserve, Delphi, and America On-line. The computer system I am connected with allows me to join over 2,500 such discussion groups (listserves), and Miguel told me that he can access 3,500 similar groups on the Usenet system to which he belongs. These discussion groups share some of the properties of the Lyceum of the last century: They are typically study groups around mutual topics of interest, entered into voluntarily by adults.

Just over half the students I interviewed were involved in these online discussion groups, sometimes to fulfill course requirements, but usually because of personal interest. There are several important similarities and differences between these electronic discussion groups and computer conferencing, besides the richer features for structured communications that the latter provides. They both share characteristics of computer-mediated communications: geographic dispersion, asynchronicity, text-based messaging, and interactivity. Students pointed out these differences: (a) online discussion groups, with many more discussants, provide greater breadth of perspective; (b) online discussion participation is voluntary, so a "vocal" minority "speak" and many members only add notes about topics of interest; (c) the public discussion groups rarely have readings or offline assignments to inform the conversation, nor are there grades or credit related to performance to insure compliance; (d) the sense of anonymity is greater in these discussion groups; (e) practices of "flaming" and "lurking"[1] are more common in network discussions; and (f) discussions sometimes give way to public exhibition of academic prowess or outrageous abandon.

Dennis, who scans 12 professional journals related to his work each month, explained the roles these listserves play in his professional development:

---

[1]*Lurking* refers to those participants who only read the electronic communications of others in an online conversation, but never contribute themselves.

Dan: Well do you feel like the networks give you information that you don't get through these publications?

Dennis: Not necessarily information that I don't get, but they give me a different insight into it and oftentimes it's a chance to converse with others who are keeping abreast of things also. It's a different perspective. . . .

Dan: Have you found some people on these networks that you relate to or that you keep a correspondence with?

Dennis: Yes. There's a few. And there is occasionally some we call for more information. It's all general broadening of your knowledge and the more minds you can pick the more effective you're going to be in your position.

Some of these students use the networks primarily for recreation—a diversion from work and studies—as Carl explained:

I can honestly say at least as far as VAX goes, I get on there at least every day. Sometimes recreationally and sometimes because I have to get the work done. . . . I don't think there's a day that goes by that I don't get on there to see if there are any messages for me, or to take a look in the bulletin boards to see what might be happening. I really enjoy getting on there for an hour or two just for a break. I'm on the system and I can have some fun with it as opposed to being on the system and I'm under the gun to get the work done.

Other students, like Len and Craig, use the networks as a way of meeting others because they feel intellectually isolated as distance students. Len belonged to 12 network discussion groups when I chatted with him, ranging from such areas as the Vietnam war, Middle Eastern and Jewish studies, to expressions of popular culture and music. Craig explained:

Sometimes I'll sit down there for three or four hours writing a paper and then I can't stand it anymore and its nice to switch to that, and I'll see other people on Bitnet or on the conference that's still going and its nice to relate to them you know. And even on Bitnet they advertise jobs they see. . . .

I know in college the connections you make are important. But at Hawks it's hard to make any connections. You don't meet anybody, but on the computer you may make some connections.

Len added, "I have been thinking about |the networks| as a way of overcoming isolation. People use networks who are isolated, to reach out to the world."

Particularly for students like Miguel, who have immigrated to the United States or are studying abroad, the networks create a means of staying in touch with their own heritage:

> I have relatives in Argentina who are connected with e-mail. That's one case. Also I have some friends from my university days there who have e-mail too. I keep contact with them. . . . Argentina has a lot of people around the world with PhDs who are working around the world. All those people are connected through e-mail. So what has happened is that there is a list-serve for people from Argentina or people who are interested in that culture. . . . It has around 1,200 people. . . . 95% [of the communication] is in Spanish. What's good about that is that 99% of these people have a high level of education so it gets really interesting. We get to talk about the country, soccer, whatever. . . . Some people are economists, some biologists, some people are computer scientists, whatever. Whoever knows about something shares it. It is like a big information family. Everybody shares what they know.

I helped a graduate assistant with whom I work, Henry (a ficti-tious name), from a less-developed African country, join listserve dis-cussions about Africa. He learned about one electronic discussion group with 200 members devoted specifically to his home country and joined it several months ago. Although almost all of the subscribers are natives of this African nation scattered all over the world, none of them actually live in the home country now—it is simply too expensive to use this kind of technology from there. Some of them use their tribal languages online. They discuss sports (particularly soccer), music, cul-ture, and politics. Henry likes to get political discussions going on the network once in a while because the others will ignore these issues if left to themselves; he is the social gadfly for the network. The "radical" things he says on the network, he told me, would not be allowed to be as freely expressed in his country, nor would he have as direct input to the social elites as he does here.

As I talked to these students about their computer conferenc-ing courses, often e-mail and listserve discussions would surface because these activities are so similar and are accessed through the same telecommunications access link. However, they are different envi-ronments, providing different types of information and learning. These students go through network discussion groups for recreation, to break down isolation, to learn, or to link to global resources to keep alive cul-tural interests.

Informal Workplace Learning

Marsick (1988) and Marsick and Watkins (1990) challenge the notion that companies should look to training to provide the bulk of learning in the workplace; rather, they demonstrate the tremendous informal and incidental learning activity that takes place at work—estimating that this accounts for over 80% of human resources learning.

Van Onna (1992) argued that learning and work are converging in the workplace for three reasons, each with a technological basis: (a) the advent of computer technology requires fluid and tacit skills that cannot be developed in formal instructional settings; (b) the expense and turnover of advanced equipment makes it difficult to build employee performance skills in simulated environments—these can only be learned on the job; and (c) newer, flexible technologies are only fully implemented when actually in use. Typically the general training skills do not meet the specialized configuration demands to operate machines or software, after they are customized. He also posited that higher levels of professionals must pursue both formal and informal training concurrently. With the rate technologies proliferate in the workplace, we should expect that those who purchase various productivity tools will learn to use them through a combination of self-instruction by reading the manuals and trial and error, as they install the innovations and apply them to their own problems at hand. This fieldnote excerpt provides an example:

> He started out telling me how he was making hardware and software transitions in his office to "Enable," a works-type software package Hawks provides free of charge to all of its faculty. He showed me the eight-inch stack of manuals that come with it and wondered aloud how long it would be until he found time to learn the stuff.

Vicky told me how computer conferencing had been used in her company for informal learning among employees:

> I've found that I've learned from other people's mistakes. Sometimes when I have very narrow thinking, and some other ideas are brought up, that really helps me look at things in a different way. And all of that is the result of people coming together and expressing their ideas. It's just a great way to learn. That's why ABC supports the idea of conferencing. To some degree they could say, "Hey, you know this could take away from your productivity, you spending all your days sitting in front of this terminal in the conferencing, in the forums." But because it encourages creative thinking and innovation and

teamwork and empowerment, they have chosen to continue it and continue to foster it and make it available on a broader basis.

Information Bulletin Boards

Another information technology that has recently come into our lives is the telephone bulletin board. Using this system, a person dials a phone number and gets a voice menu when the system answers. Using a printed list they have on hand or by following instructions, individuals punch in a code on the touch-tone phone to reach the information or services they desire.

My local newspaper latched onto this technology in a big way; they established a full-fledged news and information service (syndicated), which they list regularly in the paper. As a free service you can dial in and get current weather, hourly news, sports, stock reports, the lottery, soap opera summaries, travel information, trivial games, children's information, agricultural extension advice, want ads, and so forth. The first two services to be included were a "personals" service for matching people in romantic relationships and a church bulletin area—information about meeting times, activities, and even short sermons. Using a touch-tone phone, you can skip around from item to item (with a three- to five-item limit per call) either forward, replay, abort, and so forth. The catch is that these services each have advertising connected with them, and the system disables the user control options during the advertising. I have enjoyed dialing into the service the couple of times I have tried it—especially for news summaries, which I often miss on the radio, or to get the latest report on a news event I am following. I also learned that this kind of system is not unique to Syracuse—most major U.S. cities now have them.

One of the latest services that is being added is a school announcement service. The newspapers have sold this service to the whole district, possibly the entire region. Whole schools can leave announcements for parents and youth about their events and services. Furthermore, individual teachers leave daily information for students about homework assignments and expectations.

The newspapers have jumped ahead and created a full-fledged commercial information service here with which nonprofit services will have trouble competing. They have kept their own entrepreneurial interests well at heart throughout the process, and I expect that the ads on these numbers will become longer, more obnoxious, and more frequent as customer usage builds. They have only followed in the seemingly irreversible lead television and radio interests took earlier in commercializing information media.

Societal Implications of Learning Visions

So far I have outlined the various learning and information technologies that seem quite active now. But there are important social implications that arise from these innovations, as this next section describes.

Creating a Global Learning Community

Especially given the examples of the Argentinean and African nations' electronic network, it appears that these communications technologies can draw the world together. Francis expressed this hope:

> I think the positives are that you get more global. Society in general will become more globally in touch because you can turn on your computer and contact [other areas of the world]. It will probably work as a factor to bring societies closer in that respect, as you can contact the different cultures and find out what you have in common and what you have as differences.

One really gets the sense of this interconnectedness through the computer network activity in which Len mentioned he is involved:

> Len: I'm able to get the information from the Israeli perspective, but haven't got it from the Arabic one, yet. But, I could do that from the network out of the University of Cairo.
>
> Dan: Is all of that in English?
>
> Len: No, most of it is, but there was an Arab on the other day wanting tutorial help with Hebrew. There is a South American network that is all in Spanish. Also, there is a weekly Chinese newsletter that requires a special Mac to display the Chinese characters. The latest controversy comes out of Spain because the networks haven't made any way to accommodate the "~" (as in cañon) symbol, when the EC was developing electronic interchange standards.

However, several students told me that they rarely learned new information on these networks that they could not obtain more efficiently from other sources. They enjoyed reading how certain writers articulated their position and would search for discussion items by specific people. The credibility of the network information can also be questionable because you may not know the professional identity of contributors to the network. Finally, this activity can be highly addictive to some. For example, Len estimated that he spent three and a half hours online a day, subscribed to 12 different discussion groups simultaneously, and received close to 350 messages a day!

Educational Changes?

A familiar adage is "the more things change, the more they remain the same." This seems to apply well to some computer conference activities. Students and teachers take on similar social roles, groups include or exclude members, common social norms are sanctioned, and typical classroom conventions replicate themselves online. For example, many academic computer conferencing environments have discussion areas that mirror that of a university campus: the classroom area, a bulletin board, a student lounge, a study hall, and so forth. As discussed in Chapter 3, students take on similar roles as those in the classroom, such as being particularly attentive to the teacher's comments. Also, as mentioned, the amount of time, frequency, and individual caring of a faculty online is appreciated by students and leads to positive conferences. My discussions with Hawks College advisors and student descriptions of their instructor's online behavior indicates that those who like to maintain close contact and provide continuous feedback may utilize the computer networks to do so, but the converse is true for those faculty members who like to be aloof and inaccessible—the technology will not force them to change; they simply will avoid using it.

Higher education courses that use computer conferencing for instructional delivery will increasingly expect students to use various online resources. Examples of this activity emerged in my fieldwork, such as: (a) Craig queried a network discussion group in preparing interview questions he would ask of a news figure; (b) Craig searched network discussions for ideas that he could use for his computer conferencing discussions; (c) Carl posed questions about medical ethics in a network discussion and reported back their responses to his computer conferencing group; (d) Melody did an e-mail inquiry about careers for a course; and (e) Miguel monitored several listserves during his course on the Middle East, following up with personal e-mail inquiries to those whose opinions intrigued him.

Possibly a sense of academic isolation draws would-be distance learners back to college campuses. Kerry, for instance, continued to drive 45 minutes to his former community college, just to mix with professors with whom he studied formerly. Len told of a similar excursion:

> I went up to school the week before last, my old school in
> [Some Town] and I hung around the library and I hung around
> the political science department, and I spoke to one of the
> astronomy teachers. As far as I am concerned about the com-
> puter networks now, they are really good as a supplement (like
> it is a 40-mile drive up there). And if I get on the computer,

especially Internet, I have access to the whole world. But, that doesn't substitute for my little library up there or my little political science department or my friends up there. I can sit down with them and have a cup of coffee. And, we can discuss all of the things we did on the computer, all the research and all. So, it ends the isolation of that little campus. But, that little campus is really where it all takes place.

Distance and nontraditional educators may tout the merits of new study schemes, but these only work well for some students—perhaps those who are intellectually and socially connected in other spheres, have supportive relationships, are self-disciplined, and can sustain their enthusiasm for obtaining a college diploma over several years—or perhaps they prefer to study separated from the conformity, didacticism, inhibitions, and inconvenience that may attend classroom, campus study. Just as computer technology did not strip the world of printed papers, neither will distance technologies take away a preferred instructional mode of many—the classroom. Hall (1991) explained how several American distance initiatives failed when technologies were not adequately supported, student demand was overestimated, and piecemeal courses were offered without leading to a college diploma.

However, distance education is growing both nationally and internationally. Ely (1992) reported that most sectors in the United States are devoting effort to distance education. Perhaps 50% of students are being touched by any of a range of interactive telecommunications technologies: audiographics, microwave, fiber optics, satellite, coaxial cable, and computer networks. The pervasiveness of distance education on a global scale is indicated in the variety of dedicated distance and mixed mode institutions. Kaye (1989) stated that over 10 million students worldwide are involved in credit courses and that many more people are involved in other, noncredit distance learning.

Dedicated distance institutions like the British Open University may have more difficulty implementing computer conferencing because (a) the current culture stresses independent learning; (b) former distance education media have promoted passive, fact learning dished out in preplanned, prepared instructional materials; and (c) the economies of scale usually reached through mass production are harder to achieve with computer conferencing. Perhaps graduate seminar situations work best (Kaye, 1989). Various universities reported student ownership of computers ranging from 30% to 80%; more students accessed computer networks from home than from the workplace (Wells, 1992). Institutions can no longer be based on a single distance education medium because of the rapid proliferation of multimedia and telecommunications technologies, according to Miller (1992). He stated that these will cause infrastructure investments that link all levels of educational institutions with attendant local, state, and national policies.

Miller (1992) and Paulsen (1991) both envision electronic universities that operate at the consortium, national, and international levels, making it possible to bring a wide variety of resources to any remote student's site. Paulsen (1991) used the example of the Electronic University Network (EUN) to demonstrate how a nine-member university consortium can share a computer network among themselves, offering their own degrees, but readily transferring credit for distance students. Indeed, Granger (1990b) showed how over 21 open universities of national scope have sprung up throughout the world, with three more being planned. Even though enrollment in current computer conferencing courses remains low (10 to 50 per class), Paulsen (1991) argued that Compuserve, with its 800,000 members, exemplifies how this distance education technology could be implemented on a large scale, using facilitation models similar to that of the British Open University's DT100 courses of 1,350 or more members. Paulsen (1991) believes that the Internet could begin to offer university courses to a global audience because it already has millions of users who access its thousands of discussion areas.

A concern is not just whether the technologies can deliver but how faculty members will gain the skills to effectively instruct through this medium. Dirr (1990) posed this issue in light of a possible faculty shortage in the mid-1990s, one that will most probably be filled by instructors who have been socialized into teaching by conventional methods. He recommends distance education policies that will help these faculty members understand distance learners, learn to use distance media effectively, and gain satisfaction from distance interactions.

Societal And Personal Issues At Stake

I am concerned about how these technologies can take over our thought and writing processes. Clues of this appeared in my discussion with Craig:

> Craig: I put WordPerfect in right away and just let WordPerfect sit there. Sometimes I'll start to read and sometimes I have to write a paper, but WordPerfect will always be there you know. The computer is always humming and I'm reading right next to it or I'm writing on the computer. Maybe I'll outline anything that comes to mind.
>
> Dan: So you use WordPerfect like a blank sheet of paper?
>
> Craig: Yeah. That's just what I do. Its getting so I just can't write right. It's a funny thing. I've lost a lot of my writing it seems like. At work when I have to write a report hardly anybody can read

> it very well. [laughter] I seem to be losing it. Everything I do is on the computer. My friend Ted is the same way. Everything he does is on the computer. It's hard to write it out longhand.
>
> Dan: And why is it hard to write longhand?
>
> Craig: Well it seems like you can be sitting down in front of that screen and you're sitting there, just sitting there and all of a sudden something comes to mind and you throw it right on the screen and something else comes to mind and you try to throw that one and you try to make sense out of it. Then maybe you'll print it out and look at it. It looks a little bit different on paper sometimes. That's the flow you use. As a matter of fact, me and my friend were talking about getting laptops because we have to go out in the car and patrol at work. We were thinking of taking a laptop computer on patrol in our security job because we have to stay out there so many hours. With a lap top we could type up things that come to mind while we are on patrol sitting somewhere.

Advocates of this technology would say that it enhances thinking and writing, enabling creativity, outlining, thought generation, and so forth. But it may mean that computer use develops dependent thought and writing patterns instead.

Len was concerned "that people can relate to someone thousands of miles away on some minuscule, obscure topic, and yet they don't know or help those in their own neighborhoods." Most of these students' families were supportive and mildly interested in their computer networking activities, nothing more. Kerry mentioned that his family showed little interest in the subjects he was studying, online or otherwise. Betty, after telling me about sharing an online assignment with her husband, described his general attitude toward her computer conferencing activity:

> Well if you knew his personality, he is interested in it, and every time I tell him something he listens, but he does not go out of his way to seek what my learning is because he works many hours. So when he comes home at 8:00 he opens the newspaper, puts on a ball game or something, then plays Nintendo for an hour. That's his relaxation at night and the last thing he wants to do is communicate with people because he communicates all day with people. So he'll listen to me, but he won't go out of his way to sit down and ask what I've learned today. I'll get on the computer at 11:00 and he'll have gone to bed because he's exhausted. He has to get up early. And I'll be on the computer at 1:00 and here he comes down the steps and he will put the Nintendo on for half an hour. Its in the same room as the computer.

But, this potential dissolution of close-hand relationships was never as pronounced as when Craig told me his joys of networking:

> As a matter of fact, one good thing about the medium, you know, the computer medium we are on, a lot of times you'll research a subject and your wife really doesn't understand it, and you'll want to talk to her about it. But this way on the computer you are able to talk to people that you have something in common with, like on our course of the constitution. And that was nice. But, you'd love to talk to your wife about it, but it just confuses Marge here, you know.

Another question arises: Does computer conferencing attract conventional learners or those already somehow connected to networks to begin with? Certainly those who had the most satisfactory learning experience with the technology were either those who were already familiar with using the online networks or those whose purpose for taking the course strongly included desires to learn to use these systems. The technology is not yet developed in such a way as to be seamlessly easy to operate, nor widespread enough that typical adult students come with the skills necessary to work with ease in a computer network environment. So, it seems that this form of distance education truly depends on greater geographic distance to support the numbers of proficient users necessary to convene a computer conference.

Perhaps a more complex question involves equitable access to this technology. Is the computer conferencing creating a greater wedge between the "haves" and "have nots" of our society? A case could be made that it is opening up opportunities for those who live in geographical regions or work in time shifts that make other study modes less possible. Miguel argued that computers are within the reach of most people:

> As a nontraditional school, they should have a mind that every teacher has to be connected via e-mail with the students. The answer that I got in part was that some students don't have money to buy a computer. But I found out that you could use the Hawks computer using a terminal if you want. You don't have to use a PC. You could really be up and using a computer for $400. And most of the time Hawks will lend you a computer.

Hawks College does not loan computers, but, like most other computer conferencing providers, they recommend purchase options, a modem loaner program, and they allow students to use computers at their units (which involves no more expense to students than those taking regular campus classes). So, on the surface, it appears that most people can access this technology.

However, several of the students expressed how fortunate they felt to be able to access the computer network, especially when they realized it was beyond the means of some others with whom they work, as Betty explained:

> I can't see why anybody wouldn't like it, unless somebody can't afford a computer. You almost don't realize it that there are people who don't have one. You think that they've come down so much in price. But a friend of mine who is a nurse and has four kids, although they are all grown, is on a limited income. She said "That's nice you're going to school.". . . But, she says, "Oh but I don't have a computer." And it just hit me that she's right. I just assume that people would do it. But not everybody can afford even a $1,200 computer, or even an $800 or $900 one. They just can't do it.

However, access is more than just "having the money" to buy into this technology. It means being aware of its existence and placing value on the information and educational possibilities it may provide. Most likely these students learned of computer networks from other friends or family members. Both Rose and Betty were first exposed to computer-modem linking when their daughters hooked it up for their own schooling. My conversation with Betty brought forth these dimensions of access:

> Betty: When you mention the computer, could it be that you are already eliminating a vast number of people because the people who will utilize the computer or utilize these discussion groups have already reached a certain level of education?
>
> Dan: I think so. Inherent in that is a certain level of literacy in terms of writing and reading, and also there is a certain level of computer literacy. You were talking about that earlier, too.
>
> Betty: And different economic groups. We take it for granted that there is a computer in the house. But how many people don't?
>
> Dan: And the other thing in that is when I was talking about the listserves, which just came to mind as I was talking to you— they are mainly located at universities. . . . So, you are right; the audience there is a certain kind of person already.
>
> Betty: I'm just curious how you would reach out to an audience who wouldn't necessarily have considered it. I just fell into it, not because I was sitting at home as a housewife, but because I was already a student and I got the information in the mail. I had the opportunity to receive the letter about the class that was starting.

Dan: And you already had a computer, and you knew how to use it . . .

Betty: And I had a modem . . .

Dan: And you had some other experiences. . . . And, it gets back to some class things. You had mentioned that we have a social class in America. . . . But, you know it really is the people that you hang around and socialize with and live around that put you in touch with this kind of information and this kind of experience. And, if you don't live around these kind of people or work around those kind of people, you don't get this kind of information, I guess.

Advocates of distance education believe that this delivery system provides more equitable access to education at a reduced cost by: (a) crossing distances to reach rural students, (b) offering courses that fit the scheduling demands of adult lifestyles, (c) providing rich resources locally through telecommunications and computer technologies, and (d) reducing or eliminating the boarding and transportation costs associated with university study (Dirr, 1990).

Although microcomputers exist in public schools and 50% of students use them (Ely, 1992), some observers report access inequities, especially among females and ethnic "minority" groups (Faddis, 1985), which also includes inner city, "disabled," and rural groups (Neuman, 1991). Schools located in richer suburban areas have many more computers per student, and computer use and software have favored males and those with high achievement to use the more advanced, appealing, and career potential types of activities (Faddis, 1985; Neuman, 1991).

Futurists, librarians, and information network observers agree that there is a current danger that urban poor and rural Americans may be left out of vital future information access (O'Conner, 1992). Why? The fiber-optic networks being built will be laid by private profit-seeking companies. They will first lay these networks in suburban areas that are being rebuilt—the same neighborhoods with residents willing to pay for the commercial, money-making entertainment programming that will be offered first. The article argued that the poor will not have access to these networked information services, when a computer with a modem costs $1,000, and public libraries in inner-city and rural areas may slowly diminish as more advanced, networked information sources become available through home access. The reality of the telecommunications is that many Americans simply do not have access now. For example, a quarter of the households below the poverty level have no telephones, and only 13% of American households have personal computers (White, 1991).

LIVING IN AN INFORMATION AGE

This section discusses ways that technologies affect our lives beyond learning—in communication, forming relationships, and in performing the everyday tasks of life.

Various Communications Technologies

> Betty: I think [the computer] is almost like a living thing to me. It's a machine, but to me it's more than a machine. The fact that it can remember what I tell it or what somebody else tells it. I just love it. To me its like a person. Its always there. It knows the answers. I just think it's a nifty thing. You know how computers are in everything now. But you don't think, for instance, that there's a computer in your microwave. You just don't think of that. That's like a nonfriendly computer. But computers that I can sit in front of the screen and it talks back to me, I just think it's great.

Emergent technologies, based on computers, telephone, and video devices, can be directly used for formal or informal learning, as described in the first part of this chapter, or they may be used more for information exchange and communication. These are often competing technologies; when students wish to communicate with their advisor, they must decide whether to e-mail, FAX, telephone, write a letter, or drop by in person—each of these being relatively more convenient, available, acceptable, or possible, depending on both party's access, skills, and preferences.

For example, a common choice is whether to use the telephone or send an e-mail message. Miguel explained why he would rather use e-mail:

> I have another guy from another university that I study with. He's directing most of my courses. And he's not in the computer, but those courses are more like computer stuff, and up to now I got away with all this stuff. But I miss not having the computer connected to him because sometimes I have a question, and it would be much much easier to confirm what I think with him. I could call or write but maybe he's busy and we play phone tag for a while. . . . And you know sometimes you feel silly asking a stupid question sometimes, that you could solve with a regular e-mail.

However, some found little use for e-mail in their relationships:

Dan: Did you find that [e-mail] was an easier way to get a hold of instructors or your advisor?

Ted: Yeah, for this course. . . . Craig and I kind of threw a few things back and forth. Of course we'd see each other at work anyways and we'd tell each other what we'd sent each other before we saw it. [both laugh]

Dan: Now I was wondering about your advisor?

Ted: She doesn't like computers. I've sent her something on e-mail and she said she got it but she doesn't like to use that thing. She said she'd rather I call. [I laugh] The phone is so much nicer.

Dan: So I guess you called the next time.

Here are some other communications technologies I have encountered lately with which many others in our society are involved:

- The Syracuse University School of Education has set up a sophisticated local area network (LAN) for sharing files, printers, e-mail, CAI modules, and so forth. It gateways into the Internet and will be accessible from faculty/staffs' homes, setting up a much more useful and powerful user interface than exists for any of these technologies in a stand-alone fashion.
- The FAX machine is available all over the world, giving no one any excuse for delaying the transmission and response of documents worldwide. These systems can be hooked to computer networks, and the latest modems boast FAX capability as an integral feature. They also are connected to photocopying machines.
- The answering machine, a common feature in homes and businesses, allows people to stay more actively in touch with those they want to and to screen others out of their lives. These systems can be quite sophisticated with passwords, touch-tone retrieval and review features, individual mailboxes for different members, voice menus, and so forth.
- Ham radio, in use for several decades, has been used by enthusiasts to communicate around the world. It has been the means of delivering distance courses, too. The distance relationships built through this technology parallel that of computer networks and pen pals.
- CB radios engulfed our country just a decade ago for truckers to keep each other informed on road conditions, speed traps, and as a way to while away the hours. Common folk also picked these up for their travel communications.

- A concurrent development to the FAX machine for document transmission is the overnight and two-day delivery postal service.
- Cable television stations and telephone companies are scrambling to introduce interactive communications for shopping, entertainment, and information to peoples' homes using fiber optics. Unlike the other communications options mentioned, these systems intend to be more of a one-way, broadcast technology and will not interconnect individuals with each other—at least not initially.

Decisions About Using Technology

It seems reasonable to view the incorporation of technology into our lives as entirely a personal decision, such as whether to buy an answering machine, computer, and modem, or whether to install cable television or various options on our phone, but in many cases it is not. Often the employees' work environment dictates what technologies they will have, such as whether they will have a phone, a computer, be connected on a local area network (LAN), have FAX machine access, and so forth.

These personal and work-enforced decisions then determine the type of technologically oriented learning in which adults can participate. If you are not placed in a position within your institution with the privileges of access to technology, you are either barred from this learning, or you may be compensated by equipping your personal life with these similar systems to stay on top of the technology—a more expensive proposition. The personal study of these technologies may be due to the individual's inclination toward "tinkering with electronic gadgets" or a ploy to gain important, career-ladder vocational skills. For example, a friend of mine, John (a fictitious name), works as a Management Training Specialist in a Fortune 500 manufacturing company. Just the other day, I asked him to give me a lift home and discovered that he had a cellular phone in his car. I was interested in the gadget, and he was eager to demonstrate it to me.

He attached the antennae to the windshield and turned it on as he drove across town (it is illegal, if I am not mistaken, to dial while driving). He was calling his voice mail system at work, located about 50 miles away. When the system answered, he ignored the automated recording voice as he quickly plugged in his extension and personal access code. The system responded that he had six new messages and started to play the first one, broadcast through the cellular phone's speaker. The first one was from a vendor in California, who wanted John to call him back; John did not pay it any heed, considering it the vendor's responsibility to connect with him. The second one was from the company Vice President of Human Resource Development, who left him an extended message telling him how much she really liked the ideas for a new promotional advertisement he was putting together; he mentally registered this as an important response because there was no need to get back to her.

I asked him, "What do you do when they leave you important information that you have to act on?" He pointed out that he now has a mini clipboard and pencil attached to his dashboard. While driving he jots down the important information he needs. These voice mail systems also have the capability of forwarding, rewinding, storing, and so forth, so messages do not get lost.

That was the end of the demonstration, but we talked about it at some length afterward. He told me why he had gotten this cellular phone, just two months ago. When the company did an inventory of the voice messaging system among mid-level professionals, they found that John had not been listening and responding to messages promptly, so his supervisor came to talk to him. John explained the reality that he was much too busy in other important activities. He suggested that they equip him with a cellular phone, as they had for other top management, so he could respond to messages during his commute. Evidently, top management personnel live an hour or so each way out of the area so they have been using this new communications strategy. His supervisor balked, but when the problem continued, John got her to agree to pay the phone charges if he bought the cellular phone system out of his own pocket. He felt he got the best out of the deal because, at 25 cents or more per call, the company's investment in his new technology will soon be greater than his own.

John told me that this has now solved his voice mail problem. Because he is rarely working in his office, he gets all of his communications completed now through this new technology. But the cost is that he has given the company two more hours a day—the commute time, which used to be his own personal time. He estimates that he collects 25-30 messages a day and can now process all of them, being selective about what he responds to or turns into an "action item" in his time management system. I asked if he ever talked "live" to others—his supervisor or this HRD VP during his commute—and he said, "No." Sometimes they leave messages on his voice mail system while he is leaving messages on theirs, but usually they do not talk "in person." However, once he got into a conversation with the HRD VP while they were both commuting into work from different directions.

How does computer-mediated communication (CMC) fit in with these other technologies? CMC is perhaps more liberating as an educational medium; its discussion possibilities free it from the "cultural imperialism" labels other distance education initiatives have received (Kaye, 1989). It incorporates possibilities for discussion and adaptation to the local community that have been advocated for several decades in the appropriate development of less developed nations (Young, Perraton, Jenkins, & Dodds, 1980). Kaye (1989) sees computer conferencing as most related to conventional types of interaction: correspondence, telephone, and face-to-face conversations. He concludes that it will only reduce postal mail; in contrast, it may actually increase phone and in-person conversations because they each offer unique advantages to computer-mediated communications.

Levinson (1990) submitted that computer-mediated communication text is very different than that on the printed page—it is always revisable, read by many at once through immediate transmission. It fills the interactivity void that all other forms of published text gave up for advantages of mass production and consumption through printing. An exception to this would be letter exchanges, but computer-mediated communication recaptures those interactive attributes. He expects a revolution in the intellectual realm to accompany computer-mediated communication in much the way printing brought enormous social, religious, and political changes earlier.

Plethora of Other Technologies

Finally, there are all of the noncommunications technologies that have emerged into the American consumer lifestyle over the past 15 years—compact disks, digital clocks, videocassette recorders, calculators, "walkmen," microwave ovens, videodiscs, personal computers, video camcorders, and so forth. Surely the proliferation of these devices cause tremendous learning to go on as consumers evaluate, purchase, and learn to use (or ignore) all the various features of these items. These technologies may serve no communication purpose, but increasingly, silicon chips equipped with fuzzy logic are creeping into our lives to optimize the efficiency of our automobiles, the lighting in our homes, and even the amount of water allocated to a load of laundry.

Societal Implications of a Technological Future

Some occupations are becoming so computer related that employees are always on the computer. Ten of these students (half) used computers at work as a major component of their jobs—some were at a keyboard constantly, like Randy:

> I operate a CAD system during the day, and that much time on
> the CRT—visual— my eyes are pretty burned out by the time I
> get on [to the computer conference] at night. And the display
> is bad, the characters and all are tougher to read than most ter-
> minals I've seen. I don't know if you've seen it or not, but they
> are very difficult characters to read. And, my eyesight is pretty
> good, so I can imagine someone with poor eyesight having a
> pretty tough time with it.

Indeed, three of the students complained about the eye fatigue
they experienced from the overuse of computers. Additional occupational hazards creep up with extended computer usage, such as carpal
tunnel syndrome and back fatigue, creating a whole field related to the
ergonomic design of these technologies and changing the work of physical therapists, lawyers, and workplace safety personnel who deal with
those cases.

Indeed, computer-mediated communication may be just another
example of the specialized consumer society that we have become. The
products we purchase, like computers, are so complicated and absorbing
that they generate a whole web of workers involved in manufacturing,
marketing, training, maintaining, programming, studying their use, and
so forth, all tied together around these gadgets. Obviously, people with
high levels of education seek out these experiences, but in some ways it
may be a matter of people owning an expensive toy and seeking another
useful way to make use of their investment. Were this two decades ago,
those engineers and accountants I saw at a predominantly white, male
Macintosh user group may have been tinkering around with their cars—
discovering the latest wizbangs, gizmos, and efficiency devices—
installing and testing them out. Perhaps this technology represents a
pseudo-productive, consumerist avocation of the middle class. It presents almost endless possibilities for learning and learning-how-to-
learn, as the plethora of computer applications create jobs in and of
themselves—computer language programmer, desktop publisher, com-
puter-aided designer, computer graphic artist, and so forth.

A Workplace Reality

Professional and management positions may now require a
firm knowledge and use of a wide variety of computer network skills.
Vicky explained:

> I use [the PROFS electronic mail system] to communicate to
> people all over the world. That's how I do my business and it's
> instantaneous. When my PROFS system goes down for a cou-
> ple of minutes, I'm absolutely annoyed. [Dan laughs] I do my

> calendar on it. I find out all about my hotels and meals, flights
> and travel reservations. I do all my expense accounts online
> and they go electronically to my manager who is in
> [Northeastern City] for a signature and then to his manager
> who is in [Southern City]. I mean, I create my presentations on
> the system, and write reports. . . . I can prepare professional
> presentations and then I send it to a plotter with a few little cer-
> tain commands and I can make my own graphics. So its very
> inexpensive and very easy for me to do.

It appears that the necessity to have technological skills only
rises to the mid-management or independent professional level in
many organizations. Indeed, many upper level managers and senior
professionals and academics pride themselves in being able to delegate to another, such as an assistant or secretary, the chores of photocopying, word processing, faxing, answering and screening phone calls,
monitoring electronic mail, and so forth. Yet, the positions to which
one can delegate communication in any of these areas has eroded
because of the sophistication and simplicity of the technologies, the
pejorative, subservient appearance of the social roles of those who
handle another's communication, and the increasing need for immedia-
cy in our communications.

However, this constant complex learning that attends technological use, may occur primarily at a certain strata of our society. What
automation has occurred in the lower skilled, low-paying service and
retail industry jobs has tended to extract human intelligence from
these positions or replaced workers with more efficient machines or
robots. A familiar example is the switch from cash registers with num-
bered keys to those with fast food icons. These eliminated the need for
workers to remember prices and calculate change.

Personal Adjustments

The faculty advisors I interviewed told me that much of the
early computer technology they experienced seemed to take simple
tasks, like balancing your checkbook with a calculator, and create a
whole software package that was much more difficult to use, more
time-consuming, and presented a learning hurdle to be overcome in
the process. They looked forward to "second-generation" innovations
that were unique for the computer, instead of simple conversion of
manual tasks. Craig told me, "You always want [computers] to go faster,
though." Francis concurred:

> I think it is a real commentary on us human beings. I mean [the
> computer network] is very fast and very effective. And, it is able

*to bring several people together on the phone, for instance;
they get online and can communicate with CONFER. But, then
you get to the point where you need to log on, and if too
many people are on the system, you can't get on the system.
You have to keep redialing. It can take 20 minutes to a half
hour to get on the system at a busy time. So, that is the frustration. So, you finally feel like microwaving—you get it and then
it is not going fast enough. I think it is a commentary on
human beings, it's too slow. You may be communicating
instantaneously with someone in [Western State], but you can't
get logged on quickly.*

However, it seems that we also want to determine our communications
activity and not have the technology determine that for us:

Laura: It's the medium now that's setting the priorities.

*Steve: It's true. The telephone has that impact also. People will
often drop a meeting that they are having face to face with a
person to take that telephone call. It is kind of a cultural bias to
other than face-to-face connections.*

*Laura: Even the FAX, usually I get that delivered to my desk
instantly, rather than putting it in my box. There's something
about the urgency of that medium.*

What initially was social pressure or personal drive for constantly
improving the speed of these technologies may give way to people
wanting more control over the communications process and not let just
the quickest technology determine that.

Len wondered why people like to reveal their inner secret fantasies on the networks behind a cloak of relative anonymity:

*[Computer networks] are a way of distancing yourself, but still
being involved, and it disturbs me. There was one woman,
Carolyn, on one of these networks, who was saying some really provocative things. . . . She was telling us that she would
soon be taking a two-week trip to Los Angeles and was going
into great detail about everything she planned on doing. And
she was asking if anyone had a young man in his 20s, at the
height of his sexual powers, who would want to experience
this with her. . . . I don't know what this person is really like,
what makes her take on this persona, or if that is really what
she is like.*

However, this persona may give way to a concern to clearly portray oneself and truly get to know others in the circumscribed communication
setting of a computer conference:

Carl: But you find that in telecommunications, people really want you to know [them], or at least it certainly was with me, because I wanted the people to know that I was 20 years in supermarket retail, I'm trying to finish my formal education, and some of my personal life, because you hope that it helps them get a certain perspective about you and your comments. As opposed to just hearing someone say something without really knowing anything about that person. You might not get a good sense about where he or she is coming from.

These communications technologies constantly exert pressure to be available, accessible to customer demand, to show our willingness to be of service at all times and in all places. For example, my brother is buying a new laptop computer so he can work on the plane, on his trips, take it to church with him, and so forth. Sales representatives at Chevron, where I used to work, were very connected; they had voice mail, cellular phones, and laptop computers—all interconnected so that they were always in touch. A sales representative could park at the side of the road between service calls, attach his laptop to the cellular phone, and dial up the company's mainframe computer to use e-mail or check customer sales data. In our world we expect a speedy turn-around—the Federal Express mail system, the FAX machine, the 9600-baud modem—we even wire our homes to send or receive FAX, e-mail, and cable services. The ultimate in connectivity is the "airfone" system, installed in the third seat of every row in a recent flight I took, allowing busy executives to stay in touch, even 36,000 feet above sea level!

However, I have yet to observe anyone making an in-flight phone call, which may be the expense of the call or the lack of privacy or intrusion of one's voice in the personal space of strangers in adjacent flight seats. Or, it may really represent a fact of life—many of us do not want to be continually available; we like private time and space that is uniquely and personally our own. That a large proportion of homes do not have answering machines and individuals choose to drop out of electronic mail communication, further evidences this. Sometimes we want time to reflect, ponder, daydream, and remain incommunicado from the hectic bustle of life, regardless of what technological possibilities for connectivity exist.

Societal Adjustments

This intense pressure for rapid communications, brought on by technology, is also changing the nature of the workplace—not necessarily a positive trend. There is pressure to make quick decisions that bring immediate, bottom-line gratification—giving the workplace a fast-paced, decisive work character. This is in direct conflict with the reflectivity and analysis often promoted in the academic literature for better workplace organizations (Marsick & Watkins, 1990; Schön, 1983).

Few of the scholars saw negative aspects to the onslaught of technology. An exception, Siegel et al. (1986) suggested that "submergence in a technology, and technologically-induced anonymity and weak social feedback might lead also to feelings of loss of identity and inhibited behavior" (p. 183). Zuboff (1988) conducted the most comprehensive research to date in her classic qualitative study of the encroachment of computerization on workplace tasks, which produced role changes and worker anomie. However, others argue that computer conferencing humanizes our interaction process: unique personalities emerge, and it brings people together more than in a classroom (Kaye et al., 1989).

Levinson (1990) supported a view of newer technologies enabling us to become more human; they do this by (a) extending the range of current communications, thereby (b) recapturing elements lost by former media. He stated: "Thus, contrary to the many critics of technology who see our world becoming increasingly artificial, I see our world becoming increasingly natural—albeit on a (life enhancing) extended basis—courtesy of technology" (p. 5). He sees computer-mediated communication as not replacing the important media that convey audio and video images—radio, telephone, television, video technologies, and so on—because these cannot capture our imaginations—the abstract which was never physical—like the written word can. The future information technologies will integrate computer-mediated communication with Hypermedia; these include all today's mediated forms, plus holographic image presentations.

One gauge of the social isolation many in our society feel is the proliferation of relationship screening services—by pay-per-call telephone, videocassette, and personals in the newspapers. As mentioned earlier, the newspapers have changed their "personals" service to match up potential lovers to now include a telephone bulletin board. Every Thursday my local newspaper prints out two pages of interested parties (one for men, one for women). Each person describes him- or herself in about 30 words, and the newspaper assigns a special phone code to each ad. You simply call a toll-free number to give a representative the information you want in your printed ad. They allow you to record your own voice greeting, and you can also get once-per-week message retrieval—to hear who has called to have you contact them—at this same number. The service I have described so far is free. The pay part comes in responding to a "personals" advertisement. You dial 900 and enter the number of the person you are interested in learning more about. At your discretion you can leave them a message to call you, or you can browse through either female or male voice messages, giving phone commands. Like computer conferencing, it is available 24 hours a day, 7 days a week, but for $1.95 a minute!

We seem to be living in an increasingly fragmented social world in which intimate, long-term, physical relationships are becoming harder to establish—in part because of the specialized, esoteric individuals we have become. People are selective about who they meet—they want a third party, a computer service, or a middle person to screen these things prior any personal interaction. They want to privately scrutinize the video, resume, computer printout, or personal phone message to decide how, when, or whether they will respond. They want that privacy with no obligation to move forward. What does this say about ourselves when we will share the most private details of our lives, views, and preferences with anonymous strangers if we can secure our own identity? Does that not indicate a fear of opening up with the real people in our lives in committed, meaningful relationships!

What does it mean to know another person and to establish a relationship? Sharing computer messages for four months on a computer conference is not enough. Just speaking to people over the phone for extended periods is not enough either. I suspect that meeting in person to see face to face what these "disembodied writers" are "really like" is not what these people seek. They want close, long-term, committed relationships with trusted individuals of their own liking. A side benefit of learning for these distance students in a computer conference has been the meeting of many people over the network. It has been an opportunity for screening others whom one might want to meet someday. But usually the distance makes this physically impossible. Even if they could meet, most of the conference participants only express desires to meet in wistful, gleaming, passing-fancy-type tones. For the most part, they have too little time in their lives to really "meet" anybody else.

Perhaps the greatest threat of technology in this information age is that it continually asks us to give up our uniquely human nature, that part that telecommunications cannot replicate. One student told me that the harm in not receiving face-to-face feedback—nods, sighs, animation, interruption, and body language—is not in our inability to know whether the other person understood the content of our message. Instead, because that expression is missing, we fail to learn vital information about ourselves—how likable, persuasive, helpful, cogent, sympathetic, articulate, convincing we are—in ways that reinforce our own view of self-worth. By expressing our views to others, we learn about ourselves. Delaying or eliminating that information in our communications reduces us on a personal level. Judy spoke along a similar track:

Judy: And again I don't even know if the phone calls would have [made the distance course successful for me] because sometimes I think we can get so insular that we can totally isolate ourselves from people and we lose a lot in that. I think part of what makes us human is how we interact with each other.

Dan: So are you saying in a way that even the phone is a little disembodied?

Judy: Yes, it is. It is. Do you get the same feeling when you talk to someone on the phone as when you see them in person?

Dan: No, I don't. And I'm thinking that we've never talked through a computer medium at all, and I feel one step closer to you because I'm hearing your voice. And yet I have no idea what you look like, and that would bring another perspective.

Judy: It does. It really does. I think these computer things are great, but I think we lose some of the human qualities. And I think we lose the value of human beings by trying to say that we are going to teach totally through this medium. Not that an aspect of it can be done, because I think that it positively can be. I think it can be a valuable tool, but it can't be all or nothing. I think there has to be a balance.

CONCLUSION

Computer-mediated communication represents just one technology that has emerged in the midst of this information age in which we live. I have used perceptions of those I interviewed and observations about the current impact of technology in the world around us to speculate on learning and living in an information society.

These students uniformly held that computer networking would increase as an educational delivery system, both because of its effectiveness and for its convenience in meeting the ever increasing demands of adult life. Yet implementing the technology may include instructor involvement at similar levels to what teaching currently requires.

The implementation of computer network resources at Hawks College illustrates some of the difficulties involved in achieving the dream of universal connectivity. Several resources on the computer network have increased usage among students and faculty: e-mail, computer conferencing, listserve discussion groups, a degree-planning database, and an online library search program. The college was largely successful in placing computers on faculty members' desks, but they are not as widely used as hoped. Student use remains low—possibly 8% of students are connected—but the individuals I studied spoke of how important these resources were for them individually, especially for corresponding with their advisors and instructors. Similarly, many faculty members' championed the use of electronic communications; whereas others viewed them as consuming time, containing redundant messages, and implying a false urgency.

The corporation in which Vicky works provided a good example of technology in use for formal training. Not only is it experimenting with computer conferencing systems, but it also uses computer-based training, interactive videodisc, video conferencing, and more traditional distance delivery media—correspondence, audiocassette, and videotape. It is experimenting with newer technologies for instruction that integrate many of these devices. It is guided in choosing between the various instructional media by rationales of matching employee skill needs to position competencies, using passive media versus telecommunications and live classes for teaching lower or higher order objectives respectively, and a structured mentoring program. Distance technologies promise to link the workplace with educational institutions.

Various technologies are increasingly being used for informal learning in adult life. These students were commonly engaged in electronic discussion groups, such as listserves, with global participation. Somewhat akin to the Lyceum of a century ago, these electronic study groups are entirely voluntary in nature. They provide a means of recreation for some of these students, allow isolated individuals to meet, and may have an international makeup, especially when focusing on the culture of a specific country. In the workplace, a plethora of technologies requires ongoing, informal learning, especially through computer conferencing networks and online bulletin board systems. Another emerging information service for informal learning is the voice bulletin board system, established by newspapers. These services offer current news, weather, sports, health and nutrition, church notices, school announcements, and personals, accessed by a touch-tone phone.

Complex issues surface when examining learning with technologies in an information age. For example, the same computer network technology that can bring people of other cultures together online to bridge and discuss their common interests can create an addictive environment that breaks down proximate social relationships. The online environment often replicates the roles, protocols, and norms found in regular educational settings. Distance education, when delivered through computer conferencing, will utilize more network resources. Perhaps this form of distance education requires large geographical dispersion just to attract the necessary numbers of interested, competent computer users. Among the social and personal challenges to learning these technologies present are their ability to transform our thought and writing patterns. Also, the wedge widens between those who have access to this technology and those who do not—not just because of financial means, but through the social networks that either value this type of learning or do not.

Computer networking represents another aspect of living in an era booming with technology. When we choose to communicate we weigh the pros and cons of many choices: in person, postal mail, telephone, e-mail, FAX, and hybrid services, such as voice messaging, cellular phones, and short-wave and CB radio. Other technologies continue to engulf our lives: digital clocks, computers, VCRs, microwave ovens, CD players, and so forth.

What social implications do these developments have? First, a technology such as computer networking can take over someone's life, both through voluntary involvement or because of workplace demands. Negative results include eye strain and joint and back difficulties when people must both work and go to school through this technology. Our specialized consumerism has created full-time jobs around building, maintaining, marketing, and training on these systems. Pressure seems greatest to use technology at middle levels of the organization, whereas intelligent functions are being removed from lower level positions, and those in higher management positions do not handle the machines first hand.

Perhaps a balanced perspective fits best because neither a positive nor negative outlook is entirely accurate, and we have an almost inevitable view that these technological changes will occur. That view suggests that the inefficient, cumbersome, and clumsy "dishes" on the technological "smorgasbord" will disappear, based on "diner" demand for the truly fine, emergent "cuisine." Social pressures to do things ever faster may give way to technologies that allow us to control the pace of our communications. Social isolation and anonymity may give way to desires to accurately portray oneself and learn meaningful things about others. The frenzy to always remain connected will evolve into work and lifestyles that allow for personal, reflective time for self-communication as well. The isolation and inability to maintain close relationships is evidenced in the rise of technologically based matching services. Distance communications cannot build the intimate, committed relationships we desire. These same devices hold the possibility of reducing our humanness by downplaying characteristics that cannot be transmitted during our interactions. Machines, hopefully, will not replace humans—and perhaps more importantly, our devotion to technology will not allow us to transform ourselves into mirror images of those devices. We will cling on to our uniquely human attributes and will demand that technology permit us to convey those to each other.

7

Alone But Together

The theory . . . helps us understand what we don't know and, therefore is the only guide to research. Research that is not grounded in
theory is wasteful. It may solve an immediate problem, but it
doesn't fulfill its promise . . . its ability to solve other problems in
different times and different places. (Moore, 1992, p. 1)

This editorial excerpt substantiates criticisms Minnis (1985) levied
against research in distance education in general. First, it remains too
narrowly focused on describing particular institutional problems.
Second, it ignores the need to build theory by taking an ahistorical and
an atheoretical position. Third, researchers make few generalizations
from it because of its context specificity. Fourth, the research "lacks
meaningful cross-cultural or comparative perspectives" (p. 190); and
finally, it relies too heavily on psychological paradigms that limit the
problem settings that researchers pursue. Minnis calls for qualitative
approaches, borrowed from sociology and anthropology, to ameliorate
these concerns.

LIMITATIONS OF DISTANCE EDUCATION RESEARCH

Authors who have tried to summarize current literature on distance
learners lament its narrow focus. Cookson (1989) noted the predilection

to converge on distance education methods and student outcomes, especially regarding persistence and dropout. Sheets (1992) suggested that is the case because the voluntary nature of this type of adult education makes program planning, administration, and evaluation dependent on adequate attendance levels. As Cookson (1989) found, "Yet to be examined in detail is the nature of the adult learning process, which attends the generation of outcomes in distance education" (p. 31). Indeed, "few studies actually dealt with the dynamics of students' acquisition of new knowledge, skills, or sensitivity" (p. 23). Sheets (1992) called for "descriptive studies . . . to focus on personal and situation factors that go beyond the traditional questions of gender, age, and educational background" (p. 21). Citing Gibson (1990), she found the influence of learning styles, resources, and maintenance of motivation on persistence, with important research ventures still ahead.

Indeed, looking at the student variables of Calvert's (1986) "Conceptual Framework for Distance Education Research," many are noticeably absent from research, such as perceived needs, learning styles, study environment, and use of materials and services. This schema also fails to include some of the themes that I found emerging in my research, such as learners' perception of the medium (in this case computer conferencing), their relations with their student peers and the instructor, their perceptions of growth through participating in education, and the affect of education on their work and family lives and vice versa.

It is difficult to make generalizations about adult distance learning because of the many, narrowly focused studies that fail to describe the computer conferencing experience or the type of students who participate with this medium. The majority of these studies employ an arms-length, objective approach to research that fails to bring investigators close enough to these distance students to gather meaningful, rich data. Hence, many of their findings become armchair speculations that try to explain the results of limited, shallow data. The qualitative data being extracted from surveys and questionnaires are superficial, often not analyzed, and disallow rich description. Also most of what poses to be qualitative research lacks systematic and rigorous data gathering and analysis; rather, it seems anecdotal and impressionistic. Often when researchers interviewed students, they conducted short, one-time sessions and therefore were not able to establish greater rapport to probe indepth about issues. Almost all of these studies begin with predefined structures the researchers have determined are important in the situation—interview questions, questionnaire items, tests, and instruments—which have inhibited important themes of the field or priorities of the students themselves to emerge.

Therefore, most of the research on distance education focuses on psychological or personal variables, constructs, and attitudes, and reports them as if these qualities exist as separate entities that can be extracted from students. Indeed, the important issues of participation, motivation, and interaction are often described as speculative interpolation of numerical analyses without any attempt to gain student perspectives directly and indepth on any of these processes. In sum, what has been needed was probing examination of adult distance students using computer conferencing, using multiple types of qualitative data, that endeavor to "thickly describe" these students' lives and points of view, while tying the research into the larger societal question of what it means to learn in the information age.

This book's research, spanning a year and a half period, used qualitative methods to fill that gap. It explored learners' perspectives of computer conferencing. These adult students were enrolled at a northeastern U.S. institution, Hawks College, and were taking distance courses via computer conferencing to meet requirements for their bachelor's degrees. The qualitative methods used for this study remain unique for studies of computer conferencing. A survey found that of the 35 research projects that were studying computer-mediated communication, this one was only one of the few that took an interpretivist approach; positivist approaches predominated (Cole, Beam, Karn, & Hoad-Reddick, 1992).

A MODEL FOR COMPUTER CONFERENCE LEARNING

Using data from the various dimensions of the research presented throughout this book, I constructed an Adult Distance Study through Computer Conferencing (ADSCC) Model (Figure 7.1.) as a framework from which to understand the dynamics of successful learning by computer conferencing. Surrounding the model is the context within which the computer conference is held, the larger institutional and societal milieu that impinges on the distance learning experience. Within this context there are three major aspects that sequentially influence the student study experience: (a) readiness—the personal and environmental factors that prepare the student for study in this instructional situation; (b) online characteristics—the unique and carryover elements that make up the computer conferencing environment; and (c) learning approach—the general and specific learning strategies students use to make the conference an effective learning experience. Each of these aspects has two dimensions. Students' success with online education in subsequent phases is primarily predicated on effec-

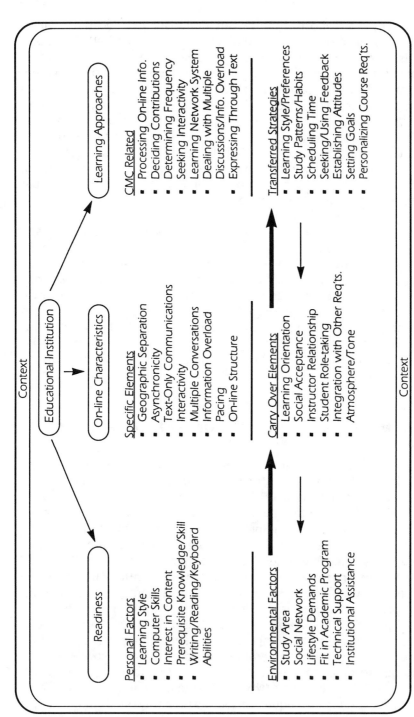

Figure 7.1. Adult distance study through computer conferencing (ADSCC) model

tively working out issues in the preceding ones (as noted by the large arrows). However, the educational institution can positively impact readiness, online characteristics, and learning approaches. The individual also can improve each dimension iteratively (shown by the small reverse arrows) as he or she uses new knowledge about learning approaches or online characteristics to enhance readiness or elements of the online environment.

Context

The overarching element of the ADSCC model—context—explains the societal and institutional milieu within which the distance course takes place. Societal elements include various access issues (class, gender, ethnic, geographic, time-related, socialization), elements of transactional distance (physical, social, intellectual, cultural), the social value of lifelong learning (especially in adulthood), and the current economic, cultural, and political atmosphere operative in society. Institutional context refers to the educational organization's mission, policies, procedures, and various initiatives to bridge these elements, as well as the institutional culture within which the course takes place.

Readiness

The distance student brings various personal factors to the learning equation that influence its success. Their learning preferences, style, array of learning strategies, and prior learning experiences affect their approach to computer conferencing. Certainly, the extent and variety of computer skills, particularly those related to basic personal computer operation and networking, stand them in good stead for this experience. Their interest in the course content affects the extent to which they will extend themselves in this learning quest. Similarly, without prior mastery of fundamental concepts and skills in the content area, their attempts to meet content demands with the computer conferencing course will be severely hampered. Finally, readiness for computer conferencing presupposes the ability to read, write, and type well; the conference can improve this, but the higher their initial development, the better chance of a successful experience.

Readiness involves external factors as well. Having a study area of solitude, space, and organization impacts course success—as does having a social network of family, friends, and associates who value your activity and support (or compensate for) you in other life roles as you pursue an education. Having space or margin for educational pursuits (McClusky, 1963) within adult lifestyle demands of work, family, and community involvement is a must. Another external factor is the centrality of the course to the student's program of study. For students new to computer conferencing, there will be some computer network learning to be done, so the ready availability of materials and personnel for technical support and training is vital. Essential, too, is institutional assistance with registration, setting up of userids, shipping course materials, adjusting course requirements, and so forth.

Online Characteristics

Upon ready entry into the learning situation, the distance student next confronts the characteristics of the computer conference. Awareness of these elements is preparatory to fitting oneself within the online environment. Distance students must recognize that their geographical separation from the instructor and other students will require higher levels of self-discipline and independence. Successful students become aware of how asynchronicity affects other elements of the conferencing environment, such as (a) the pace of online discussions; (b) the plethora of multiple, simultaneous discussions; (c) the potential to become overloaded with information; and (d) that interactivity depends largely on participation frequency and the volume and structure of contributions. Becoming a productive member of a computer conferencing course begins by knowing the various discussion areas—their purposes and the protocols for structured communications. Distance students observe the strengths and limitations of text-only communications as they can build on or compensate for those.

However, many of the characteristics of the online conference are not directly related to the medium but have been brought into this instructional environment by the teacher and students (often purposefully) from past successes with other formats. The learner's orientation to the meaning of learning predicts whether interaction, reflection, collaboration, experiential, or discovery components will be viewed as important or necessary. Likewise, establishing a social environment and meeting the norms of acceptance within it leads to successful conferencing experiences. Instructor's and students' role expectations, the boundaries of relationships, and respective responsibilities are carried over from other learning experiences. Students should become aware of how this online component fits into the larger instructional activities and requirements of the course. Finally, instructor style and participant makeup will also influence the intellectual atmosphere of the conference.

Learning Approaches

Only as distance learners become aware of how the medium's characteristics and carryover social elements affect online dynamics and learning can they address these. Many learning approaches relate specifically to the computer conferencing medium itself, such as: (a) learning technical procedures to effectively participate online; (b) processing the online information; (c) deciding when to contribute and how best to present one's thoughts online; (d) determining a frequency of reading and writing on the conference, primarily to follow multiple discussions, avoid information overload, and achieve maximum interactivity; (e) inviting further interactivity through timely contributions that solicit response; and (e) learning to express oneself accurately and concisely through text.

Additionally, the learning approaches distance students bring to bear on the computer conferencing course experience are often general strategies transferred from other settings. Arriving at this setting with a particular learning style and instructional preferences, they seek to find ways to express these. Likewise, having already found various study patterns and habits effective in other study settings, they will try to apply them here. Because computer conferencing requires different scheduling changes for distance and regular students, they will need to make those time adjustments to be successful in this environment. Other individual learning approaches include: (a) seeking feedback on performance or understanding and using that to shape successive learning; (b) establishing an attitude or instructional climate that is conducive to learning; (c) setting personal goals during one's study; and (d) personalizing the course to meet one's own expectations, needs, and interests.

As noted earlier, the large arrows on the ADSCC model indicate that readiness precedes the experiencing of online characteristics—the perception of which allows students to create effective learning strategy responses. Yet, the process is also iterative (represented by the small arrows). Once students understand the online environment, they can modify both personal and environmental readiness factors to facilitate learning—such as developing computer skills or negotiating with those they live with for better study arrangements. Likewise, learning approaches can positively affect online characteristics; for example, when someone attends frequently and makes effective contributions she or he heightens interactivity and reduces elements of information overload and asynchronicity. When a student reaches out to encourage and support a less active individual, this affects the social climate of the conference.

Finally, the educational institution can enhance student experiences online through a variety of ways. They can prepare students in gaining prerequisite skills for online study, thereby making them aware of the demands and support they will need. Similarly, the institution can explicitly state up front the elements of the conferencing environment, as well as the social and role expectations involved in online study. Learning strategies for the electronic course can be taught directly, without students seeking to create their own approaches without guidance. Hopefully, the ADSCC model presented here can guide administrators, instructors, and students' efforts in recognizing and working within the dynamics of computer conferencing courses for successful learning experiences.

IMPLICATIONS

This book's research is valuable in extending the knowledge base, providing practical applications, and indicating areas for further research.

Extending the Knowledge Base

Revealing the Distance Student

Distance learners are often characterized as lonely, isolated individuals seeking education to escape the intellectual famine of their life situation. This study revealed primarily active, successful adults with happy social and intellectual relations who have been able to make it thus far in life without a university diploma, but who are hoping for something more. Social networks, especially within the family, sustained their degree pursuit. Instead of being reduced to a potpourri of psychological constructs, these adults are self-determining individuals who pursue education for a variety of reasons, despite intense lifestyle demands. The "distance" in the equation is often the institution's isolation from those it serves—in really understanding them. The academic literature on distance education, likewise, is filled with teacher and institutional injunctions for improved practice, not based on a firm understanding of its clients—a void this study has begun to fill.

Challenging Distance Education Notions

This book presents important instances that ask us to reshape our understandings of distance education. A primary attribute of computer conferencing is its group orientation. The interactivity of the conference is among group members, more than between them and the instructor. Harasim (1990b) called this the many-to-many communication (as opposed to the conventional one to one of distance education). Certainly this attribute runs counter to two of the definitional attributes of distance education, as discussed in Chapter 1.

Thus, because of its group nature, computer conferencing also allows very competitive or collaborative learning environments to flourish—not typical aspects of distance study. These students under the guidance of an instructor can learn in both ways, discovering and creating individual knowledge together. Distance comes in various amounts among and between all in that learning environment—a much larger and more complex equation. Bridging all of the transactional and physical distances between them exponentially compounds the complexity of the situation. And because of people's inability to monopolize the conversation, even the instructor, the group learning tends to level out the hierarchical relations often found in classes or learning groups.

Perhaps not a distinguishing characteristic, but a certain mindset about distance education is that the providing institution stands in the center, delivering instruction to students scattered geographically around it in various fixed locations. This notion holds true for the various forms of correspondence study and is only beginning to be challenged in audio/video conferencing when instructors choose (depending on equipment capabilities) to teach from remote site locations. However, with computer conferencing, remote site locations may be any home, office, or hotel room on a telephone network, for those whose occupations involve much travel, such as Vicky and Randy. Or it may be primarily remote in time, like in the case of Harry who lives in the same town as the Distance Education Center. Perhaps it is the instructor who teaches from moveable locations, like David did several times in his courses. Temporal distance with computer conferencing becomes more fluid than rigid, more moveable than stationary.

As with other telecommunications technologies, characteristics of computer conferencing call into question distinguishing attributes of distance education (Barker et al., 1989). Moore (1991) tried to fit computer conferencing within the context of distance delivery media, yet some scholars classify it as a totally new domain for learning, completely redefining distance education itself (Harasim, 1989; Kaye, 1989; Mason & Kaye, 1990; Paulsen, 1993). Aspects of my study further support these assertions. However, it questions whether properties of interactivity, collaboration, and reflection were inherent or necessarily fostered by the medium. Many learners (perhaps a majority) experienced these characteristics, but for some the experience was fairly passive, competitive, and totally spontaneous. Perhaps the paradigm of "distance education" will become so completely challenged by various attributes of various technological media that the term itself will cease to effectively define our future instructional environment (Miller, 1992).

Explaining Learning Approaches

Students involved in new forms of study develop approaches to this work that make it effective and successful for them. They tailor their lifestyle, attitudes, information processing skills, study habits, time schedule, and physical and social environment to get it to work for them. Corroborating Blumer's (1969) view of human thought and action, the learning approach revealed by this study shows people involved in directing their actions, individually and collectively, around shared understandings of their world. They each carry cultural, philosophical, physical, and psychological luggage with them (to say nothing of the everyday demands of the adult working world), but within those structures they are able to shape the learning experience to meet their own ends. They prefer institutions like Hawks State that allow them to individualize their education, capitalize on their experience, and flexibly pursue a degree.

Two important contributions this study makes to the scholarship on learning approaches are, first, that media, such as computer conferencing, play a strong role in determining learning strategies. For example, with computer conferencing, students must deal with an entirely different set of media-related challenges: asynchronicity, text-only ambiguities, multiple conversations, information overload, participation frequency, and information processing. Second, it argues that learning skills are incidentally learned and subconsciously held. Because these process skills are rarely the focus of student attention, in their quest to master objectives, learn content, and fulfill assignments, students rarely seek to build and refine their learning strategies in a concerted fashion.

Showing the Role of Online Relationships

In creating computer conference learning environments, both teachers and students seek to recreate the classroom world with which they are familiar. They structure the conference like an electronic campus. The social norms of politeness, courtesy, and ostracism prevail. The inaccessible, distant, pedagogical classroom relationship can also be recreated in this environment. The promises of computer conferencing for increased reflection, collaborative learning, and intellectual amplification have begun to be realized but are largely dependent on the individuals who meet in this "electronic classroom," the instructor's approach to teaching, the design of the course, and not the classroom itself.

Computer conferencing has the potential to bring together more participants from wider geographical regions, lifestyles, social strata, and with diverse personal characteristics than other media, and it encourages them to interact with each other online. Although polar positions and frictional dynamics occurred in these conferences, they led to important learning—that of understanding others' perspectives and adjusting ones' own accordingly. Online relationships form to support these students, especially those who feel intellectually isolated, but they rarely last beyond the computer conferencing course.

Online Learning In An Information Age

Computer networks have the potential to bring about relatively quick information exchanges with knowledgeable adults all over the globe who share like interests and needs. They allow individuals to pose and answer questions and are modern-day study circles— Lyceums for global collaborative learning. These information technologies pervade the workplace, constantly challenging workers to acquire new skills, and they also convey information and present opportunities for training. We take it for granted that these technologies are the inevitable mainstay of our future progress.

However, these telecommunications on an individual basis may strip us of our humanness—reducing ourselves (and that portrayal) to the text we can type. In the social realm it separates those networked individuals from meaningful neighborhood relationships they might develop instead. The social implications run deeper as well. No one knows how to harness the willing laborers who want meaningful work and whose jobs are to be replaced by this computer automation. Those of poorer means or less education are barred from information gathering and sharing activities, further wedging apart the "haves" and "have nots." A more optimistic outlook finds distance education providing more equitable access to information technologies and necessary employment skills. Perhaps people will be able to control electronic communications to create periods of secluded reflection and foster closer relationships.

Applications in Practice

Applications of Findings About Distance Students

Increased understanding of both the internal (personal) and external (environmental) elements that operate in the learning of distance students' lives can inform distance education practice. Individualizing instruction (Granger, 1990a; Hiemstra & Sisco, 1990) must attend to the wider issues of student development than just intellectual attainment of knowledge. Part and parcel with the instruction should be opportunities to apply new learnings in workplace tasks and career development, especially as many of these adults work in challenging positions during their education. For those who have less meaningful positions or feel intellectually isolated, the institution could look to computer conferencing or social events on a regional level to create more affiliation and engender camaraderie.

Degree programs need to enable adult students to independently address job enlargement, promotion, or career changing as part of their education because this was the primary reason most of these students had for returning to school. This study also indicates that social networks, especially within the family, improve or inhibit individual degree ambitions and progress. Perhaps advisors could work with students in determining their network of supports and how they will be affected by their schooling, particularly looking at negative impacts and how they can be ameliorated.

Applications of Findings About Computer Conferencing

Institutions will need to look more closely at participation rates, interactivity, technical support issues, learning orientations, and the collaborative atmosphere of computer conferences, in order to improve their computer conferencing efforts. Individualizing instructional approaches can recognize that not all students learn effectively through this medium, and they may want to structure other activities, for example, correspondence, telephone sessions, or tutorial time, for those students who would rather learn through other media. Also, computer conference design can anticipate the dissipation of discussion during assignment due dates and holidays and plan for official suspension of graded online activities during these periods.

The extent of interactivity depends on participation frequency, group size (to influence the amount of information presented), and the nature of one's online contributions. Perhaps the best way to assist learners to maximize their learning through heightened interactivity is to make these elements explicit in preliminary student study materials. These could contain suggestions for involvement frequency and the crafting of messages so as to further conversations and invite dialogue. Course design and moderation patterns need to be modified to maximize the interactivity of the conference, not to dissipate discussion more broadly than the number of students available to carry on conversations in various nooks and crannies of the conference. For large conferences, small group work or smaller moderated sessions can provide more personal interaction than large sections overloaded with messages.

Technical support remains a problem, exacerbated by distance, but somewhat inherent in the "user hostility" of current technology and students' inordinate focus on tasks, assignments, and content to the exclusion of the tools for effective online work. Beyond an initial in-person session, added support, and provision of clear instructions, the practical further step might be to create a brief listing of skills—a checklist—that will let students know precisely what technical knowledge and skills they need to master for various online course requirements. Also, explicit time should be allotted near the beginning of the course for them to gain the necessary skills as they are new to this technology.

Students come with different orientations to learning and opinions of what a successful instructional experience will be for them. Because computer conferencing fosters discussion, active participation, and perhaps reflection, interaction, and collaboration, the importance of these elements to the learning process needs to be brought up and emphasized. Students will attempt to incorporate these elements more into their own learning if they understand their importance to the learning process. Along with this explanation needs to be discussion of the value and purpose to learning of other elements in a more holistic distance education experience,that is, one that combines texts, video- or audiocassettes, broadcasts, field trips, interviews, and network resources besides the online sessions.

These various learning aspects which computer conferencing encourages, coupled with its current limitations of text-only transmission and its inability to support large or small numbers of participants, easily suggest the types of content, tasks, and groups suited for this environment. These include current affairs topics and courses in the humanities and social sciences that encourage reasoning, issue taking, and discussion. Many applied fields, such as education and social work, seem equally suited. However, when content is fixed, such as for the performance of procedural tasks or the taking of a closed-item test, instructional approaches become more one way, and do not suit this medium well. Highly visual, auditory, or kinesthetic subjects (art, music, drama, dance, speech, and perhaps science) or those with laboratory components may be difficult to teach with this medium. Multimedia and holistic approaches to distance education may overcome most of these limitations. When computer conferencing courses attract students with related background experience or content knowledge, as many adult students possess, insightful discussion will most likely result; so upper division seminars or graduate study seems ideally suited for computer conferencing. Courses with 10 to 25 participants seem best for this environment, but one of these courses I studied had only four participants and seemed successful, given everyone's determined and frequent involvement.

Collaboration may be an ideal to foster generally, but this study called into question whether it was universally appropriate. This research showed effective learning also occurred in a competitive conferencing environment. Instead of assuming that collaboration is an inherent component of the medium, it needs to be explicitly fostered in course design, materials development, and instructor preparation. The instructional design should look at online group activities that provide teamwork and task completion through shared involvement, matching students in ways that enhance learning. As with learning orientation, course materials should explicitly address the role, importance, and strategies students should take to promote collaborative experiences. Finally, instructors may want to examine their teaching style to see if they can facilitate a collaborative or competitive instructional environment, seeking out assistance if they find themselves lacking.

Applications of Findings About Learning Approaches

The question remains: Can generic, useful LHTL skills be identified and taught, or are these so idiosyncratic, individual, and context specific that the effort is futile? I believe that the learning approaches these students exhibited can be extracted, and although their generalizability to other media may be minimal, they nonetheless can be useful in enabling other students to successfully deal with online courses. Some of these include:

- Learning how to use the personal computer and conferencing application to an adequate level of mastery and having a technical support system readily available.
- Planning to be engaged in the computer conference several times a week to stay involved in current discussions and make the medium more interactive and engaging.
- Making at least one contribution (or more) every time they read through the computer conference.

- Reading through all unread messages within a specific branch and taking notes before responding.
- Seeking to reference other people's comments, synthesizing them, and keeping one's own notes within the context of the current discussion.
- Placing notes in appropriate discussion items.
- Using role playing, analogies, and humor to enhance learning and the online atmosphere.
- Finding a comfortable way to process the online information and respond, either spontaneously online or by printing out the conversation, reading it offline, preparing responses, and uploading those. Recognizing the tradeoffs each approach makes.
- Keeping most communications short, task or topic specific, and clear.
- Keeping an informal and clear writing style that aids online communication, which is predisposed to textual ambiguity.

Applications For Administrative Policy Formation

Several students in this study complained that they got a different experience than they bargained for in taking the online course—ranging from initial impressions that computer aspects were only a minor component, to difficulty with the amount of work they had to exert for these course credits. Institutions should assess these expectations and make sure their communications to students accurately describe the course, prerequisite skills, and special requirements for participation.

Instructor performance varied in the frequency, involvement, and follow-up given to students (as they did on other dimensions, such as instructional style). This study recommends that enthusiastic, attentive instructors be employed to teach the computer conferencing courses, especially as they become firmly established, in order to create both faculty and student advocates of this instructional system.

Finally, because this research revealed that gaining access to computer conferencing technology involves more than the money to buy a computer and modem (aspects of access the institution seems to be addressing), administrative policy efforts should look at informational, instructional, and socialization aspects of this issue as well. Perhaps more publicity about these courses could reach out to underrepresented groups. As these students take university courses, perhaps they could be advised toward taking those courses in which they can develop the necessary prerequisite technical skills and familiarity to work effectively in a computer conferencing course. Offering courses in content areas that appeal to these students may increase their participation as well.

CONCLUSION: TOGETHER YET APART

For both those students taking courses through a mixture of independent study formats and those studying solely at a distance, the computer conferencing course brought a "togetherness" they had not experienced in the same way before. Some students who live isolated lives found great joy and excitement in interacting socially with others online. Others, who were actively engaged in social roles both in their work and family, found that lively discussions on the conference with other students made their classes more meaningful personally and enhanced their learning. Still others did not feel a camaraderie on the computer conference; rather, they found that this component of the course consumed their time and energy, and they made few online acquaintances.

Aspects of computer conferencing itself are isolating, such as separation by time and distance from other participants. Living so far apart, there are rarely opportunities to meet in person; phone calls are expensive, so aside from the conference, students perform their study activities on their own. Because they study at different times, students are rarely connected to the discussion concurrently, and the text-based nature of the online seminar further distances students from their disembodied counterparts.

Yet students are brought together by the computer conference, as they frequently interact with others, post meaningful messages, give insights, and receive feedback from others. Some students found it recreationally satisfying to find out "what was going on" in the conference everyday. The conference learning I observed, whether by collaboration or competition, was only possible in a group situation when students came together online.

Learning-to-learn on the computer conference was done in isolation—modifying one's daily routine to accommodate this mode of study, transferring strategies that had been successful in other situations to the new online learning environment, and inventing individual, sometimes idiosyncratic, strategies for processing information and contributing online. Yet, even here, students were connected, asking and receiving assistance in the computer conference, sharing their successful learning approaches with others, and adapting similar techniques they learned about online.

Perhaps more than any other medium, computer conferencing brings together diverse students and encourages them to share their perspectives with one another, exposing their differences, while working toward commonalty. Whether friendly or hostile exchanges, these encounters lead to important learning by all parties. Online relations can be formed by some who might otherwise be set off by physical appearance, coming to know others before prejudices color those bonds. However, despite the meaning and important purposes these relationships serve during the conference, they dissolve afterward. Ultimately conferees are left alone and are too distant or busy to meet face to face or sustain continued or enhanced friendships.

Although I examined the technological aspects of living and learning in an information age, the social implications of these changes to our relationships remains central. Technology brings dimensions of control over communications—to decide how, when, and whether we will interact with others. To isolate us, these developments may ask us to interact more with technological devices than with other humans. They may invite us to use media as screening agents that bar us from establishing and maintaining committed relationships. They may beckon us to trade our real-time, physical relationships with those in our neighborhoods for asynchronous, electronic associations with unseen hosts living in foreign lands. However, we may choose to chart a different course—to meaningfully and honestly express ourselves online, to regulate our use of technology, and to use these tools to form and sustain relationships in a world as divided as ever by distance, time, culture, economic means, and the pace of living and working in the adult world.

Appendix:
Research Methodology

An emerging discipline, distance education will grow only to the extent that its research base incorporates divergent and competitive methodologies from a number of disciplines. (Minnis, 1985, p. 197)

The methodologies this author indicated are the qualitative approaches of ethnography, case study, and grounded theory as they have been successfully used in anthropology, sociology, and other areas of education. Morgan (1984) also claimed that "studies adopting qualitative methodologies are under-represented in distance education" (p. 255). Merriam (1989) argued that the most lasting research contributions to adult education have been qualitative; some of these include Fingeret's (1983) study of the social networks of illiterate adults, Houle's (1961) research on the continued academic learning of non-degree-seeking older adults, and Mezirow, Darkenwald, and Knox's (1975) investigation of adult basic education programs. Besides the well-known and accepted forms of qualitative research—the grounded theory and ethnographic approaches—Deshler and Hagan (1989) explained how newer qualitative methodologies of interpretive, naturalistic inquiry, concept-linguistic analysis, phenomenology, hermeneutics, participatory research, and critical theory are gaining credence in adult education. Both distance and adult education fields have come to appreciate qualitative research.

OVERALL CONCEPTUAL APPROACH

The methods I used for this book are qualitative, primarily based on those from the Chicago School of Sociology, which are heavily influenced by symbolic interaction (Blumer, 1969), with elements of feminist and postmodern (Bogdan & Biklen, 1992), ethnographic (Spradley, 1980), and grounded theory approaches (Glaser & Strauss, 1967).

Symbolic Interaction

Blumer (1969) best described the symbolic interaction perspective for qualitative research. He challenged researchers to "respect the nature of the empirical world and organize a methodological stance that reflects that respect" (p. 60). This perspective holds that meaning resides in the shared interactions individuals and groups have about objects in their world. The primary purpose of research is to describe these meanings to the outside arena.

Blumer believed that qualitative research approaches could best capture these shared meanings because the researcher was immersed in a naturalistic setting during the inquiry—not sequestered away from the empirical world, conjecturing from hypotheses-testing procedures, relying on operationalized variables, and being subservient to a scientific protocol. Some other premises Blumer (1969) stated about the symbolic interaction approach are worth noting:

- Human societies and group life exist in an environment of action.
- Social interaction involves actors engaged in behavioral dialogue, each imputing meaning on others' words and deeds, which in turn allow the individual to decide his or her own next act.
- The world consists of objects (physical, social, and abstract) that have different meanings to individuals and groups— meanings that are in a constant flux of negotiated change.
- Humans direct their actions from the inside out—the individual directs her or his actions. This stance rejects the notion that external or internal psychological or sociological variables, such as motives, drives, needs, attitudes, social status, and role taking, unconsciously and predictably shape human behavior.
- Symbolic interaction interlinks the actions of groups and societies. "[I]t is the social process in group life that creates and upholds the rules, not the rules that create and uphold

group life" (p. 19). Organizations operate from the process of symbolic interpretation from various participants within them. Current actions of individuals, groups, or societies arise from an historical context of past responses.

Other Qualitative Approaches

Developing overarching concepts and relationships that can theoretically and parsimoniously describe relations and meanings is often seen as the ideal aim of academic research inquiry (Moore, 1992). This has been a primary aim of my research as well. Rather than seek to develop formal, grounded theory (Glaser & Strauss, 1967), this research endeavor, in an applied field, is more concerned with establishing substantive theory, "which deals with a particular limited domain of inquiry" (p. 67). However, there are other purposes and approaches to investigating the human experience that I sought to employ. First, the ethnographic approach, arising out of anthropology, seeks to provide "thick description" (Geertz, 1973) that meaningfully captures the essence of what transpires in a setting and the interactions among groups. Often that expression cannot be reduced to summary statements and concepts without losing important meanings and relationships (Spradley, 1980; Wolcott, 1988). My approach also shares common elements with Eisner's (1991) conception of educational criticism and connoisseurship—a stance that other disciplines' contributions, particularly those of art, music, and literature from the humanities, have as much to offer in elucidating our knowledge of educational realities. I agree that a nonscientific, yet disciplined inquiry has much to offer.

Aspects of feminist and postmodern methodologies for qualitative research provided me with important insights. First, studying issues about gender in fieldwork has sensitized me to these dynamics in fieldwork relations and created an awareness that, being male, I may not have complete access to the gender-related information and perspective of my study (Warren, 1988; Wax, 1979). Useful aspects that are advocated by this perspective are that researchers should reflect about themselves, enter their feelings into the research equation, and locate themselves within their study, making their relative position evident to those they study (Warren, 1988). From participatory research approaches, I have come to see those I study as collaborating with me in developing useful knowledge (McTaggart, 1991). The ability to be eclectic is a strength of qualitative research, encouraging me to apply my own hunches, techniques, and experiences into the inquiry.

THE QUALITATIVE RESEARCH PROCESS

Qualitative research methodology takes a strong process orientation. The qualitative research paradigm posits active engagement of the researcher in a reflective, observational, analytical inquiry that involves the total self—thoughts, feelings, and commitments to an activity with systematic rigor. The endeavor is somewhat like baking bread—the exact number or sequence of the loaf ingredients is not as important as the intensity and combined affects of the process—mixing, rising, kneading, and baking—in some order to achieve a useful product.

The phases I followed were similar to the constant comparative method outlined in Bogdan and Biklen (1992):

1. Initial Fieldwork
2. Initial Analysis
3. Thematic Fieldwork and Analysis
4. Critique of Others' Scholarship
5. Coding and Theorizing
6. Results and Reporting

Each of these phases are discussed next, but one caveat is first in order. None of these phases are discrete because data gathering, analysis, and comparison with other research studies happen throughout the process. These phases indicate areas of concentrated activity in which other tasks took a "back seat."

Initial Fieldwork

In the first chapter I described how I began the study and entered the field. I realized that beyond gaining initial consent, it was important to continually renegotiate a beneficial consent relationship throughout the study (Wax, 1980). Becker and Geer (1957) noted the advantages of participant observation over interviewing, so I tried to incorporate these into my fieldwork as well, however difficult. I met in person with those participants who lived within a two-hour drive of my home; I tried to watch them in their homes or at work actually accessing the computer conference and interacting with the online session. The rest I interviewed by phone, some several times. Most of these students lived within 400 miles of me, but one (and an instructor I worked with later on) lived in the West.

My primary subjects were nine adult students involved in a distance education course on the Constitution, taught at Hawks College during Fall 1991, with additional data taken from 11 other students at the College during Summer 1992. Additionally, I interviewed a small number of instructional personnel associated with the conference—moderators, mentors, technical support people, and administrators—for their distinct perspectives. However, these interviews were held primarily to get a feel for the larger, institutional perspective, because I sought to "level the hierarchy of credibility" somewhat by telling the learners' typically untold perspective (Becker, 1970). In total, I interviewed 20 students and conducted a total of 38 research sessions (either observations or interviews), holding follow-up interviews with several of the students. Qualitative researchers usually choose their subjects through purposeful and snowball sampling techniques rather than through random sampling (Bogdan & Biklen, 1992). However, I was fortunate to be able to interview every student who agreed to participate in my study, focusing my attention in follow-up sessions on those subjects who provided the richest initial interview or following theoretical sampling techniques to look for negative cases (Glaser & Strauss, 1967).

Research Purposes

Research serves several purposes: It can substantiate or refute existing theories; it can be the basis for providing models of reality in a discipline; it can seek to resolve some pressing problem; it can fill a void in a discipline's knowledge base; it can describe phenomena so as to illuminate alternative routes for practice; or it can be a means of grappling with conflicting ideas and concerns in which the researcher is particularly interested. The intent of this research was also multifaceted. The major thrusts of this effort were:

- To investigate the life situation of adult learners who are seeking a university degree through distance study. I wanted to explore the effect of their current work and family life on that pursuit and vice versa. I was curious about their reasons to pursue a college diploma at this stage in life and why they were achieving it through distance study.
- To examine their perceptions of the value of education, the utility of a college degree, and the viability of these goals through distance education.
- To explore student views of computer conferencing—the nature of this medium, its assets and limitations, especially for learning, information exchange, and the social environment of schooling.
- To look at the learning approaches adult students take or

develop when using this medium, in contrast to their approaches to study in conventional courses. I suspected that this new instructional environment would require them to change or develop new learning strategies and information processing procedures.

- To investigate the nature of online relationships that emerge during a computer conference course. How intimate and viable are these? What advantages do they offer, and what limitations?

- To discover the fit of this experience within a larger societal context, grappling with such issues as the use of telecommunications technology to learn in an era of information, the social implications of these forms of study, the extent that they replicate existing forms of the educational process, the extent they are openly accessible, and whether these technologies reduce or widen distance between people.

This book will contribute to distance education scholarship by holistically addressing the distance learner's experience with learning, particularly with the computer conferencing medium, using research methods that have not been systematically and rigorously applied to this task previously.

Collecting Data

I kept detailed fieldnotes of each research session, the bulk of which were transcribed nearly verbatim from audiocassette recordings. Geer (1964) explained how "untrained observers . . . can spend a day . . . and come back with one page of notes and no hypotheses" (p. 384), whereas the competent fieldworker will have many notes and numerous questions that both narrow and enlarge the study.

My fieldnotes were central to this study, so I briefly describe here their format and the way I processed them. Each interview began with essential identifying information—location, time, subject, researcher, and duration. The first part of the notes contained descriptive information about the interview—why I chose this subject, some of my objectives for the session, description of the setting, and so forth. The second part detailed the discussion we undertook during the unstructured interview. These notes occurred in dialogue form with occasional observer comments. I disciplined myself to write out essential impressions and contextual material the same day as the interview so I would not forget them, also listening to the taped session and immediately writing up portions that were unclear or less audible.

Initial Analysis

Initial analysis refers to the analysis done while still in the field, which helps the researcher assess progress to date and prepare for further fieldwork in areas of hunches, insights, or unresolved topics that require further probing (Bogdan & Biklen, 1992). At the conclusion of each set of interview notes I included a section on observations, insights, and hunches that arose from the interview; this might also help to summarize some of the key points. I also formulated a list of follow-up questions and issues in the last section. I would review these and the comments I made on the notes as I marked them in preparing for subsequent interviews, especially with the same subject.

Often weeks or months later, I would read over each set of field-notes, using a pen to indicate areas of importance and commenting on insights, hunches, or follow-up possibilities. I would mark fieldnotes before a follow-up interview as a preparation step. One vehicle for keeping one's own perspective, opinion, and related experience in constant focus throughout the research process is through writing research memoranda. These included significant findings, follow-up questions, insights, excerpts, and themes. Also, Wiseman (1974) explained that the writing of these documents occurs more frequently from the middle to the end of the research process, and this was the case in my study. These ranged from summaries of fieldwork to date, decisions I made in fieldwork themes, reflections on my own computer conferencing experience, insights from conversations with faculty or books on qualitative research, to observations about the various information technologies and their inclusion in adult lifestyles.

Thematic Fieldwork And Analysis

Thematic fieldwork and analysis began after I had completed studying the Constitution course more completely through interviews, numerous memoranda, and document review. Also, I had primarily concluded my preliminary review of related scholarship (Step 4) before embarking into the field once more, but that occurred concurrently throughout this phase. The thematic fieldwork and analysis phase involved developing coding categories, coding the data, analyzing data using the computer, focused fieldwork during this period, and leaving the field.

Coding categories provide a schema to assemble extracts from fieldnotes and eventually become major themes for writing (Bogdan & Biklen, 1992). Glaser and Strauss (1967) described how researchers develop coding categories:

> The analyst starts thinking in terms of the fullest range of types or continua of the category, its dimensions, the conditions under which it is pronounced or minimized, its major consequences, its relation to other categories, and its properties. (p. 106)

I read through my fieldnotes and jotted down ideas for possible categories. Roughly 200 items emerged. I used the topics of my themes as major categories and clustered related subtopics under these; both of these became coding and subcoding categories respectively. Wiseman's (1974) approach of differentiating between foreground and background categories in order to determine which categories to further analyze, combine, and sequence was useful. I was then ready to begin coding my field data. However, the coding scheme continued to be shaped and refined by further coding and analysis activities.

During coding the researcher reads through all fieldnotes, classifying segments that are associated with each coding category. Segments are not coded exclusively for one code only, and usually an excerpt denotes two or more codes (Bogdan & Biklen, 1992). During this thematic analysis phase I coded all of my fieldnotes to just the specificity of the 26 coding categories. At this stage they were ready for computer entry.

Tesch (1991) reported that a majority of qualitative researchers now use computers to assist them in analyzing their fieldnotes. I used such a computer program for data analysis that allows the researcher to highlight and select (with the mouse) portions of electronic fieldnote copy to extract into a database of like instances—one for each category. When the computer program extracts the data, it keeps essential original source information for later reference. This reduces the labor-intensive photocopy, cut-and-paste activities that accompanied qualitative research analysis until recently.

My intent when I reentered the field was to study similar adult students taking other distance courses from Hawks College, to see if their experiences corroborated or diverged from my preliminary work with the first group. Also, I expected to enlarge the database from which I was studying online learning. I undertook this approach with the intent of narrowing my focus to the "foreground" categories I identified (see later). I contacted Hawks again and learned of two online summer courses that were about to begin. I got the instructors' consent and cooperation to help me in the study. I interviewed the students in these courses who agreed to be studied and followed up with a second interview with four students who were most involved with computer conferencing. I also contacted four students from the initial, Constitution, course to find out about changes in their lives, their current impressions of the computer conferencing medium, and for details on some of the thematic areas in which I was interested.

Glaser and Strauss (1967) spoke of "data saturation" as the time to leave the field, meaning that the researcher has reached a point of significantly diminishing returns in gaining any new insights from informants, especially after applying negative case, theoretical sampling techniques. Bogdan and Biklen (1992) wrote similarly that often qualitative researchers involved in large studies need to leave the field when they have gathered extensive field data for dedicated reflection and analysis. Hence, when the second group of students I was studying had completed their online courses for summer semester, this seemed to be a natural cutoff point to leave the field.

Critique of Others' Scholarship

Becker (1986) used the metaphor of building a desk to describe how a literature review should be used by the qualitative researcher. It provides the overall context and content for its contribution, but it is incumbent on the scholar to place it appropriately, as one would a new drawer in an existing desk, and to add the finishing touches—the hardware, stain, and varnish. At the same time as I was pursuing my thematic analysis, I read in some detail scholarship on adult learning, distance education, and specific studies about student use of computer conferencing. This review was useful for fitting my fieldwork and its themes into the larger picture of my discipline and for examining other scholarship surrounding computer conferencing.

I tried to approach the literature review as if it were research data and I was doing participant observation—critically analyzing it and not accepting its assumptions at face value. In this approach, each article became another piece of field evidence; my work was to place it within the context of all the rest (Becker, 1986).

Coding And Theorizing

During this phase, most of the fieldwork is over and the researcher works to organize and analyze the data collected. The specific activities I was involved with during this stage were: (a) incorporating all of the research data—fieldnotes, memoranda, documents, and so on—into the analysis process, (b) finalizing coding categories and doing more complete coding by subcode category, and (c) building analysis and summary tables to aid in examination and reporting.

After transcribing and marking all fieldnotes, I began the formidable task of doing the same with memoranda, documents, e-mail messages, and so forth, and entered all of these with my second set of interview notes into the computer program. I used it to sort and print "fat stacks" of the 17 foreground categories I hoped to analyze in depth. I then read through all of this categorized field data, coding each instance by a corresponding subcode, combining, eliminating, and tailoring these subcategories to match my field data.

Finding the printed excerpts for each coding category unwieldy, and feeling a strong need to be able to chart each individual's perception through all of my coding categories, I constructed a matrix analysis table for each of the 17 foreground codes. This table listed all the individuals on one dimension by the subcode categories on the other. Each cell of the matrix summarized the person's response to that category and listed the page number in the printout, so that I could easily read and incorporate the original into my writing.

Another useful table I constructed was the summary table. This table categorized all students by various dimensions: view toward the computer conferencing experience, instructional format preference, technical background before taking the course, existence of a support network, depth of online relations, view of self, socioeconomic class, sex, age, and location. Using a simple sort procedure, I was able to study relationships among these variables as needed in my analysis.

Results and Reporting

This book presents the finished product of the research endeavor—the outcome of the results and reporting phase. As Morgan (1984) noted, qualitative research has a generalizability of its own:

> This type of research has generalisability [sic], obviously not in a statistical sense, but in a phenomenological sense. The readers or users of the findings can recognise[sic] a relevance to themselves and to their own contexts. This type of research aims to raise people's awareness of activities and events in particular settings so that links and parallels can be drawn to inform practice in other settings and new contexts. (p. 265)

I chose to write the study in the first person, using active voice and avoiding jargon (Becker, 1986). Eisner (1991) posited that expressive language and interpretation are defining features of qualitative research. Darkenwald (1980) explained how the written presentation is so integral to presenting qualitative findings:

> The theory is discursively developed in narrative form as categories, and their relationships are defined, elaborated, and illustrated by the data (for example, incidents from field reports) used

to generate them. Thus, the most useful and natural form for the presentation of a grounded-theory analysis is a running discussion that permits full elaboration of the situation or problem under study. (pp. 67-68)

Based on examples of published qualitative research (Best, 1990; Erikson, 1976; Goffman, 1963; Liebow, 1967; Rist, 1978; Rubin, 1976; Wiseman, 1979), I worked to weave my analytic commentary and related scholarship with fieldnote excerpts in chapters of this book.

References

American Society For Training And Development (ASTD). (1992, November/December). *National report on human resources.* Alexandria, VA: Author.

Apps, J.W. (1988). *Higher education in a learning society: Meeting new demands for education and training.* San Francisco: Jossey-Bass.

Apps, J.W. (1989). Providers of adult and continuing education: A framework. In S.B. Merriam & P.M. Cunningham (Eds.), *Handbook of adult and continuing education* (pp. 275-286). San Francisco: Jossey-Bass.

Barker, B.O., Frisbie, A.G., & Patrick, K.R. (1989). Broadening the definition of distance education in light of the new electronic telecommunications technologies. *The American Journal of Distance Education,* 3(1), 20-29.

Becker, H.S. (1970). Whose side are we on? In H.S. Becker (Ed.), *Sociological work* (pp. 15-26). Chicago: Adline

Becker, H.S. (1986). *Writing for social scientists: How to start and finish your thesis, book, or article.* Chicago: University of Chicago Press.

Becker, H.S., & Geer, B. (1957). Participant observation and interviewing: A comparison. *Human Organization,* 16, 28-32.

Best, J. (1990). *Threatened children: Rhetoric and concern about child-victims.* Chicago: University of Chicago Press.

Blumer, H. (1969). *Symbolic interaction.* Englewood Cliff, NJ: Prentice-Hall.

Bogdan, R.C., & Biklen, S.K. (1992). *Qualitative research for education: An introduction to theory and methods.* Boston: Allyn and Bacon.

Boshier, R. (1988). Socio-psychological factors in electronic networking. *Canadian Association for the Study of Adult Education: Proceedings of the Annual Conference*. (ERIC Document Reproduction Service No. ED 299 461)

Brookfield, S.D. (1983). *Adult learners, adult education, and the community*. New York: Teachers College Press.

Brookfield, S.D. (1986). *Understanding and facilitating adult learning*. San Francisco: Jossey-Bass.

Burge, E.J. (1992). *Computer mediated communication and education: A selected bibliography*. Toronto, Canada: Distance Learning Office, Ontario Institute for Studies in Education.

Burnham, B.R., & Walcott, L.L. (1991). Tapping into motivation: What learners find motivating in instruction at a distance. *Proceedings of the 7th Annual Conference on Distance Teaching and Learning, 7*, 200-207.

Calvert, J. (1986). Research in Canadian distance education. In I. Mugeridge & D. Kaufman (Eds.), *Distance education in Canada* (pp. 94-100). London: Croom Helm.

Candy, P.C. (1990). How people learn to learn. In R.M. Smith & Associates (Eds.), *Learning to learn across the life span* (pp. 30-63). San Francisco: Jossey-Bass.

Candy, P.C. (1991). *Self-direction for lifelong-learning: A comprehensive guide to theory and practice*. San Francisco: Jossey-Bass.

Coldeway, D.O. (1988). Methodological issues in distance education research. *American Journal of Distance Education, 2*(3), 45-54.

Cole, S.L., Beam, M., Karn, L., & Hoad-Reddick, A. (1992). *Educational computer-mediated communication: A field study of recent research*. Unpublished paper, Ontario Institute for Studies in Education, Toronto, Canada.

Cookson, P.S. (1989). Research on learners and learning in distance education: A review. *The American Journal of Distance Education, 3*(2), 22-34.

Cookson, P.S. (1990). Persistence in distance education: A review. In M.G. Moore (Ed.), *Contemporary issues in American distance education* (pp. 192-203). New York: Pergamon Press.

Cross, K.P. (1981). *Adults as learners*. San Francisco: Jossey-Bass.

Darkenwald, G.G. (1980). Field research and grounded theory. In H. Long, R. Hiemstra, & Associates (Eds.), *Changing approaches to studying adult education*. San Francisco: Jossey-Bass.

Darkenwald, G.G., & Merriam, S.B. (1982). *Adult education: Foundations of practice*. New York: Harper & Row.

Davie, L. (1989). Facilitation techniques for the on-line tutor. In R. Mason & A.R. Kaye (Eds.), *Mindweave: Communication, computers, and distance education* (pp. 74-85). New York: Pergamon Press.

Deshler, D., & Hagan, N. (1989). Adult education research: Issues and directions. In S.B. Merriam & P. Cunningham (Eds.), *Handbook of adult and continuing education* (pp. 147-167). San Francisco: Jossey-Bass.

Dirr, P.J. (1990). Distance education: Policy considerations for the year 2000. In M.G. Moore (Ed.), *Contemporary issues in American distance education* (pp. 397-406). New York: Pergamon Press.

Eastmond, D.V. (1992). Effective facilitation of computer conferencing. *Continuing Higher Education Review, 56*(1&2), 23-34.

Eastmond, D.V., & Ziegahn, L. (1995). Instructional design and the online classroom. In Z. Berge & M. Collins (Eds.), *Computer-mediated communication and the online classroom* (Vol. 3, pp. 59-80). Cresskill, NJ: Hampton Press.

Ehrmann, S.C. (1990, April). Reaching students, reaching resources: Using technologies to open the college. *Academic Computing, 4*(7), 10-18.

Eisner, E.W. (1991). *The enlightened eye: Qualitative inquiry and the enhancement of educational practice.* New York: Macmillan.

Ely, D.P. (1992). *Trends in educational technology 1991.* Syracuse, NY: ERIC Clearinghouse on Information Resources, Syracuse University. (ED number pending.)

Erikson, K.T. (1976). *Everything in its path: Destruction of community in the Buffalo Creek Flood.* New York: Simon and Schuster.

Experiential learning cycle. (1990). San Diego: University Associates.

Faddis, B. (1985). *Computer equity.* ERIC Digest. Syracuse, NY: ERIC Clearinghouse on Information Resources, Syracuse University.

Feenberg, A. (1989). The written world: On the theory and practice of computer conferencing. In R. Mason & A.R. Kaye (Eds.), *Mindweave: Communication, computers, and distance education* (pp. 22-39). New York: Pergamon Press.

Fingeret, A. (1983). Social networks: A new perspective on independence and illiterate adults. *Adult Education Quarterly, 33,* 133-146.

Fleming, M., & Levie, W.H. (1978). *Instructional message design: Principles from the behavioral sciences.* Englewood Cliffs, NJ: Educational Technology Publications.

Florini, B.M. (1989). *Computer conferencing: A technology for adult education* (Tech. Rep. No. 1). Syracuse, NY: Syracuse University Kellogg Project.

Florini, B.M. (1990). Delivery systems for distance education: Focus on computer conferencing. In M.G. Moore (Ed.), *Contemporary issues in American distance education* (pp. 277-289). New York: Pergamon Press.

Garrison, R.D. (1989). Distance education. In S.B. Merriam & P.M. Cunningham (Eds.), *Handbook of adult and continuing education* (pp. 221-232). San Francisco: Jossey-Bass.

Geer, B. (1964). First days in the field. In P.E. Hammond (Ed.), *Sociologists at work* (pp. 372-397). New York: Basic Books.

Geertz, C. (1973). *The interpretation of cultures*. New York: Basic Books.

Gibbons, M. (1990). A working model of the learning to learn process. In R.M. Smith & Associates (Eds.), *Learning to learn across the lifespan* (pp. 64-97). San Francisco: Jossey-Bass.

Gibson, C.C. (1990). Learners and learning: A discussion of selected research. In M.G. Moore (Ed.), *Contemporary issues in American distance education* (pp. 121-137). New York: Pergamon Press.

Gibson, C.C. (1991). In, but for how long? Factors affecting persistence in the early months of distance learning. *Proceedings of the 7th Annual Conference on Distance Teaching and Learning, 7*, 208-212.

Glaser, B., & Strauss, A. (1967). *The discovery of grounded theory*. Chicago: Aldine.

Goffman, E. (1963). *Stigma: Notes on the management of spoiled identity*. New York: Prentice-Hall.

Gooler, D.D. (1990). Changing the way we live and learn in the information age. In R.M. Smith & Associates (Eds.), *Learning to learn across the lifespan* (pp. 307-326). San Francisco: Jossey-Bass.

Grabowski, B., Suciati, & Pusch, W. (1990). Social and intellectual value of computer-mediated communications in a graduate community. *Educational and Training Technology International, 27*(3), 276-283.

Graddol, D. (1989). Some CMC discourse properties and their educational significance. In R. Mason & A.R. Kaye (Eds.), *Mindweave: Communication, computers and distance education* (pp. 236-241). New York: Pergamon Press.

Granger, D. (1990a). Bridging distances to the individual learner. In M.G. Moore (Ed.), *Contemporary issues in American distance education* (pp. 163-171). New York: Pergamon Press.

Granger, D. (1990b, July/August). Open universities: Closing the distances to learning. *Change: The Magazine of Higher Learning*, 45-50.

Grint, K. (1989). Accounting for failure: Participation and non-participation in CMC. In R. Mason & A.R. Kaye (Eds.), *Mindweave: communication, computers and distance education* (pp. 189-191). New York: Pergamon Press.

Gundry, J. (1992). Understanding collaborative learning in networked organizations. In A.R. Kaye (Ed.), *Collaborative learning through computer conferencing: The Najaden papers* (pp. 167-177). New York: Springer-Verlag.

Harasim, L.M. (1987). Teaching and learning on-line: Issues in computer-mediated graduate courses. *Canadian Journal of Educational Communication, 16*(2), 117-135.

Harasim, L.M. (1989). Online education: A new domain. In R. Mason & A.R. Kaye (Eds.), *Mindweave: Communication, computers, and distance education* (pp. 50-62). New York: Pergamon Press.

Harasim, L.M. (1990a). Bibliography on educational CMC. In L.M. Harasim (Ed.), *Online education: Perspectives on a new environment* (pp. 229-264). New York: Praeger.

Harasim, L.M. (1990b). Online education: An environment for collaboration and intellectual amplification. In L.M. Harasim (Ed.), *Online education: Perspectives on a new environment.* (pp. 229-264) New York: Praeger.

Harasim, L.M. (Ed.). (1990c). *Online education: Perspectives on a new environment.* New York: Praeger.

Harasim, L.M. (1991). Teaching by computer conferencing. In A. Miller (Ed.), *Applications of computer conferencing to teacher education and human resource development. Proceedings of the International Symposium on Computer Conferencing* (pp. 25-33). Columbus: Ohio State University.

Hall, J.W. (1991). *Access through innovation: New colleges for new students.* New York: Macmillan Publishing.

Hatfield, T.M. (1989). Four-year colleges and universities. In S.B. Merriam & P.M. Cunningham (Eds.), *Handbook of adult and continuing education* (pp. 303-315). San Francisco: Jossey-Bass.

Hawkins, J. (1985). Computers and girls: Rethinking the issues. *Sex Roles,* 13(3,4), 165-177.

Hiemstra, R., & Brockett, R.G. (1991). *Self-direction in adult learning: Perspectives on theory, research and practice.* New York: Routledge.

Hiemstra, R., & Sisco, B. (1990). *Individualizing instruction: Making learning personal, empowering, and successful.* San Francisco: Jossey-Bass.

Hiltz, S.R. (1986). The "virtual classroom": Using computer-mediated communication for university teaching. *Journal of Communication,* 36(2), 95-104.

Hodgkinson, H. (1991, August 14). *Responding to new demographic realities: Challenges for the field of distance education.* Keynote presentation at the 7th Annual Conference on Distance Teaching and Learning. Madison, WI.

Houle, C.O. (1961). *The inquiring mind: A study of the adult who continues to learn.* Madison: University of Wisconsin Press.

Kaye, A.R. (1989). Computer-mediated communication and distance education. In R. Mason & A.R. Kaye (Eds.), *Mindweave: Communication, computers and distance education* (pp. 3-21). New York: Pergamon Press.

Kaye, A.R. (Ed.). (1992a). *Collaborative learning through computer conferencing: The Najadn papers.* New York: Springer-Verlag.

Kaye, A.R. (1992b). *Learning online: A review of typical applications.* Unpublished manuscript, British Open University, Institute of Educational Technology, Milton Keynes.

Kaye, A.R., Mason, R., & Harasim, L. (1989). *Computer Conferencing in the Academic Environment* (CITE Rep. No. 91). Milton Keyes, Great Britain: Institute of Educational Technology, British Open University. (ERIC Document Reproduction Service No. ED 320 540)

Keegan, D. (1986). *The foundations of distance education.* London: Croom Helm.

Kennedy, D., & Powell, R. (1976). Student progress and withdrawal in the Open University. *Teaching at a Distance,* 7, 61-75.

Knapper, C. (1988). Lifelong learning and distance education. *American*

Journal of Distance Education, 2(1), 63-72.

Knowles, M.S. (1984). *The adult learner: A neglected species* (3rd ed.). Houston: Gulf Publishing.

Levinson, P. (1990). Computer conferencing in the context of the evolution of media. In L.M. Harasim (Ed.), *Online education: Perspectives on a new environment* (pp. 3-14). New York: Praeger.

Liebow, E. (1967). *Tally's corner: A study of Negro streetcorner men.* Boston: Little, Brown, and Company.

MacGregor, J. (1990). *Collaborative learning: Shared inquiry as a process of reform. New directions for teaching and learning* (No. 42). San Francisco: Jossey-Bass.

Mackerron, J.L. (1984). *Conditions that affect participation in distance education at selected institutions producing and using television-assisted instruction in the United States.* Unpublished doctoral dissertation, Syracuse University, Syracuse, NY.

Manninen, J. (1991, August 19-21). Computer conference as learning environment: Experiences from computer-mediated facilitating. *Nordisk konferance om fjernundervisning, opplaering of dataformidlet kommunikasjon,* Oslo, Norway. Proceedings, pp. 81-85.

Marsick, V.J. (1988). Learning in the workplace: The case for reflectivity and critical reflectivity. *Adult Education Quarterly,* 38(4), 187-198.

Marsick, V.J., & Watkins, K.E. (1990). *Informal and incidental learning in the workplace.* New York: Routledge.

Mason, R. (1988). Computer conferencing: A contribution to self-directed learning. *British Journal of Educational Technology,* 19(1), 28-41.

Mason, R. (1990). *Home computing evaluation. Use of CoSy on DT200, 1989* (CITE Rep. No. 99). (ERIC Document Reproduction Service No. ED 320 541)

Mason, R., & Kaye, A.R. (Eds.). (1989). *Mindweave: Communication, computers and distance education.* New York: Pergamon Press.

Mason, R., & Kaye, A.R.. (1990). Toward a new paradigm for distance education. In L.M. Harasim (Ed.), *Online education: Perspectives on a new environment* (pp. 15-38). New York: Praeger.

McClusky, H.Y. (1963). The course of the adult life span. In W.C. Hallenbeck (Ed.), *Psychology of adults.* Washington, DC: Adult Education Association.

McCreary, E.K., & Van Duren, J. (1987). Educational applications of computer conferencing. *Canadian Journal of Educational Communications,* 16(2), 107-115.

McTaggart, R. (1991). Principles for participatory action research. *Adult Education Quarterly,* 41(3), 168-187.

Merriam, S.B. (1989). Contributions of qualitative research to adult education. *Adult Education Quarterly,* 39(3), 161-168.

Mezirow, J. (1990a). How critical reflection triggers learning. In J. Mezirow (Ed.), *Fostering critical reflection in adulthood* (pp. 1-20). San Francisco: Jossey-Bass.

Mezirow, J. (1990b). Preface. In J. Mezirow (Ed.), *Fostering critical reflection in adulthood* (pp. xiii-xvi). San Francisco: Jossey-Bass.

Mezirow, J., Darkenwald, G., & Knox, A. (1975). *Last gamble on education: Dynamics of Adult Basic Education.* Washington, DC: Adult Education Association of the USA.

Miller, G.E. (1992). Long-term trends in distance education. *DEOS News—The Distance Education Online Symposium,* 2(23).

Minnis, J.R. (1985). Ethnography, case study, grounded theory, and distance education research. *Distance Education,* 6(2), 189-198.

Moore, M.G. (1989). Editorial: Three types of interaction. *American Journal of Distance Education,* 3(2), 1-6.

Moore, M.G. (1991). Computer conferencing in the context of theory and practice of distance education. *Proceedings of the International Symposium on Computer Conferencing* (pp. 1-9). Columbus: Ohio State University.

Moore, M.G. (1992). Distance education theory. *American Journal of Distance Education,* 5(3), 1-6.

Morgan, A. (1984). A report on qualitative methodologies in research in distance education. *Distance Education,* 5(2), 252-267.

Neuman, D. (1991, December). Technology and equity. ERIC *Digest.* Syracuse, NY: ERIC Clearinghouse on Information Resources, Syracuse University.

O'Conner, R.J. (1992, November 26). The great electronic divide. *Syracuse Herald Journal,* pp. 1, 16.

Olgren, C. (1991). Learning strategies and knowledge outcomes: The quality of learning in an independent study course. *Proceedings of the 7th Annual Conference on Distance Teaching and Learning,* 7, 79-84.

Paulsen, M.F. (1991). The electronic university: Computer conferencing in mass education. *DEOS News—The Distance Education Online Symposium,* 1(20).

Paulsen, M.F. (1993). The hexagon of cooperative freedom: A distance education theory attuned to computer conferencing. *DEOS News—The Distance Education Online Symposium,* 3(2).

Perry, W.G. (1970). *Forms of intellectual and ethical development in the college years: A scheme.* New York: Holt, Rinehart and Winston.

Peruniak, G.S. (1988). Life situation and prior learning of adult learners studying at a distance. *Canadian Association for the Study of Adult Education: Proceedings of the Annual Conference.* (ERIC Document Reproduction Service ED 299 461)

Phillips, C. (1990). Making friends in the electronic student lounge. *Distance Education,* 11(2), 320-333.

Rice, R.E. (1982). *Human communication networking in teleconferencing environment.* Unpublished doctoral dissertation, Stanford University, Department of Communication, Palo Alto, CA.

Rist, R.C. (1978). *The invisible children: School integration in American society.* Cambridge, MA: Harvard University Press.

Roberts, L.H. (1990). Educational goals and self-concepts of distance learners at Empire State College (Doctoral dissertation, Nova University, 1990). *Dissertation Abstracts International,* 51, 11A.

(University Microfilms No. AAC9109556, 3602)

Robinson, R. (1992). Andragogy applied to the open college learner. *Research in Distance Education*, 4(1), 10-13.

Romiszowski, A.J. (1992). *Computer mediated communications: A selected bibliography* (ETSBS. No. 5). Englewood Cliffs, NJ: Educational Technology Publications.

Rose, A.D. (1989). Nontraditional education and the assessment of prior learning. In S.B. Merriam & P.M. Cunningham (Eds.), *Handbook of adult and continuing education* (pp. 211-220). San Francisco: Jossey-Bass.

Rubin, L.B. (1976). *Worlds of pain: Life in a working-class family*. New York: Basic Books.

Rumble, G. (1986). *The planning and management of distance education*. New York: St. Martin's Press.

Säljö, R. (1979). *Learning in the learner's perspective I: Some common-sense conceptions* (Rep. No. 76). University of Gothenburg, Institute of Education, Gothenburg, Sweden.

Schön, D.A. (1983). *The reflective practitioner: How professionals think in action*. New York: Basic Books.

Scollon, S. (1981, December). *The teacher-student role in instructional telecommunications*. Paper presented at the Annual Meeting of the American Anthropological Association, Los Angeles, CA. (ERIC Document Reproduction Service No. ED 239 792)

Sheets, M.A. (1992). Characteristics of distance education students and factors which determine course and program completion: A review. *New Horizons in Adult Education*, 6(1), 3-14.

Siegel, J., Dubrovsky, V., Kiesler, S., & McGuire, T.W. (1986). Group processes in computer-mediated communication. *Organizational Behavior and Human Decision Processes*, 37, 157-187.

Simons, P.R.J. (1992). Theories and principles of learning to learn. In A.C. Tuijnman & M. Van der Kamp (Eds.), *Learning across the lifespan: Theories, research, policies* (pp. 159-171). Tarrytown, NY: Pergamon Press.

Small, M.W. (1986). Learning strategies of adult distance students. *Australian Journal of Adult Education*, 26(1), 18-26.

Smith, R.M. (1982). *Learning how to learn*. Chicago: Follett.

Smith, R.M. (1990). The promise of learning to learn. In R.M. Smith & Associates (Eds.), *Learning to learn across the life span* (pp. 3-29). San Francisco: Jossey-Bass.

Smith, R.M. (Ed.). (1988). *Theory building for learning how to learn*. DeKalb, IL: Educational Studies Press.

Smith, R.M. (1992). Implementing the learning to learn concept. In A.C. Tuijnman & M. Van der Kamp (Eds.), *Learning across the lifespan: Theories, research, policies* (pp. 173-188). Tarrytown, NY: Pergamon Press.

Spradley, J.P. (1980). *Participant observation*. New York: Holt, Rinehart and Winston.

Tesch, R. (1991). Introduction to special issue on computer-assisted qualitative analysis programs. *Qualitative Sociology*, 14(3), 225-243.

Van Onna, B. (1992). Informal learning on the job. In A.C. Tuijnman & M Van der Kamp (Eds.), *Learning across the lifespan: Theories, research, policies* (pp. 125-136). Tarrytown, NY: Pergamon Press.

Vision of IBM human resource performance in the year 2000. (1990, January). In *Ports Of Entry: Major Case Studies Of Distance Education, National Satellite Videoconference*. Madison, WI: Seventh Annual Conference on Distance Teaching and Learning.

Warren, C.A.B. (1988). *Gender issues in field research*. Newbury Park, CA: Sage.

Wax, M. (1980). Paradoxes of "consent" to the practice of field work. *Social Problems*, 27(3), 272-283.

Wax, R.H. (1979). Gender and age in field work and field work education: No good thing is done by any man alone. *Social Problems*, 26(5), 509-522.

Wells, R. (1992). *Computer-mediated communication for distance education: An international review of design, teaching, and institutional issues* (ACSDE Monograph No. 6). University Park, PA: The American Center for the Study of Distance Education.

Whipple, W.R. (1987, October). Collaborative learning. *American Association For Higher Education Bulletin*, pp. 3-7.

White, C.S. (1991, May). Information technology and the informed citizen: New challenges for government and libraries. ERIC *Digest*. Syracuse, NY: ERIC Clearinghouse on Information Resources, Syracuse University.

Wiseman, J.P. (1979). *Stations of the lost: The treatment of skid row alcoholics*. Chicago: University of Chicago Press.

Wiseman, J.P. (1974). The research web. *Urban Life and Culture*, 3(3), 317-328.

Wolcott, H.F. (1988). Ethnographic research in education. In R.M. Jaeger (Ed.), *Complementary methods for research in education* (pp. 187-289). Washington, DC: American Educational Research Association.

Young, M., Perraton, H., Jenkins, J., & Dodds, T., (1980). *Distance teaching for the third world: The lion and the clockwork mouse*. London: Routledge & Kegan Paul.

Zuboff, S. (1988). *In the age of the smart machine*. New York: Basic Books.

Author Index

Subject Index